CREATIVE DISARRAY

From the library of

Carolyn

DEDICATED IN GRATITUDE

to cherished colleagues on the faculties,
trustees, members of the staffs,
and students preparing for ministry
in the schools
where I have been privileged
to spend my years of teaching —

NORTHWEST CHRISTIAN COLLEGE, 1946-1950
CHRISTIAN THEOLOGICAL SEMINARY, 1950-1973
THE ECUMENICAL INSTITUTE, Chateau de Bossey, 1954-1955
UNION THEOLOGICAL SEMINARY IN THE PHILIPPINES, 1965
THE SCHOOL OF THEOLOGY AT CLAREMONT, 1973-1982
LEXINGTON THEOLOGICAL SEMINARY, 1987

CREATIVE DISARRAY

Models of Ministry in a Changing America

Ronald E. Osborn

Chalice Press
St. Louis, Missouri

Biblical quotations, unless otherwise noted, are from the *New Revised Standard Version Bible*, copyright 1989, Division of Christian Education of the National Council of the Churches of Christ in the USA. Used by permission.

Library of Congress Cataloging–in–Publication Data

Osborn, Ronald E.
   Creative disarray : models of ministry in a changing America / by Ronald E. Osborn.
   1. Pastoral theology—United States—History. 2. Clergy—Office.
I. Title
BV4006.073 1991   253'.0973   91-29001
ISBN 0-8272-0462-0

Printed in the United States of America

CONTENTS

PREFACE

This book addresses the diverse and conflicting expectations that hamper the work of ordained ministers, restricting freedom to serve. Perplexing both to ministers and to members, this confusion underlies much of the unease in contemporary church life. Discussions of the problem frequently end in frustration.

My thesis is this: Our history has imposed on us a burden of diverse, even contradictory, expectations, impossible for any mortal to fulfill. Only as we clearly formulate a guiding concept of ministry of our own, assimilate to it those features from other patterns that are essential to ministry, make it plain to those with whom we work, and decline any contract that does not consent to it as valid, can any of us who minister find integrity and freedom—or even raise a legitimate set of standards by which to measure the effectiveness of our work.

To some extent, our particular gifts and inclinations rightfully will shape our concept. Even so, the work of defining it requires informed theological reflection in responsible interaction with the Christian community and especially with those we try to serve. We who seek to minister dare not take on this task as a private fling at self-fulfillment, nor is it proper for individual members to set up themselves as a court of final appeal.

Where does a minister or congregation find guidance in working out a concept of ministry that has biblical integrity, theological dimension, responsibility to the needs of the church, and responsiveness to the unprecedented situation in which we are called to minister today? While others may approach the troublesome reality of clashing expectations from the perspective of scripture, theology, psychology, or social dynamics, I propose to come at it through my discipline as historian. By examining how this vexing complication arose out of the diverse expectations of the American churches, I believe we can discern more clearly the nature of our difficulty and then move together to resolve it.

Therefore this book invites you to consider varied forms of ministry that have loomed large in the American churches and to reflect on the concepts associated with each. Here I use the term *ministry* to refer to the work of those ordained servants of the church whom it charges with the maintenance of its integrity and appoints as its public representatives. While assuming the corporate ministry of the whole Christian people (which I have treated elsewhere[1]), this essay has a more restricted focus. Even so, I have found active lay leaders in the churches no less interested in the issues raised than are ministers and seminarians.

The book's story line plots the way in which good people unwittingly transfer expectations and concepts related to a particular form of ministry over to another. Because such a diversity of models has appeared on the American scene, a tangle of unrelated hopes and expectations snares the minister's work in confusion and frustration for both pastor and people. Jesus told of a net cast into the sea that brought in a great catch containing all manner of fish (Matt 13:47-50). In the case before us, it is time to sort out this slithering, gasping jumble, to disentangle the squirming shapes from one another. Accordingly, I have undertaken to systematize, even at the risk of oversimplifying, what has happened under the pressures of American life to the ways we try to do ministry and the ways people feel about it.

The project began several years ago with a request from my colleagues in the School of Theology at Claremont, Dean Joseph C. Hough, Jr. and Professor John B. Cobb, Jr., to write a historical paper on the concepts of ministry in America for discussion by our faculty.[2] During a memorable summer on the Oregon coast, far from theological libraries, I pondered anew the development of ministry in this country. My thinking gradually took shape around a proposition that I had not seen developed in any systematic way, and the models described in the following chapters began to stand out with increasing clarity. I took back to Claremont a manuscript that has been discussed, enlarged, revised, annotated, and refined across the intervening years.

These chapters grow out of a lifetime of involvement and reflection. As a lad already drawn to ministry, I eagerly seized every opportunity to listen to my father and his ministerial colleagues in their good-humored shop-talk; that was sixty years ago. Through college and seminary and my early years as a pastor, a company of radiant spirits walked just ahead of me and beside me. I recall their names in silent gratitude.

After an idyllic first pastorate, forty years of my ministry were spent in teaching—a brief stint as editor, a short while in college, more than thirty-two years in seminary—and now eight years in active retirement. During all that time, the life of the church and the concerns of the parish have remained at the center of my attention. From service as an interim minister in a score of churches and as a member of pastoral search committees in two congregations, I have heard hundreds of laypersons express their hopes regarding the kind of minister they longed for. In general courses in church history I have tried to keep congregations and pastors in the picture—a feat not always easy to bring off, given the preoccupation of scholars and writers of textbooks with popes and archbishops and theologians and councils. I have repeatedly offered such courses as Historic Models of Ministry, the History of Preaching, and the History of the Cure of Souls. Ministerial biography has been for me a favorite form of reading. Serving on denominational and ecumenical commissions on ministry, I have learned much from some truly great colleagues and have written historical and theological essays on the subject. But the approach and the typology used in this book are new.

A select group of close friends let me talk through the argument and gave good counsel about it in its formative stages: Jay R. Calhoun, Edward Dyer, Prudence Osborn Dyer, Linda Langsdorf Johnson, Pastor Rudolph Johnson, Naomi Jackson Osborn, Donald D. Reisinger, and Keith Watkins. Faculty colleagues at Claremont, and at Christian Theological Seminary, where I presented some of this material as lectures, commented helpfully, as did delegates to an assembly of Shared Ministry in Utah, a company of regional leaders gathered in Little Rock for a consultation of Disciples on evangelism, and groups of ministers meeting for study or retreat in various states on the Pacific Slope. A few curious or accommodating friends have read the manuscript and improved it by their suggestions. These include Jay R. Calhoun, Howard C. Clinebell, James O. Duke, David Griffin, Joseph R. Jeter, Jr., John M. Mulder, Robert A. Thomas, and especially David Polk, editor of Chalice Press, whose encouragement spurred me on to the completion of this project and who named the book.

To all of these my debt is great, as well as to those historians, biographers, theologians, sociologists, pastors, teachers, editors, and fellow church members whose discussions of ministry I have read or heard. Some of their ideas lodged in the back of my mind so long ago that the source can no longer be recalled, but my intention is to give credit for the work of others when using it. To all the intellectual and spiritual benefactors indicated in these paragraphs I express deep gratitude, and especially to my wife, Nola, who while learning to cope with the peculiarities of the minister she consented to marry has given constant support and unfailing encouragement.

Hunter Beckelhymer, David I. McWhirter, James Blair Miller, Martha Nesmith, and Randi Jones Walker gave helpful bibliographical assistance, for which I am grateful, as also for the courtesies of the librarians at the Disciples of Christ Historical Society, Northwest Christian College, the School of Theology at Claremont, and the University of Oregon.

Each of the forms of ministry discussed in the following pages has had importance in its time and, through its legacy of expectations, continues to affect our work today. Yet, as H. Richard Niebuhr concluded concerning the models he analyzed in his memorable work *Christ and Culture*, none is completely valid to the exclusion of the others, and perhaps none is to be wholly rejected. Even so, his own preference was clear. My attitude is similar toward the models presented here. Each was shaped in Christian response to individual and social needs at a specific historical moment. Each has possessed, therefore, at least for a time, essential elements of validity. Each, however, is subject to certain limitations, even perils, especially when carried uncritically into a different situation. Some forms particularly appeal to me. That will be clear enough. A few trouble me. That too will be clear.

This book will fulfill its purpose if it helps its readers think their way through to greater clarity concerning ministry, to arrive at a concept that has validity for them as well as relevance for our time, and then sets them free for the joyful practice of ministry or the equally demanding task of working faithfully with their ministers, sustained by the integrity of a sure purpose, the comradeship of Christian minds, and a firm reliance on the grace of God.

Ronald E. Osborn
Eugene, Oregon
Pentecost, 1991

THE PROBLEM OF
MINISTERIAL IDENTITY

In the far-off days of my childhood, before the rise of neo-orthodoxy, we used to hear preachers of our tradition proclaim that unbaptized children were free from sin. But despite our alleged innocence, some of us who had not yet reached the "age of account-ability" found ourselves locked in mighty struggles with temptation. And we did not always win. The serpent set a trap for us in the little store on the corner—at the candy counter. For there among an agonizing variety of sweets too seductive for our own good, our friendly neighborhood merchant displayed an alluring game of chance. A large box of small chocolate creams, separately wrapped in foil and retailing for a penny apiece (about twice the going price), supported on an overarching cardboard frame an immense, irresistible candy bar.

With all the guile of the huckster's art, a sign offered the bar as a prize—ABSOLUTELY FREE!—if the cream we chose had a pink center.

No wailing sirens. No flashing lights. After all, those were simpler days. Nevertheless, the display seized our undivided attention, as the serpent fascinates the bird before it strikes. While our inward battles raged, the strains of "Yield Not to Temptation" fell ever more faintly on our childish consciences. We passed most of our days without so much as touching any spending money, and when once in a blue moon we clasped a copper coin in our tingling fingers we deemed ourselves incalculably rich. But if a penny was our fortune, the only way to enjoy it was to blow the whole thing.

We knew we weren't supposed to waste money on something not good for us, much less stoop to gambling. But there in the spotlight that giant prize fairly glittered. At last, all fidelity to virtue gave way. We paid our money and we took our choice.

1

No, I never once drew a pink center. I never knew anybody who did. What we got inside the shiny foil was the thinnest of chocolate creams, gone in much less time than it had taken to overrule our consciences.

After a few such sallies down the ways of the world, we decided that our father was right after all: "You can't get something for nothing. Nobody ever got rich from gambling." Before many years had passed, I was myself a student preacher warning against games of chance—and careful not to confess the sins of my lurid past.

In our small church college the nearest thing we had to a free-thinker used to counter our prudential moralizing with the argument that everything in life is a gamble. Whether you sow wheat or drill for oil or put money in the bank at 3 percent interest, he said, you're taking a chance, and he was right on all of those counts. Whether he was right in his generalization that everything in life is a gamble, I leave to those more subtle in ethical analysis.

But this much I have concluded, after long and intimate involvement with the American church. The situation of a minister seeking a compatible congregation or of a search committee looking for "the right minister this time" is frighteningly like that of the innocent child handing over its last penny in hope of picking the pink center. It is a game of chance, and you may try again and again without winning the prize.

Confusion in Definition

Why is it so hard to find the right fit in ministry?

Pity the poor search committee shopping for a minister. The box is full of foil-wrapped creams that look pretty much alike: graduate of a good seminary, three enthusiastic letters of recommendation, a reasonable amount of experience, the age bracket on which the committee has set its mind this time around. Ministers used to come without exception in blue wrappers, but now more and more come in pink. Still, our denominational leaders assure us, the color of the foil has nothing to do with what's inside: As ministers, male and female are equally qualified.

To your committee struggling to make the right choice, your regional minister or other judicatory official will suggest a number of persons to consider, but will not pick just one of them for you. So you agonize through an ordeal of indecision, remembering past disappointments. How do you decide? Maybe by the candidate's present position. Perhaps by running statistics through a computer. Possibly by believing too eagerly the strongest letter of recommendation. Maybe by throwing darts at a board. Undoubtedly, you pray. At last you make the fateful choice. Nervously you unwrap your selection. Will it have a pink center this time?

Now let me complicate the analogy. This enterprise is far more complex than selecting one pink cream out of a gross of pale centers. The problem lies in our unspoken assumptions about ministry, our unsystematic and unavowed diversity in our conceptualizing of a "good minister." It is as though the centers came in two dozen different flavors, and each member was looking for a different one. One person wants a cherry center; another, strawberry; another, raspberry; another, peppermint; another, lemonade; and one wants champagne. But everyone designates the desired flavor by the color "pink."

Because the fantasies sound so much alike, because everyone speaks longingly of finding a pink center, each person takes it for granted that the expression denotes the particular flavor he or she has in mind. The members hear themselves agreeing simply because all are determined to find "a good minister this time." The hard fact is that they are not all looking for the same flavor, but they do not know it.

A *good* minister? What is that? A massive study conducted by the Association of Theological Schools discovered that, apart from an almost universal agreement on integrity of character and ability to get along well with people, there is no broad consensus in the American church on what a good minister is or ought to be.[1]

Now saying that there is no agreement is quite a different matter from asserting that there is overt dissension stemming from a clear-cut disagreement-in-principle. With everyone on the committee and in the congregation assuming that everyone agrees with one's own notion of what a good minister is, it comes out only gradually and painfully, and often too late, that not everyone sees eye to eye after all. We are dealing with notions, not clearly defined concepts—notions deriving from one's impression of a minister one once knew who was "just right."

It all adds up to a sorry sum: Even within a single congregation, American notions of proper ministry are so diverse that no mere mortal, indeed, no divinity, can accommodate them all. No theological curriculum can be devised to prepare a student to meet all the expectations. The diversity is so widespread as to make it unlikely that the members of any seminary faculty can agree on a single controlling model of ministry capable of giving unity and direction to its educational program.

And what of the poor minister? If no clear concept of ministry obtains within the culture generally, within the church at large or any given congregation, within theological education or even within a particular seminary, is it any wonder that confusion as to vocational self-understanding troubles many a minister?

A New Thesis

Ever since sociologist Samuel W. Blizzard conducted his celebrated studies on the dilemmas of the American minister, the prevailing consensus has held that the problem of stress and burnout arises from tension between the priorities of the minister and those of the congregation that pays the minister's salary.[2] The nub of the problem, Blizzard maintained, was simply this: The tasks the minister believes are most important and most enjoys doing are valued least by the people and are crowded out of the minister's week, whereas the tasks the minister regards as least significant and likes least are those by which the congregation measures success or failure and which eat up most of the time. This analysis is still, I believe, widely accepted and undoubtedly contains much truth.

One may question, however, the uniqueness of parish ministers in struggling with such dilemmas. My years in the Groves of Akademe convince me that professors suffer the same kind of pain in the preemption of their time by matters they least enjoy and consider least significant, whereas opportunities for meaningful relationships with individual students get crowded out of their schedule and truly important scholarly commitments suffer delay after delay "until the next sabbatical" or until retirement. Granted, most professors do get study leaves, whereas most pastors do not. But that difference hardly explains the evidently higher level of professional distress among ministers.

One observes the same kind of tension between what one finds satisfying and what one has to do in the work of attorneys, physicians, engineers, homemakers, actors, and store clerks. Every job or profession under the sun has its quota of drudgery and ill-tempered demands from apparently insensitive superiors or a sometimes boorish public, whereas the truly significant aspects of one's work—the point at which one most keenly feels a sense of calling—are often crowded to the edges or off the edge.

A historian with nothing better to do could readily compose an essay on the tendency to frustration and discouragement on the part of ministers through the centuries. Though many a servant of God has cried, "Woe to me if I do not proclaim the gospel!" (1 Cor. 9:16), that same servant has at least at times suffered feelings of total inadequacy, rejection, and failure. Sixteen hundred years ago, Bishop Ambrose of Milan found it necessary to rally his disheartened priests who felt the urge to drop out of the ministry for a life with fewer harassments and financial limitations. He could imagine the heavenly host suffering similar temptation: "Do we not believe that the angels themselves groan in the performance of their various functions amid the toils of this world, as we read in the Apocalypse of John?"[3]

But one can characterize the unease of ministers in other times and places—where ministry itself was often honored—as arising from the tension between the demands of their heavenly calling and the realities of their earthly task. Though the demands were often great, the expectations represented a broad consensus within the church. The uniqueness of our problem lies in the clash of expectations projected on us.

Here I propose a new look at ministry in America, an analysis historical in nature rather than sociological. And I suggest a somewhat different thesis from Samuel Blizzard's to explain the widespread unease among ministers. It does not deny the validity of his thesis and is not inconsistent with it, but locates the crux of the problem at a different point. Blizzard's thesis presented the problem as a conflict among priorities. I see it as a question of role definition, of social and institutional identity.

My thesis holds that our problem in ministry in America today is the problem of great expectations joined to hopeless confusion over basic definition. No clear consensus prevails in America as to what a minister is or ought to be. The question lies deeper than frustration over priorities: It arises from perplexity as to essential identity.

From the beginning of our checkered history, diverse types of ministry have flourished in America, increasing in number with the passing decades, and all of these have left conceptual relics in the mixed bags of our expectations. Moreover, each bag is different from all the others. No class of seminarians, no faculty of theological professors, no college of bishops, no conference of regional ministers or "bishop-type" officials, no staff of ministers, no board of congregational officers, no pewful of parishioners is likely to discover a common conception of ministry among its members.

Our crisis in ministry is conceptual, arising from our lack of a common understanding as to "goals, norms, and values."[4] How can you and I agree as to my effectiveness in my ministry when we measure it by different standards based on different conceptions of what a minister is? If a person's identity is a social creation (as maintained by the distinguished philosopher and sociologist George Herbert Mead[5]), it is no wonder that many a young minister in America struggles with a serious identity crisis, for neither the church nor society at large agrees on what it means to be a minister.

Let me offer, in support of my thesis, two affirmations from my discipline as historian. The first is factual, the second theoretical.

Effects of Diversity

First, the fundamental source of our confusion and unease is a diversity that has been the hallmark of ministry in America since colonial times. In fact, our cultural heritage in this land is characterized by extreme diversities in many aspects of our common life. Yet, despite our vague awareness of this historical truism, the discovery of particular instances now and again takes us by surprise, as do the radically different concepts of ministry and the expectations they produce. We all know that in various strains of American life one way or another of conceiving the essence of ministry has prevailed. But we have yet to come to terms with the effects of that diversity.

Consider that when a new concept of ministry takes over, remnants of the old concept commonly linger on in the religious consciousness—or at least in the unconscious. Even when a particular institutional form is acknowledged to be outmoded or is overtly repudiated, expectations associated with it continue in the popular mind, only to be projected onto some subsequent form for which they have little or no relevance and with which there may be no basis for authentic compatibility.

We clearly see this resiliency in the two evident marks of holiness associated with the shaman, the most primitive form of ministry in the archaic world. The shaman was authenticated as a sacred person by a crisis of vocation and by subsequent experiences of spiritual ecstasy. The first involved a vivid interior vision of the unseen world, accompanied by behavior recognized in the tribe as that of one marked out for this distinctive role. The later occasions of ecstasy renewed the original encounter with the spirit-world.[6]

In due time shamanism gave way to priesthood, a form of ministry on which the warrant of holiness was bestowed by the religious institution. Like the shaman, the sacred powers of this new kind of mediatorial ministry derived from the divine realm, but, unlike the shaman, they came through institutional processes. They were not directly attainable through individual genius or personal experience.

Here are two radically different forms of ministry sustained by two radically different channels of holiness. Yet in pagan and in Christian society alike, a *priest* who possessed those two primitive signs of *shamanic* holiness—the experience of being "called," and subsequent direct encounters with the unseen—has commonly enjoyed an extra measure of effectiveness among the people. This endures despite the fact that these marks of shamanic holiness are in no way essential or even relevant to the essential holiness of the priest.

As you rightly perceive, these same two marks of holiness persist in the expectations that many American Protestants in mainline churches project upon their ministers today. They hold particular importance in the contemporary charismatic movement.

The first effect of diverse forms of ministry, then, is residual, as a new concept of ministry responsive to a new situation in society is required to carry a burden of irrelevant expectations associated with an earlier model.

The second effect is pervasive or contaminant. When two quite different concepts of ministry co-exist in a pluralistic society, the popular mind within one tradition may absorb expectations appropriate to the other, and these expectations may become so powerful as to reshape the ministry of one group after the image of the alien form. The process is deceptive in that it may receive little theoretical articulation. In fact, at the crucial moment of mutation the guardians of the tradition may well deny that any real change is taking place. But the untheological forces of popular expectation, the pressures of society, and the denomination's bureaucratic demands overwhelm the capacity of the theological tradition to resist, and sometimes radical change occurs despite all protests and denials.

Consider two examples of pervasion or contamination, both interacting with the residual effect, and both associated with the urbanization of nineteenth-century America. For Methodists Bishop Asbury had established itinerancy as virtually the essence of ministry, and for Disciples of Christ Alexander Campbell had defined the "essential and immutable ministry" of the apostolic church as that of local elders serving collegially as the pastors and teachers of a congregation. The rationale supporting such ministries carried great plausibility on the frontier and in rural America, because they worked amazingly well.

In the towns and cities, however, the greater success of those denominations maintaining a settled pastor full time with one flock could not escape the notice of ordinary Methodists and Disciples. New expectations stirred; time made ancient good uncouth. Despite all the theology and sacred rhetoric of those who pointed to the old paths, itinerancy gave way to a settled ministry—at least temporarily settled!— in Methodism, and eldership shrank in significance among Disciples as the "one-man pastorate" became the norm for successful congregations.

These two drastic changes in the pragmatic polity of Methodists and Disciples are well known to anyone familiar with their history. But the point of my argument is that however well these two radical mutations may be known as historical facts, the theological and ethical understanding of the polity was slow to show a corresponding change.

As Methodists told their own sacred story, they continued to glorify the marvelous efficiency of the old itinerant system among scattered frontier communities and the self-sacrificing exploits of the circuit riders in backwoods America. Where did the young Methodist minister turn for a personal concept or image of ministry? The tradition and the moments of stirring emotional resonance in Annual Conference evoked the memory of a form of ministry that the pragmatic mind of the church had declared to be now irrelevant.

Where was one to find an ideal *model* of Methodist minister as settled pastor? One's common sense rationalized the new situation, one argued for it on pragmatic or sociological grounds. But Methodist theology, Methodist piety, Methodist tradition, and Methodist emotion still magnified the form that Methodist practice had now deliberately repudiated. The minister had to develop a new ethos in the same way that the new form had been acquired—by osmosis.

A similar problem in clarifying vocational self-identity confronted the young preacher who accepted a settled pastorate among the Disciples. Campbell had inveighed against the "kingdom of the clergy" and against salaries for ministers. For much of the nineteenth century, what "professional" leaders there were served under the title of evangelists, converting the unbaptized and setting new congregations in order. What on earth, then, was one of these new-fangled, resident, salaried pastors? The opposition in Texas didn't make things any easier by referring to them as "stall-fed preachers."[7]

For a long time, Disciples insisted that the minister was one of the elders of the congregation (but, do not forget, an elder-with-a-difference!). No sacramental distinctiveness marked this new form, for the local elders had been ordained to preside at the Lord's Table and still continued to do so while the minister received the bread and cup like any other member of the congregation. One learned to think of oneself as a pastor by associating with others in the same work, whether Disciples or ministers "of the denominations," by reading the Lyman Beecher Lectures and religious journals, and by meeting the expectations of one's members. But it was a century after the change occurred before Disciples attempted a common theological formulation of what they had so long been practicing in the broad light of day.

A remarkably similar example of such confusion occurs in scripture, in the first book of Samuel. The old tribal confederacy—rallied in times of crisis by a charismatic leader to defeat the enemy, then content that she or he should "judge" Israel until death intervened—no longer seemed sufficient to cope with the power of the Philistines, the Amalekites, and other rivals. So Samuel anointed Saul as Israel's first king.

Here was a new form. But was it good? Some thought so; in their stories God commanded Samuel to anoint Saul to the royal office. Others thought not; in their stories a faithless people demanded a king, Samuel resisted, and God at last reluctantly consented to the innovation. Which notion was right? The book does not say. The compiler preserved both traditions, and for generations these conflicting views of monarchy disturbed the peace of Israel. Most people wanted a strong king. But most of them also resented the taxes, the military draft, the levy of forced labor, and the pretensions of the royal family. And some disliked a particular ruler. Their conflicting hopes, expectations, and disapprovals rumbled through the national consciousness for generations.

In either of the two American traditions just mentioned, Methodist or Disciples ministers who wanted an understanding of their identity as settled pastors had to pull it out of the common air. From their theological tradition they had learned one concept based on a form that, in an earlier time, had corresponded to the realities of history. But in the actual world of their ministerial practice they were expected to play out quite another role, for which the denominational doctrine and ethos gave little help. They had to acquire a new self-identity in the same way the new form had been acquired, absorbing it from outside traditions.

Difficult as that task was, it was compounded by the *mixed expectations* of the constituency. For the congregation projected on their minister not only alien hopes and demands, based on their perception of the unfamiliar form as "successful" (the reason why they had adopted it). They also continued, however illogically and unconsciously, to project hopes and demands associated with the traditional form of ministry that they themselves had chosen to replace. A minister should not be concerned about personal income, for example; the circuit riders had been self-denying soldiers of the cross, and the old-time elders had served without recompense. In such a situation, what was the concept of ministry? It was a mixed bag.

Now the point of my contention is that the crisis of ministry today is precisely such a crisis in vocational self-identity as we have just reviewed, except that it is far more complex. Instead of being caught between the expectations and demands associated with two different forms, the old and the new (the traditional "horns of a dilemma"), today's minister is tangled in a thorn-thicket of expectations derived from at least half a dozen forms of ministry out of the American past and almost as many more from the current scene. In such a context, how can we speak of a concept of ministry? Confusion prevails in the mind of the minister, the congregation, the theological seminary, denominational officials, and the secular community.

A generation ago a book by two psychiatrists entitled *The Three Faces of Eve* attracted a wide readership.[8] It was a troubling story of confused identity. Eve was a woman who at different times thought of herself as strikingly different persons. She suffered indescribable agony from the conflict among these multiple personalities. As one or another assumed dominance, Eve became that person, enduring the unique pain peculiar to that identity. It was a new "face." She was not playing with masks, but suffered the misery of uncertainty as to who she really was. Only through long and patient effort did her therapists succeed in helping her climb to a level of self-understanding that enabled her to discover her true identity.

It should be clear by now why the title first chosen for this book, while still in manuscript, was *The Many Faces of Ministry*.[9] For many a minister today is hopelessly confused by conflicting expectations derived from a number of quite different forms of ministry. There is no escape from the pain until one discovers for oneself one's true ministerial identity. This book is designed to assist that process.

An Invitation to Reflection

My second affirmation as historian is theoretical, a central item of faith with those who practice my discipline. For we who spend our lives in the study of the past hold that the story of any development, honestly told, clarifies understanding and thus facilitates responsible action. That is the working faith of the historical profession. In a sense the historian is a kind of social psychotherapist, trying to help the patient bring up from the unconscious those buried memories of a long-forgotten past that may be the festering source of a current problem. This second affirmation is simply a particular application of that item of faith.

I am firmly convinced that reflection on the history of ministry in America will help us to understand our confused situation and thus to come to terms with it. I cannot prove this assertion, but you can test it as we think through the prevailing models of ministry in American history and the expectations emanating from them that still swirl about us.

Three terms recur throughout the following pages: *form, concept,* and *model*. By *form* I mean to designate a particular pattern of ministry as it was actually practiced. It is a behavioral phenomenon, subject to observation by historians, sociologists, anthropologists, and other empirical scientists. By *concept* I refer to the ideas, expectations (both positive and negative), and emotional responses that attach to a given form. The term embraces both the theology and the ethos associated with it. The term *model* includes both of the other two terms: the *form* and the attendant *concepts*.

Such a model represents what Max Weber would have called an "ideal type."[10] Alasdair McIntyre uses the term "social character" to designate a vocational form with its attendant concepts. It molds the ethos of the person in the given role, and, because of its importance to the life of a period, becomes a door into the understanding of the people and institutions of an era.[11]

While not every minister before our time would have conformed precisely to one ideal type alone, I propose that the expectation of the people and the minister's own sense of social identity tended to coalesce in one or another of the models—until our own time, when the melange of expectations deriving from the plethora of models left church members confused and ministers frustrated.

Clearly none of the forms emerged as the invention of a lone genius, but rather as the product of a generation or more of ministers and faithful Christians, responding either intuitively or analytically—or both—to a new situation and the clamorous needs of their time. As emphases suggestive of a new form of ministry proved more and more effective, increasing numbers of ministers would devote their energies to them and begin to articulate these concepts, with the result that a new model was established. It is unlikely that any one person today possesses sufficient insight or knowledge of the new world now emerging to be able to prescribe a model of ministry likely to become dominant in the twenty-first century. But all of us may improve the effectiveness of our service by giving thought to the matter.

Form, concept, model—these are elusive notions, concerning which social psychologists and the staffs of the national polling organizations might collect data subject to statistical analysis. That I have not done. My formulations of the various models in our American experience derive from observation and reflection.

A particular concept of ministry can crystallize into *doctrine*, which the denomination confessing it may come to regard as an essential of the faith. Consequently the separated churches have given their attention primarily to theology when discussing the issues regarding ministry that presumably separate them.[12]

If my analysis is correct, however, we may well conclude that the truly devastating differences in the concept of ministry obtain *within* denominations, congregations, and ministers themselves, and that in this respect our separated churches, whatever their doctrines of ministry, suffer distressingly common problems. This condition arises because the expectations associated with a particular concept of ministry loom larger in practice than does its theological component. While not wishing to ignore that theological component of each model of ministry,[13] this book will emphasize the expectations that accompany it in practice. Our concern is not abstract propositions, but the way in which each model has left a deposit of expectations that often litter the ground on which the minister tries to serve.

Each form with its attendant concepts I shall designate by a single word, e.g., Saint. For emphasis and clarity I capitalize the term for each of the dominant forms of ministry. Each major part of the book concentrates on a given century, with an introduction to the period, a chapter for each of four predominant models of ministry in that time, with special attention to the way in which concepts associated with it affect ministry today, and a conclusion augmented by summary reflection.

Because the earliest churches in America inherited a Christian tradition already long and varied, and because experience here has been complex from the beginning, it is doubtful that any sizable proportion of ministers ever perfectly embodied one model alone, with no influence from the others. Still, I try in each case to describe the form in its ideal purity or integrity, even at the risk of caricature, for the concepts associated with it often presuppose such purity as a fact of history; the power of the expectation is not limited by the way things really are.

The ambiguities inherent in each model arise because it is a human construct, i.e., an emergent in history, and therefore the outcome of a particular set of circumstances. In these ambiguities we see illustrated anew Dante's perception that our particular vices are the defects of our particular virtues.[14] I therefore commend no model as perfect, nor do I totally reject any—though I may come close in one or two instances.

My intention, then, is to trace the dominant models of ministry that at one time or another, in one tradition or another, have prevailed in America. We shall observe how each particular form related to the society in which it flourished, and what new historical trends caused it to wane. Our primary concern is to inquire how the various concepts of ministry inform contemporary church and society, as well as the outlook of ministers themselves, to confuse or to clarify, to accuse or to reassure.

Finally, I hope to suggest the task that confronts those of us ordained to the high calling of minister. That task is no less than a responsible effort to determine the dominant emphasis in our own model of ministry, to appropriate from other models such elements as may be supportive, to acknowledge more explicitly the validity—or at least the rationale—for the expectations derived from other forms that people project on us, and to decide how we will articulate honestly and persuasively the concept of ministry that commands us and reject with clarity and pastoral understanding those alien elements which we cannot accept.

PART

I

Ministry Cast
in an
American
Mold

THE EIGHTEENTH-CENTURY SETTING

From that October day in 1492 when Christopher Columbus planted a great cross, along with the arms of Castile and Aragon, on the island he named Holy Savior—San Salvador—colonialism prevailed in the New World for more than half its subsequent history, the imperial powers of Christian Europe laying claim to various parts. The incursion of Europeans into the Western hemisphere brought with it exploitation of the land and oppression of the peoples, yoked with an impressive effort to convert the oppressed to the faith of the oppressor.

In the service of that faith, Christian ministry established itself in the Western hemisphere in a variety of forms. For the most part, these derived from the common heritage of Christendom or, even more broadly, of religion in general. But though not invented in the eighteenth century, the peculiar circumstances of time and place cast them in a distinctive American mold. These heroic models of two hundred years ago made a large impression on the colonial scene and left a sizable legacy of expectations. Their mummies and ghosts still haunt us.

The variety of forms that ministry assumed derived in part from the strange diversity of cultures striving to gain a foothold along the seaboards, in the valleys of the great rivers, and at the edge of the wilderness. Recall the territorial claims of the imperial powers, along with their religious professions and that of the peoples whom they subjugated.

The Rival Empires...

At the end of the eighteenth century, Spain still ruled the greater part of the Western hemisphere: the major islands of the Caribbean, the bulk of the territory now comprising the contiguous forty-eight states, Mexico, Central America, and most of South America. This great Catholic power ceded Louisiana to France in 1800 and the Floridas to the United States in 1819; it lost the vast land it called Mexico to the free nation that took that name in 1823. Mexico in turn lost Texas to the Lone Star Republic in 1836 and ceded that great stretch of territory comprising New Mexico and California, along with parts of Colorado, Arizona, Utah, and Nevada, to the United States in 1848.

From the beginning, the Spanish crown undertook to convert the peoples of the colonies to the religion of the cross. The first effective patterns of Christian ministry in the New World were established by the priests and padres in the service of the Catholic kings Ferdinand and Isabella and their successors.

The other great Catholic power was France, which claimed the valleys of the St. Lawrence, the Great Lakes, and the Mississippi. In 1763 France ceded Canada and all its lands east of the Mississippi, except for New Orleans, to Britain, and in 1803 Napoleon sold Louisiana to the United States, giving the young nation a vast interior empire reaching to the Continental Divide. Wherever the French explorers and trappers went, priests of the Jesuits or other missionary orders went with them, sometimes even preceding them.

Preoccupied with civil wars over dynastic ambitions and religious claims, England came late to the race for empire, but its internal struggles impelled many of its people to flee to the New World, there to establish homes that became permanent settlements. Many of these adventurers and refugees brought their pastors with them—Anglicans, Roman Catholics, and dissenters of various persuasions. England yielded its lands east of the Mississippi and south of the Great Lakes to the United States in 1783, but pursued its dreams of a Pacific empire nearly halfway through the nineteenth century. Not until 1846 did the English-speaking rivals settle the question of the Oregon boundary—and settle it amicably at that, conceding to the United States a vast domain that includes western Montana and Wyoming, along with all of Idaho, Washington, and Oregon.

Unwilling to forgo the prize for piety or for greed, other Christian powers entered into the contest for empire. For a time, Holland boasted impressive estates and towns along the Hudson, but lost them to England in the 1660s—not, however, before leaving churches and ministers of the Reformed faith on these shores. Sweden likewise undertook a colonial venture in the valley of the Delaware but lost out to the Dutch in 1665, after having established some permanent settlements committed to Lutheranism. Early in the nineteenth century, Russian fur traders worked their way down the Pacific coast, establishing claim to land as far south as California and building great timber churches that still convey the mystic faith of their Orthodox founders. Most of these settlements soon gave way to their imperial rivals, but Russia held Alaska until 1867, when it was sold to the United States.

...and Their Victims

Overrun by conquerors from Christian Europe, the scattered peoples already living in the Western hemisphere found themselves decimated by a combination of forces they were not equipped to deal with: a more advanced technology, superior weaponry, unfamiliar concepts of land ownership and treaties, the continued violation by the new powers of these solemn agreements, the destruction of their food supply, the enclosure of the open range, epidemics of hitherto unknown diseases, the cynical use of hard liquor to reduce them to dependence and helplessness, and, concurrent with all these, well-intentioned efforts to convert them from their ancestral faith.

Some Native Americans undertook to establish a dignified coexistence with the invaders and some put up spirited and heroic resistance, which was finally broken by the United States Army in a series of "Indian Wars" ending in 1891. With much of their population annihilated and the economic base for their traditional culture destroyed, their old way of life was irrevocably lost. Despite all that, their ancestral religion persists, either as a distinctive faith or as a strain of peculiar coloration within a profession of Christianity. Tribal rituals and beliefs even appear to be making a comeback, as the dominant white society increasingly accepts the implications of pluralism and concedes its guilt toward the peoples who inhabited the continent before the coming of the colonial powers.[1]

From the outset, the major economic problem in exploiting the riches of the Americas was the supply of labor. As aristocrats by aspiration if not by birth, the European conquerors undertook through their conquests to gain admission to the privileged class. Following unsuccessful attempts to turn the Native Americans into serfs after the feudal pattern they had known in Europe, they began importing blacks kidnapped from Africa to serve as slaves. The oppressive institution spread throughout the colonies, as Portuguese, Dutch, English, and Yankee captains grew rich on the trade. So there came to these shores unwilling immigrants from Africa, brutally cut off from familial, cultural, and religious roots, all but dehumanized by the attitudes and institutions of those who held them captive.

For a time the European colonists made little effort to convert the slaves to Christianity, alleging their lack of an immortal soul or fearing that baptizing them into the faith might necessitate their emancipation. In time, for reasons that defy logic, the people in bondage became an earnest Christian community. Both before and after their profession of biblical faith, important elements of the African spiritual tradition persisted. It would appear that some aspects of "ministry" in African tribal religion—though not in Islam, as far as I know—continued in the black church.[2]

From Uniformity to Diversity

Within any particular beachhead of European empire in the New World, a uniform pattern of ministry tended to prevail, since each outpost of settlement undertook to bring over the essential features of the society from which it came, including its established church. Diversity in form appears most strikingly in the contrast between imported and indigenous religion. But ministry soon developed greater complexity in the British colonies.

Granting a considerable degree of religious freedom from the outset, Maryland, Rhode Island, and Pennsylvania consequently experienced increasing variation in ministries. But by the eighteenth century, some decades before the Revolution, an explosion of religious diversity occurred throughout the colonies. A number of elements contributed to it: a large increase in immigration, with people coming from many nations; the movement of settlers through natural corridors provided by river valleys, which ignored the neat geometry of the colonial boundaries described in the charters; the rise of new movements within Protestantism; the slow growth of toleration. Up and down the Atlantic seaboard, Anglicans, Presbyterians, Congregationalists, Baptists, Quakers, Roman Catholics, Lutherans, Moravians, Jews, and others gained new footholds in close proximity to one another.

If this all too brief sketch of the colonial religious scene seems distressingly complex, it has served its purpose. For out of this welter of competing cultures and diverse forms of religion came the models of ministry that first prevailed in America. Though we may seldom give thought to the matter, our concepts of vocation and the expectations with which people confront their ministers today are haunted by these mummies and ghosts of ministry past.

Forms of Colonial Ministry

From our perspective, as we survey three and one-half centuries of colonial religion on this continent, the diversities of ministry overwhelm us. Yet without doing violence to the remarkable variety, we may perceive a limited number of basic types that recur with only slight differences from denomination to denomination and even from religion to religion. In eighteenth-century America, the major concepts of ministry clustered around four such forms. Rather than the antiseptic designations employed for technical studies in anthropology and history of religion, I use familiar Christian terms with some emotional resonance in the tradition, intending, however, sufficient elasticity to cover similar religious offices in various faiths, to some of which the chosen term will be foreign.

These four eighteenth-century types are: *Saint, Priest, Master,* and *Awakener*.

Model 1

SAINT

Saint means *holy one*. That is the etymology. In such a primal sense the word here designates that person to whom a given society looks for ministry precisely because it perceives in the woman or the man evident marks of holiness, of having been touched by the divine. In Judaism and early Christianity, holiness had an essential ethical component, with emphasis on style of life. Our English versions of the scriptures use the terms *holy woman* and *man of God* with this sense. Yet both here and in religions that may link ethics less tightly with spirituality, the Saint is perceived as one who lives especially "close to God."

Understanding sanctity in this biblical way, the eighteenth century was less reticent than our own in using the language of holiness or godliness[1] and in regarding the role of living example as a crucial element in the ministry of one who is in obvious communication with the spiritual realm. In this emphasis on lifestyle, the holy man or woman perpetuates the earliest known form of ministry.

This oldest of ministries goes back to the hunting and gathering peoples before the invention of writing. In eighteenth-century North America, most of the indigenous population, both Indian and Eskimo, continued at this stage, as had many of the unwilling immigrants from Africa until seized and shipped as slaves. Scholars commonly designate such an acknowledged holy one among the archaic peoples as *shaman*, a title used by Siberian tribes ethnically and culturally related to the American Indians.

The shaman bore the mark of divine vocation to ministry, commonly received during the crisis of an illness. Its essence was the capacity for ecstasy, the release of the soul from the limitations of the flesh to a direct engagement with the spirits of the unseen world. The shaman's ministry consisted of crossing the rainbow bridge to accompany the soul of the dying to its final abode or journeying to the unseen realm to bring back the soul of one who had evidently just died. The prominence of this ministry of healing gave rise to the term *medicine woman* or *medicine man*.

The first Europeans to encounter such shamanic types looked upon them with hostility and condescension, considering them demon-worshipers who preyed upon the superstitions of a childlike folk and engaged in patent trickery in order to demonstrate their powers. Only rarely before the twentieth century did outside observers discern in at least some shamans those remarkable gifts of spiritual sensitivity and insight that characterize some of their number. Perceptive scholars have come to recognize the shamanic vision and narrative of experiences in the other world as an important source of primitive mythology, art, poetry, ethics, and religion.[2] Fortunately, some tribes of American Indians managed to resist the onslaught of the European and American intruders until the coming of modern anthropologists, historians of literature, and historians of religion. As a result we have some knowledge of the ministry of shamans among the Native American peoples.

Our information concerning indigenous religious leadership among eighteenth-century blacks in America is far more limited because of the depredations of the slave trade. Captives brought from Africa were separated from family and tribe, cut off from culture and religious tradition, overseen with brutality and suspicion. Who was there to note with sympathetic insight and record with sensitivity the visions of the spiritual genius among them to whom the call came in the manner of the ancestral shamans?

Yet, while little effort was spent in trying to convert the slaves until the beginning of the eighteenth century, some black preachers arose among their oppressed people in late colonial times. Though we know the names of only a few black religious leaders before the national period, some were already demonstrating impressive power. Bishop Asbury prized the assistance of Harry Hosier—widely known as "Black Harry"—as colleague and exhorter, and there were others who spoke with great effectiveness to their fellow slaves.[3]

We may fairly surmise that an important element in the charismatic power of such Christian leaders among the slaves was the familiar mark of holiness which had everywhere characterized the shaman. A striking trait of black preaching, as long as we have known anything of it, has been the preacher's gift of "vision," the ability to perceive and memorably describe the reality of the spiritual world. The typical dialogic style of preaching termed "call and response" evoked answering participation from the hearers as the heightened feeling and natural eloquence of their orator caught them up into the spiritual world of the preacher's own experience.

In the case of the Spanish padres and nuns, the title Saint denotes holiness after the pattern long established in Christian tradition: an experience bringing a conviction of divine vocation and a response of unreserved self-giving in that complete obedience to the way of Christ intended to prepare one for the beatific vision.

The spiritual quest of the medieval monks had led to a life of withdrawal from the world and to the discipline of monastic cell and chapel. But the seekers after holiness who came to the New World belonged to the serving orders—Franciscan, Dominican, Jesuit, Recollect, Sulpician. With a renunciation as complete as that of any anchorite or monk before them, the friars and nuns went into the world they had renounced in order to serve humanity by preaching the gospel and working in missions, schools, and hospitals. If they fell short of the Christian perfection they sought it was in an assumption they shared with Europeans generally, perceiving themselves as members of an advanced Christian race intended by God to teach and rule and civilize an ignorant, childlike, savage people. As a result they did not hesitate to exercise domination over their charges in a transplanted feudal regime, living at a level of comfort and gentility which few Indians could ever hope to achieve and sometimes imposing on them rules and punishments far too harsh to comport with our gentler notions of sainthood. But the cruelty we perceive as a personal fault was rather a flaw in the context in which they had been formed.

Nevertheless scores of nuns and friars, French as well as Spanish, gave themselves in heroic devotion to serve the children of the American wilderness. Stand in an old mission in California or Arizona and read the simple inscriptions on the stones in the crypt or the churchyard—a name, perhaps a birthplace half a world away (Seville, Barcelona, some country town), dates of birth and death. Some of these saints lived to advanced years. Others perished before they were thirty. But all renounced self and home and kindred to give themselves in service. One may read the record along the California chain of missions, in Arizona, New Mexico, Texas, Florida, throughout Latin America, and for the French in Quebec, Montreal, St. Louis, and New Orleans.

From the outset, such holy men and women rose to the defense of the Indians—Antonio de Montesinos within twenty years of "discovery," Bartolomeo de las Casas later in the sixteenth century, Junipero Serra in the eighteenth. Padre Serra was forging the first links in the California chain of missions in the very decade that the thirteen

Atlantic colonies won their independence from England. A naive statue of this man at Mission San Gabriel shows him in a Christlike role, with Indian children gathered in his protective arms.

The uprooting of the indigenous peoples from their villages to a mission compound, the pursuit of those who ran away, the flogging of those who were caught, all strike us as they did the Indians—as cruelty ill becoming one human being toward another, more befitting a bully than a saint.[4] But the padres saw themselves as divinely appointed to the task of Christianizing and civilizing a childlike folk and responsible for employing the disciplinary measures commonly used in their time by rulers and parents. The presumption that the faith they professed and the culture they represented should rightly supplant all others, no matter how arrogant or unjustified it may seem in our radically different context, was axiomatic to the "civilized mind" of their day. The cruelty we perceive as a personal fault was rather a flaw in the context that had formed them.

We see, of course—we superior, cynical, unholy moderns—that the missionary enterprise was inextricably linked with imperialism, that the missionaries deliberately or unwittingly prepared the way for the advance of that so-called civilization that would obliterate the Native American way of life. We recognize that the missionaries went to the whip for discipline, even while thinking of themselves as defenders of the mission Indians against the political authorities. Granted, the padres failed of perfection according to the standards of our hindsight. Granted, events took a course they had neither desired nor anticipated. (Remember Theodore White's dictum that history is the record of what happens to good intentions.) Yet for all their limitations, they brought a humane and idealistic touch into a dramatic clash of cultures and sought to grace the life of their time with the holiness they so earnestly desired.

Not a few friars suffered violent deaths, unresisting, in ultimate devotion to their faith. The martyrologies recounting the death of Juan de Padilla in New Mexico or of Jean de Brebeuf at the hands of the Iroquois are wholly consistent with those of the early Christian centuries on which they were modeled. That self-giving was the ultimate mark of the holiness they sought, and places them firmly in the category of Saint.

Protestantism also had its saints, their holiness marked for the most part by a sobriety of life and restraint of manner which accorded with the distinctive heritage of the Reformation.

In eighteenth-century New England the early severity had softened since the ardor of the Great Migration, and the prosperity engendered by the Protestant virtues had lured the newer generation into more secular preoccupations and even delights. But despite the compromises of the Halfway Covenant, New England preserved the memory of the Pilgrims and especially of that great company of saints who began arriving in Massachusetts in 1630 to establish a Holy Commonwealth.

The Puritan requirement of an experimental knowledge of election as a condition of church membership produced a laity and a ministry with a powerful sense of vocation and evident signs of it. If their subsequent engagement with the spiritual world was dominantly intellectual—we should say dogmatic—rather than mystical, their preoccupation with things divine was total and their delight in the ways of God their supreme source of joy.

Even in the eighteenth century the ministers in this tradition had too lively a sense of sin to regard themselves without reproach, but they idealized their clerical predecessors, as Cotton Mather did in his *Magnalia Christi Americana,* and as Samuel Danforth had already done in his celebrated election sermon of 1670, *Errand into the Wilderness.* Unworthy though one knew oneself to be, there was no question but that the model for ministry in the Puritan tradition was the Man of God, the embodiment of holiness, the Visible Saint. The title page for a volume of John Cotton's sermons published in 1659 had attributed them to "that holy and judicious man of God."[5]

Perhaps the closest Christian approach to the open spiritual aristocracy of shamanism was found in the early Quakers of England and America. Rejecting traditional churchly concepts of ministerial orders and ordination, members of the Society of Friends sought the inner light and accepted the ministry of all those in whom that light had evidently shone. Their worship consisted of waiting on the Spirit, their instruction of listening to those whom the Spirit moved to speak to the others. Their daily walk followed the ways of simplicity and gentleness, marks of that holiness set forth in the Sermon on the Mount.[6]

Their ministry of testifying to the Spirit involved women as well as men. In the seventeenth century George Fox, the founder of the Society, had conducted a spiritual mission in the colonies. In the fateful year of 1776, responding to a call received in a vision, a young woman in Rhode Island named Jemima Wilkinson began to prophesy to "a dying and sinful world." For forty-three years she continued her ministry as "Publick Universal Friend," a living embodiment of holiness.[7]

Another powerful force for holiness was Pietism, a movement to replace the barrenness of Protestant scholasticism with a deeper spirituality, demonstrated in a lifestyle befitting disciples of Jesus, sustained by prayer and Bible study in small groups, and expressed in a new fervor for evangelization throughout the world.

Pietism came to America in various forms, most notably in those companies of Moravians who settled in Georgia, Pennsylvania, and North Carolina. Like the Quakers they pressed the call to holiness upon all who fell under their influence and obviously expected it of those who practiced ministry among them. Count Nicholas von Zinzendorf himself came to the colonies in 1741, preaching a warm and demanding spirituality and calling unsuccessfully for the union of all German-speaking Christians in the New World. Perhaps the largest contribution of the Moravians to the spread of scriptural holiness was their profound influence on John Wesley and, through him, on the development of Methodism in Britain and America. But the real story of American Methodism comes in the nineteenth century.

The most spectacular manifestation of the marks of holiness in colonial Protestant ministers came in the Great Awakening. In 1734 revival burst upon Northampton, Massachusetts, as its people trembled under the preaching of Jonathan Edwards. While Edwards himself was an intellectual who wholly integrated mystical inclination with the rational discipline of a powerful theological mind, the excitement which erupted among the people during his preaching broke through the accustomed restraints of social discipline and rational control. The enthusiasm of direct spiritual encounter with the convicting and converting Spirit of God continued for some months, and spread throughout the colonies. In the same decade the celebrated London preacher George Whitefield began his preaching tours of America, speaking to vast crowds from Georgia north to New England, winning many converts, and releasing shock waves of religious excitement.

Preachers less stable than Whitefield and less intellectual than Edwards got into the act, and the antics of these fanatics drew criticism from cooler heads in the churches, ironically arousing intense emotion among the rationalists. From that time on, American ministers have tended to register with one camp or the other, and only a few have managed the powerful synthesis of the spiritual with the intellectual that characterized early Puritanism and Edwards himself.

In 1740 Gilbert Tennent preached a fateful sermon on "The Danger of an Unconverted Ministry."[8] In it he insisted on the absolute need for a personal experience of conversion and call for anyone undertaking to preach. He admonished laypeople to examine the sermons of their ministers and, if they found them lacking in this essential, to seek out for themselves ministers who possessed the evident marks of holiness. Charles Chauncy countered with a sermon "Enthusiasm Described and Cautioned Against," but Tennent's plea continued to impress the greater body of public opinion in American religion, it would appear, even in the twentieth century.

Tennent's emphasis introduced a vigorous assertiveness into the expectations of American church members regarding their ministers: "Do they offer what *I* value?" Even in circles where holiness has evaporated, that assertiveness nevertheless continues. The American minister is under pressure to meet the people's expectations.

Reflections on the Saint

Whatever our personal experience of vocation may or may not have been, whatever our personal set of priorities for emphasis by the minister, whatever our personal definition of spirituality, we have to accept the fact that the model of the Saint, the holy one called in an experience of crisis and continuing to manifest the marks of direct contact with God, has released powerful expectations in American Christianity. Ever since the eighteenth century—in fact, ever since the days of our hunting-and-gathering ancestors—many people have understood the shaman or Saint to be the essential model for religious leadership. They want to know that their minister is in direct touch with God and that God deals directly with and through the person who claims to speak in the divine name.

The popular mind sometimes resorts to trivial, even irrelevant canons of spirituality that it deems authentic. A widespread prejudice against read sermons or prayers or printed liturgies prompts churchgoers to ask: "How can your words come from your heart if you have to read them from a book or a worship bulletin?" Some people demand signs—miracles, twitches, shouting, prancing, a holy tone, an unctuous manner, the use of particular phrases, speaking in tongues, the gift of healing—as the mark of sanctity. A surprising number of church members, and even of outsiders, seems certain that the minister's prayers will avail when there is no other hope.

Most devastating to the minister is the demand for perfection of life on her or his part, accompanied by an unreadiness to accept the ministry of one whose human weakness or limitation betrays imperfection—flouting the rules of pietistic lifestyle, undergoing divorce, falling before carnal temptation.

This concept of the minister as perfect flies in the face of universal human experience and the Christian doctrine of human nature. Nevertheless it remains a powerful force, imposing great loneliness on the minister who tries to fit the mold. It makes many ministers hesitant to acknowledge before their people their own humanity, limitations, and struggles. Thus it robs preaching of that element of honesty required for any proper conveyal of the gospel and turns ministerial careers into a nervous game of "Let's pretend." It lays on many a parson a heavy burden of guilt and amplifies a clerical sense of need for a support group of one's peers in which one can honestly speak the secrets of the heart without fear of evoking disillusion or reprisal.

It is natural for a modern minister to cry out against the popular expectations and to lament the widespread practice that Langdon Gilkey has characterized as making the contemporary minister into the congregation's scapegoat.[9] By all means, let us honestly and kindly disabuse the people of those faulty notions which would persuade us to try to live a lie within their imaginations.

Yet it must be added that not a few introspective Protestants find themselves attracted to a ministerial vocation under the illusion that it will offer greater opportunity than a secular career for cultivating their personal spiritual lives. Such passive-dependent types seem to imagine the church as an ever-watchful mother who will protect them from the harsh demands of the cruel world outside. Anyone who has served in the ministry even for a brief time could disabuse such dreamers of their illusions; neither the Catholic priesthood nor the Protestant ministry offers much opportunity to withdraw from society in order to pursue the quest for holiness. The would-be monk must seek out a monastery.

Even so, people look for signs of holiness in their ministers, despite their seeming unawareness that this popular desire necessarily conflicts with other demands they make—for skillful management of the institution, for outstanding "production" to improve the statistics. Moreover, the discomfort that some people feel in the presence of a minister arises from the ancient perception of the holy woman or man of God as someone clearly different from themselves, whose manner of life casts their own under judgment.

Despite all the pressures and problems just mentioned, the model of the Saint is not obsolete. Consider the appeal of the guru to thousands, even in our secular society. Because a "holy man" is such a novelty in these cynical times, the media frequently bestow instant celebrity status, and not a few exotic "saints" have milked their curiosity value for their own financial advantage. But may not that very possibility inform us that many people still find themselves attracted to a person who, like the shaman, gives evidence of communication with the divine and speaks a spiritual wisdom at odds with the secular axioms of our existence?

The twentieth-century church has not been without its saints. With only a little thought one can readily name a score of prominent contemporaries whose lives have borne the mark of holiness: Pope John XXIII, Thomas Merton, Dorothy Day, Sadhu Sundar Singh, Mother Teresa, Archbishop Romero, Dom Helder Camara, Dietrich Bonhoeffer, Dag Hammarskjold, Muriel Lester, Suzanne de Dietrich, Georgia Harkness, Howard Thurman, Benjamin Mays, Clarence Jordan, Alan Hunter, Toyohiko Kagawa, Mae Yoho Ward, Kirby Page. The ideal of holiness, even within the life of the world, continues to exert its appeal.

At its best the model attracts us at our best. A group of ministers from a western state, recently asked to note their ideals for their own ministry (without prompting as to a desired answer), testified to the continuing appeal of the vision of saintliness. More than any other concern, they wrote down something like "proclaiming Christ in faithfulness." And immediately after that came "communion with God" as an expression of spirituality and of the desire for personal growth.

No program of ministerial education can produce without fail the authentic Saint, defined in accordance with shamanic marks of holiness.[10] The experience of ecstasy that brings on the crisis of vocation or renewed contact with the spirit-world may be induced in some persons by long periods of fasting and prayer, by the excitement of the ritual dance or the camp meeting, by the ingestion of certain drugs. But it is a different mode of perception from that of the classroom, where knowledge of the tradition is conveyed and critical thinking is developed.

The medieval church worked out patterns of priestly formation that sought to shape the personality of the future minister—whose essential holiness, let us remember, was imparted by the church through ordination—into a mold formed by expectations of saintliness. Much of this discipline was adapted from the monastic rule. Most contemporary Protestant seminaries confess their inability to achieve observable results along such lines; they may even disavow the idea of "formation," but sometimes with wringing of hands and a confession of frustration. By contrast, a few schools for the training of ministers major in stamping their students with certain traditional signs of "holiness"—a recognized vocabulary, mode of dress, lifestyle, or clerical manner. A widespread popular understanding of theological seminaries seems to assume the prevalence of this latter pattern.

If the difficulties and ambiguities prompt us to dismiss for ourselves the demand of holiness, to discard the essential element in the model of the Saint, we diminish our ministry. It has then lost something of primordial importance.

Model 2

PRIEST

The second major form around which concepts of ministry still cluster in America is the figure of the Priest.

As noted in our introductory chapter, a crucial shift occurred in the religion of the archaic world as shamanism gave way to priesthood. This development occurred as agriculture succeeded hunting and gathering. With the building of cities and the growth of kingship in antiquity, priesthood grew in importance. City, monarchy, and temple emerged in mutual interdependence and flourished together.

Holiness, the gift of communicating with the divine and making manifest its power, was still the essential mark of ministry. But as we have seen, holiness now flowed through the religious institution, and it was the institution that declared the Priest holy. Signs of the special priestly status and function included distinctive dress (in daily life as well as in religious ceremony), a distinctive mode of sexuality (ranging from virginity to sacred prostitution, from castration to symbolic marriage), and an archaic style of speech.

The priests conducted the ceremonies believed to appease the gods, to invest the coronation of the king with divine favor, to bring down the blessings of heaven on the city-state and its people. They gave instruction in right behavior, with warnings of dire consequences for those who violated the code. They conducted rituals for the stages of passage in a person's life and for regaining the favor of the offended gods. They composed and conducted the liturgies for the sacred observances. They also taught the mysteries of religion considered appropriate for the laity to know.

Priests constituted the first educated class, for the practical demands that society made on religion led to their acquisition of considerable learning. They developed the art of writing and amassed

29

an impressive knowledge of mathematics, astronomy, agriculture, history, medicine, law, and stagecraft, as well as of ritual and theology. They made significant contributions to the development of the arts, especially music and architecture. Priesthood was one of the earliest professions, though admission to it was frequently restricted to members of a particular clan or group. To repeat an earlier point, entrance did not require an ecstatic experience of deity or mystical sense of call. More likely it derived from birth into a priestly family and from an extended course of education (or indoctrination).

In the ancient world, orders of female priests were common, as well as orders made up exclusively of males, but particular states might well limit the office to one sex or the other.

In eighteenth-century America priesthood no longer flourished among the indigenous peoples. It had reached impressive levels of wealth and splendor in Mexico, Central America, and Peru before the coming of the Spaniards. Though the conquistadores devoted their utmost energies to pillaging objects made of gold, no matter how sacred, and to destroying the magnificent temples and other artifacts used in worship, some of the beautiful sacred texts from the Maya and the Aztecs escaped destruction and are now available in translation.[1] Archaeologists continue to recover precious objects from those vanished cultures, including religious texts.

Among the Indians north of the Rio Grande, priesthood, though not universal, had begun to emerge in a number of tribes.[2] It held no place in the religious customs brought to America by the blacks from Africa.

Christian priesthood in its medieval form came to these shores in various mutations. Roman Catholic priests held an important place in the Spanish and French efforts to establish footholds in the New World. For the most part the earliest arrivals were a special brand of priests, not so much parish pastors as chaplains to expeditions of exploration and conquest, or missionaries to the Native Americans. Having experienced an intense sense of calling and having dedicated their lives to service in one of the preaching orders, they had been granted ordination in order to carry out that commitment.

In the English colonies, Roman priests found acceptance only in Maryland and Pennsylvania, where they were permitted to minister, working primarily among their own people in parish church and chapel rather than in an apostolate to the Indians. Similarly, the Orthodox priests in the Russian settlements on the California coast directed their ministry primarily to their own people, although some missionary work was undertaken in Alaska.

Anglican priests in Virginia, the Carolinas, Maryland, and New York, with a scattered presence elsewhere, also served as parish clergy. They tended to be more Protestant in outlook than most Anglicans have been since the Oxford Movement of the nineteenth century. After the work undertaken by agents of the Society for the Propagation of the Gospel met with minimal success among the Indians and the black slaves, the missionaries turned increasingly to preaching among the settlers of British descent. Traveling throughout the British colonies, they established Anglican churches not only in areas destitute of ministers but even in New England, the very citadel of Puritanism.

One of the chief problems of the colonial church was the difficulty of securing an adequate supply of qualified and effective ministers. The shortage of priests was especially painful among the Anglican parishes. Moreover, a striking contrast with the normative situation of Christian priests elsewhere marked the priesthood in the eighteenth-century colonies. Nowhere in the vast region now occupied by the United States was a bishop to be found, nor had there ever been an episcopal see in these parts. Now, according to catholic ecclesiology, the bishop as successor to the apostles is the true pastor of all the faithful within his diocese, and the parish priest is delegated to represent him in congregations that he can visit only occasionally. Here that doctrine was strained to the breaking point.

The French and Spanish at least sent bishops to the New World, but their sees were in the Caribbean, Mexico, or Canada. The bishop of Havana made a pastoral visitation to the converts in Florida in the sixteenth century, and the bishop of Durango in Mexico traveled north into New Mexico in the eighteenth century. But none came to California. The French established no cathedral in colonial Louisiana. A Russian archimandrite in the Aleutians, called back to Irkutsk for consecration as bishop of Alaska, drowned while attempting to return by sea to his diocese.[3] All the Anglican churches and priests in the colonies belonged to the enlarged diocese of the bishop of London. With his many responsibilities in the capital of the British Empire, he had his hands full and consequently managed to spare little attention for the condition of ministry on the far side of the Atlantic.

American priesthood developed, then, in an anomalous situation. Canon law forbade priests to fulfill certain essential sacerdotal functions, reserving these to the bishop, for he alone possessed the fullness of priesthood. But the bishop was able only rarely among the Spanish, never among the French or the British, to visit this corner of his diocese and here fulfill his pastoral ministry. In order to receive confirmation or ordination a Christian living in the colonies destined to become part of the United States had to travel to Mexico or England or France. In such circumstances the fabric of sacramental religion was strained to the point of unraveling.

For the most part the distant bishops failed to understand the situation in the colonies. One particularly striking example illustrates the problem. About A.D. 1000 a lonely priest among the Norse in Greenland had sent an inquiry to the pope asking if rye bread and beer might be used for the eucharist since wheat and grapes would not grow there and the supply ships were often delayed in coming. Rome answered no, thus condemning a people whose religious life centered in the sacrament to months, even years, without it. But how could the far-off bishop surrounded by glittering chapels and crowds of priests in a land rich in corn and wine comprehend a situation so alien to everything he had ever known?

Not only did the distant bishops fail to understand; they often had little interest in the churches in the colonies. Even when they tried to exercise their pastoral responsibility, their mode of doing so was inevitably that of an authoritarian administrator insisting on obedience rather than that of a shepherd who knew his sheep, not to mention the dangerous terrain of their wanderings. Thus the American priest lacked that close relationship with a pastoral bishop that forms the heart of priestly ministry.

Fear and resentment of arbitrary episcopal *power*—for so many previous centuries exercised in affairs of state as well as within the church—gave rise in the British colonies to rabid anti-catholicism and even forthright anticlericalism. Any slight rumor that a bishop was about to be sent to these shores threw consternation into colonial hearts.

Despite such difficulties, the colonial priest served the continuity of the church in a ministry of great symbolic force. Not only did his office assert the oneness of the worshiping congregation with the mystical body of Christian faithful reaching back through the apostles to the Lord Jesus Christ himself, but his ministrations also linked the pilgrims and exiles in these remote parts with the familiar rituals of home. A bronze bas-relief at Jamestown depicts the Reverend Robert Hunt serving the eucharist to the colonists on the first Lord's Day after their landing in 1607, and the vine-covered brick tower of the old church still stands as witness to the importance of priestly ministry to those first Virginians. That ministry centered in an ordered liturgy and the sacraments.

Priestly ministry required education in liturgics, theology, and canon law, as well as examination by the bishop and ordination at his hands. It was exceedingly difficult therefore to raise up a ministry from the Christian community in America, and the long voyage to

England could be perilous. Early in the eighteenth century a young American just ordained by the bishop of London was lost at sea when his ship went down in the Atlantic.

No women served as priests in any of the Christian communities. Neither the Romans nor the Anglicans raised up a priesthood from among the Native Americans, or even from the Mexican people in the old Spanish border provinces, nor did any black priest serve at any catholic altar in America. All the priests in the eighteenth-century colonies were males of European descent, and all but an infinitesimal few were also of European birth.

With all the difficulties under which they labored, the priests of the various catholic traditions firmly transplanted the church they had known into the soil of the New World. Despite the hostile conditions arising from the anti-clericalism of the Enlightenment and the dominance of Reformed Protestantism in the eighteenth-century British colonies, the catholic churches flourished in the New World, survived the anti-catholic movements of the nineteenth century, and won a place of influence in American life. Because they continued to embody a concept of ministry long established in Christian history, they kept green in the popular memory expectations concerning religious leaders which continue to be projected on ministers today. Their presence also stimulated certain anticlerical prejudices which have not yet abated.

Reflections on the Priest

Because priesthood in the eighteenth century flourished most vigorously in those "established" churches that maintained official alliance with their respective governments, providing religious ceremony for occasions of state and receiving various degrees of financial aid and social preference from the secular power, the social radicals who contended for democracy often took an anti-clerical stance.[4] Church and hierarchy appeared to them as bulwarks of oppressive regimes and the privileged class, and their perception was not inaccurate. It was the ministers of the "free churches," some of them radical and all of them without priestly rank, who gave most vigorous support to the cause of freedom and equality. Even in more recent times, priesthood and hierarchy have frequently sided with privilege and power. (Perhaps the real offense of "liberation theology" is its inspiration of priests and even bishops to take up the cause of the poor in their spiritual and economic struggle).

The most clear-cut vestige of priesthood today is the concept of the minister as substantially different in nature from the laity. The notion of priestly "character" indelibly impressed at ordination lingers even in liberal Protestant churches. An atmosphere of awe sometimes attends the ritual of ordination, or quiet panic momentarily seizes a group at the sudden realization that a minister has come upon the scene, and red-faced apologies are blurted out. In these shadows lurks the ghost of priesthood past, whose haunting presence can still make for ministerial loneliness.

Equally disquieting to anyone whose faith centers in the belief that a personal God has chosen to be revealed most fully in the person of Jesus of Nazareth, and consequently is made known today through the loving ministry of persons acting in the spirit of Jesus, is the notion, derived from common ideas of priesthood, that a minister's essential contribution is the performance of an appropriate ritual act—as though the act possessed efficacy in itself apart from being a compassionate, relational deed of human helpfulness representing God and God's faithful people in loving response to a human need.

In *All the Way Home*, the dramatization of James Agee's story *A Death in the Family*, the minister who comes to the home fills a distant, purely ceremonial role. His relation to the bereaved is purely formal; no slight intimation of a spark of empathy arcs between the parson and the mourners. The orphaned lad suffers miserably in his aloneness, which the pastor makes no obvious attempt to break through. Yet it may be that the black-clothed minister likewise suffers in *his* aloneness, sitting there so irrelevantly at the edge of the family circle until time to perform his ritual.

Other fictional presentations of bereavement (e. g., *Our Town* or the Bogdanovich film *Paper Moon*) frequently depict the minister in the same merely ceremonial, almost inhuman role; the ministration is a distant performance, not a warm, much less impulsive, act of human friendship and sharing in grief. For some people the notion that the ritual ceremony conducted by the priest makes things right *ex opere operato* has its positive side, despite its tendency to rob the minister of standing as a genuine person in authentic personal relationship with the persons for whose benefit the service is offered. When the time comes for the ritual, they believe that the words and actions of the Priest will square things with God. It is hardly a matter for wonder that many moderns, assuming such a misconception to be the teaching of the church, turn against religion or that many ministers resist being cast in such a priestly role.

Not far removed from the misconception just mentioned is the widespread notion that while the minister may be highly educated in such arcane specialties as theology and liturgics and biblical history, this learning is of no earthly use in any practical situation. Not a few of our contemporaries, including a high proportion of church members, assume that a minister lacks any basis of informed competence to discuss issues of public importance. Witness the all-but-unanimous condescension of journalists toward the Catholic bishops when they issued their pastoral letters on nuclear weapons and on economic justice. Clearly, it was implied—if not flatly stated—the good pastors were out of their depth.

Such prejudice prevails, lamentably enough, among many academics who still think of ministers either as ignorant country hicks snapping their galluses or as ethereal monastic types learnedly disputing how many angels can dance on the head of a pin. Ministers I know best, graduates of historic liberal arts colleges and first-rate seminaries or divinity schools, many with the advanced degree Doctor of Ministry, revel in the intellectual comradeship of cultivated and informed persons and in the interplay of keen minds in honest discussion. Yet such ministers frequently find themselves in situations of loneliness resulting from ignorant presuppositions about their education and interests.

The custom of calling on a minister to pray on public occasions gives evidence that concepts clustering about the form of the Priest linger in the common mind. At luncheon clubs, at the opening sessions of legislatures, at political conventions, at the meetings of all sorts of subgroups in local congregations, the minister can expect to be called on to pray. Sometimes it seems that the only public occasion when it is deemed appropriate for a layperson to pray is one at which no minister is present. Such thinking is a relic from the days when priests officially represented the spiritual power, and everyone else deferred to them.

The force of all these expectations inherited from the concept of Priest bears upon many ministers with a great deal of discomfort and embarrassment. On occasion we even think to ourselves, "I hope this person doesn't find out I'm a minister." It is not that we want to do anything shady; it's just that we cannot endure being seen through the distorting spectacles of such expectations. And after the cat is out of the bag, we sometimes feel compelled to establish the point that we do not fit the widely held stereotype of ministry. Small wonder that some ministers now and then indulge in an off-color story or a shot of vulgar language as a pathetic assertion of normality: "Hey, look, fellas, I'm human too!"

Surely much of the resistance to the ordination of women to Protestant ministry arises not from the questionable Pauline prooftexts legalistically quoted to rationalize the prohibition, but from the collective image of appropriate ministry derived from centuries of exclusively male priesthood.

Another lingering legacy of medieval priesthood is the assumption, taken as an all but universal rule of order in Protestant churches, that only an ordained minister may officiate at the eucharistic table. No shred of scripture from the New Testament points to such exclusive practice. The ecclesiology of all the Protestant churches denies a spiritual distinction between ministry and laity. In very few discussions are reasons adduced to support this exclusive rule of order; it is simply assumed to be self-evident. Believers just take it for granted that ordination means the imputation of the exclusive right or power to minister eucharistically. In various ecumenical encounters my efforts to elicit substantial discussion of this issue have resulted in nothing more than gasps of horror at the thought of questioning the almost universal assumption.[5] It derives from the concept of the Priest as endowed by the institution with that official holiness presumed to be essential for the conduct of public religious ceremony.

The term *clergy* itself, so overworked today in ministers' references to themselves, derives from a pattern of thinking that for centuries separated Christians into two distinct classes, priesthood and laity, often using the term *church* in an exclusive sense to designate the former. Until recently, Americans have disliked the term *clergy* because of unacceptable concepts of church, ministry, and society which it long implied. The democrats of our eighteenth-century Enlightenment rarely, if ever, used it in a complimentary sense. Neither did the frontier folk from that time till the passing of the Old West. Some egalitarian groups like Disciples of Christ rejected the word as unscriptural and—as if that were not reprehensible enough!—as undemocratic and divisive.

Yet in less than a generation "clergy" has become a preferred term of self-reference and self-affirmation in ministerial jargon. Hardly anyone not connected with professional ministry ever uses the term in a positive sense, but *we* employ it as though the title conveyed enormous prestige. About the time it crept into our working vocabulary we had our consciousness raised regarding sexism in language, and ministers seized on an even more ludicrous expression. So now on approaching the end of my ministry, I plaintively ask: Having begun as a preacher, must I go out as a *clergyperson*? God forbid!

Presumably ministers clutch at the term *clergy* not out of commitment to the hieratic and hierarchical concepts it implies, but because it seems to designate ministry as a profession. That is hardly the most rewarding concept we can appropriate for our ministry from the notion of minister as Priest.

At the very least, however, we can call to mind several elements in the model of the Priest that call for a more positive assessment.

First, the ceremonial aspects of religion properly point away from the celebrant as an individual and toward God. Even though one's ministry is commonly carried out within a small and intimate fellowship where everyone is personally acquainted and where strong personal relationships give meaning and depth to the symbolic actions, any minister will be summoned at times to step outside that limited circle and minister to a stranger. I was called to the bedside of a young mother at the point of death. Neither of us had ever seen each other, and her weakness prevented any effort at small talk or getting acquainted on a human basis. But she knew that I came as a minister and when she received the broken bread and the cup, she knew that they were the emblems of the Savior's dying love. In such a situation one realizes the profound strength, even necessity, of the model of the Priest, even though it may not carry all the fullness of one's understanding of ministry. As a representative of the church, authorized to conduct its most sacred acts, the Priest meets human need with the holy power of God.

Because society has long understood the Priest as holding an office devoted to the service of God and of human beings in their need, many people are conditioned to turn to a minister in time of extremity. Particularly telling was the widespread practice among the Forty-Niners of addressing any minister in the mining camps as "Father." Using the term may have served to ease the homesickness of lonely youths who had rushed off to California in search of gold and had no one else to turn to. Perhaps in a territory dominated by the Catholic Church, Protestants addressed their preacher as "Father" in a defiant assertion of religious equality. In any case, the priestly model at its best embodies parental concern for the injured and the lost, offering friendship the stranger can trust.

Always the teaching responsibility of the Priest must be remembered. (We shall consider examples from colonial America in the treatment of the next model, the Master.) Catechizing neophytes in the basics of Christian faith, instructing a congregation in the knowledge of scripture and tradition, guiding persons in proper behavior, schooling the young in the cultural heritage—all these are crucial elements of the priestly task. Because the Priest is a teacher of righteousness, it is a mistake to set this form of ministry over against that of the Prophet, as though the two were necessarily at odds. Biblical scholarship has made it quite clear that the priests of Israel conserved and inculcated in new generations the inspired message of the prophets. They did so not only in the formal, didactic tasks associated with their calling, but also in the liturgies they composed and conducted for the people. It might even be argued that without the priests who came after them the prophets would have been forgotten. They set the visions of justice and shalom at the heart of Israel's worship, directing the thoughts and commitments of the people toward the achievement of God's purpose.[6]

The Priest remains among us, continuing the most venerable model of ministry carried on through the religious institution and imposing its burden of expectation on every minister. As every reformer or iconoclast knows, the model is not free from the danger of distortion and misuse. On the other hand, it is committed to the service of God through care for human beings in their deepest needs and to the maintenance of the faith through the structures of history. Would-be prophets do well not to discard this model out of prejudice, but to examine it with openness and charity of spirit.

MASTER

For a model of ministry as learned profession, we can find no loftier example than the form that reached its apex in colonial New England, the minister as Master.

Here we use the term *Master* to mean authoritative teacher, as in "schoolmaster." It derives from the Latin *magister*, which in academia underlies all our master's degrees and in ecclesia provides the word *magisterium* for the teaching authority of the church. In Christian Europe the two Latin words *magister* and *doctor* long had a similar meaning: The degrees they designated conferred the right to teach. Since the rise of the medieval university, the master of arts or the doctor of philosophy was a scholar entitled to membership in a faculty.

Ministry conceived as defined by this capacity for teaching is as old as the sages of Oriental wisdom and the rabbis expounding the scriptures of Judaism. The ideal flourished in the ministry of Christian scholars at Alexandria and Antioch in late antiquity and again at the cathedral schools and universities of medieval Europe. It was institutionalized in the Reformed ministry of Calvin's Geneva and Knox's Edinburgh. In Scotland down to our own time the minister was affectionately and deferentially addressed as *dōminie*; the schoolmaster rated the only slightly less respectful form *dôminie* (distinguished by a short accent on the initial syllable). The derivation from the Latin *dominus* is obvious. The concept of Master prevails wherever the minister is understood as the qualified and authorized teacher of an authoritative body of knowledge in which it is the duty of the people to receive instruction.

In the magisterial concept of ministry, the essential ingredients are an authoritative scripture or body of tradition and a person authorized to teach it. The encounter with the holy occurs neither in ecstasy nor in rite but in engagement with the divine reality conveyed through the sacred text. (Here the reader may note a striking correspondence between our three American forms of Saint, Priest, and Master and the three historical stages noted by the late Urban T. Holmes III in the early development of Christian ministry: in the ancient church, the Sacramental Person; in the Middle Ages, the Sacramental Rite; in the Reformation, the Sacramental Word.)[1]

Because transcendent holiness is for the Reformers encountered supremely in the sacred text, knowledge of that Word is the fundamental requisite for ministry. One need not receive a miraculous call conveyed in ecstasy; indeed, the impression that one has been called to preach by virtue of having received a mystical vision may be mistaken. What is essential is a love for the scripture, a knowledge of the scripture, a manner of life according with scripture, and the ability to convey the message of scripture faithfully to others.

Preparation for this form of ministry most clearly employs the pattern of education established in the secular university. It involves the study of ancient languages and literatures, history and philosophy, logic and rhetoric—those disciplines clearly necessary for the understanding and interpretation of the sacred text—as well as of scripture itself and the arts of ministry. More fully than any other of our eighteenth-century models, that of Master incorporates the Christian ideals of Renaissance humanism.

Even the shamanic and priestly ministries had exercised significant teaching functions. In the oral culture of the American Indians, after the crisis of vocation, the neophyte shaman needed to appropriate a large body of religious lore, and older shamans gave instruction in this tradition. As noted in the previous chapter, the Priest also had to master a considerable body of knowledge. Yet with both shaman and Priest, a large part of what they learned was kept from the general populace. Even though both types imparted some instruction to the people, the power of their ministries rested in their possession of secret knowledge.

The Black Preacher

The oral cultures of Africa, by contrast, made use of two kinds of public office that combined in America to elevate the black minister, even during the days of slavery, to a remarkable teaching role. We have already noted the shamanic heritage of black religion and the power it conveyed to traditional black preaching. The tribes of West Africa also possessed an important secular figure, the *griot*, made famous by Alexander Haley in *Roots*. This person was the living repository of knowledge important for the life of the tribe, especially genealogical information; he could recite the "oral text" of this tradition for hours on end and did so when the needs of the people required.

In the horrors of capture, the Middle Passage, the slave market, and gang labor in the fields, the black immigrants were cut off from their ancestral language and much of the substance of their ancestral culture, though the faint survivals in the black church and in voodoo are of considerable importance. It appears that the old role of the *griot* or storyteller converged with that of shaman in the majestic office of the black preacher, who enhanced the dignity of those antecedent forms with the knowledge of the Christian scripture. Its moving narratives, its archetypes, its rhythmic cadences, its sublime vocabulary, and its unconquerable hope became the intellectual and spiritual preoccupation of the black preacher. This knowledge was not arcane information to be held in secret. It was good news to be proclaimed.

If ever a case study was wanted for that extreme position held by some in the Reformed tradition which insisted that Christian faith was the religion of only ONE Book, it may be found in black religion in America. One could argue that the black church, even in the days of slavery when few blacks were permitted to learn to read, was as profoundly biblical as that of the Bible Commonwealth in New England—or even more so. Under the most demeaning conditions of oppression its people were sustained in dignity and hope by the word of their preachers concerning the Lord God who came down to deliver his people from slavery, who sent his beloved Son Jesus Christ to die for sinners and to prepare for his people an eternal home in heaven.

The Spanish Padre

In the experience of Roman Catholics in colonial America, as we have seen, the traditional teaching office (the episcopal *magisterium*) was not present, and the rigorous life of missionaries on the far frontiers offered few opportunities for that scholarship normally found among the friars and priests of old Europe. The situation called for hardy pioneers, builders, and shepherds of souls. Yet the intellectual splendor of the Spanish Renaissance shone in the minds and spirits of those tough and wiry padres. In the deserts of New Mexico, Arizona, and California they built magnificent churches, drawing the plans, overseeing construction, and painstakingly teaching their Indian charges the arts of carpentry, masonry, metal work, sculpture, and painting as they went along; importing bells from Lima and installing organs[2]; and flanking their golden rococo altars with wonderfully spiritual *santos* carved from wood and great canvases of holy scenes, some shipped from Europe, but some painted on the spot. In the holy liturgy they wore magnificent vestments, some of which came from the deft fingers of schoolgirls instructed by nuns in the convents. Besides all this, the padre was tutoring his charges in principles of agriculture, irrigation, animal husbandry, milling, harness-making, and other essential crafts. Like other missionaries of the modern era, the padres thought of themselves as teachers of Christian civilization.

As for the intellectual side of education, they undertook to teach the children to read and write and cipher, though such schooling did not go far, the primary emphasis falling on vocational skills. All this activity is necessarily impressive, however, when we recall that the Spanish missions were generally understaffed. If the padre ran his domain like an autocrat, it could well have been because he was the lone European for miles around, his assistants being Indians or *mestizos* who had come from Mexico bearing a tradition of Christian faith and culture which for them reached back only one of two generations.

Some of the padres earned the admiration and friendship of the occasional British or Yankee trader who settled down in the Mexican border provinces to stay, and the first American mountain men to reach Mission San Gabriel after crossing the desert were dazzled by the elegant formal gardens with fountains, the prosperous fields and vineyards and orchards grown under irrigation, the abundant meals of domestic meats and vegetables and fruits, the elegant wines and brandies, the evening concerts of music with European instruments— all offered with unreserved hospitality.

Under the more settled conditions of urban life in New Orleans, French nuns conducted well-ordered schools and hospitals. In the Spanish colonial capital the University of Mexico, founded in 1551 with an interest in the education of priests, was already a venerable institution by the eighteenth century. Its founders and teachers for generations were friars and priests. From its classes came a significant number of teachers and intellectuals to root the cultural tradition of Christendom in the soil of the New World. Unfortunately, however, the native sons of Mexico were slow to enter the priesthood, and the padres who pioneered the work in the border provinces which are now part of the United States were all born in Europe.

Never forgotten in the midst of all this other teaching activity on the part of the padre in the mission was his work as catechist. Because of language barriers, the first converts to be baptized had a woefully limited understanding of the content of the Christian faith and even of what they were doing in receiving its initiatory sacrament. But soon the children of Christian parents filled the mission compound, along with many more children from the surrounding villages, all of them readily speaking Spanish as a second language. These the priest regularly instructed in the catechism, and by the time of confirmation they had a significant knowledge of Christianity. Though many of the indigenous tribes died out as victims of diseases carried by their civilizers, communities of Catholic Indians remain to this day in the Southwest.

Of far greater effect was the emergence of *la raza*, a new race of Christian people combining the Western cultural tradition with that of their ancestors on this continent. Descendants of Spanish traders, soldiers, and colonial officials who married wives and established permanent homes in the New World, these *mestizos*, in time called Mexicans, appropriated the fervent Christian piety of their Mediterranean ancestors. Despite the unfortunate alliance of the Roman Catholic Church with the wealthy oppressors in Latin American society until fairly recent times, that church represents great spiritual power in the culture and life of this new people.

Teacher in the Pulpit

Throughout the course of Christian history one will not find a form of ministry conceived as essentially the work of the Christian teacher to surpass that which prevailed in the Bible Commonwealth. This magnificent ideal of the magisterial pastor draws heavily, of course, on the model of those great bishops of the Patristic Age—Basil the Great, Gregory of Nazianzen, Gregory of Nyssa, John Chrysostom, Cyril of Alexandria, Ambrose, Augustine, Hilary—who for all their administrative responsibility were yet the pastors and teachers of a congregation. It draws even more directly on Calvin and Bucer and the pattern of ministry that developed in the Reformed tradition, an ideal espoused also by the Presbyterians of the middle colonies.

But nowhere in the history of the church had the course of events combined to produce a population so zealous in informed Christian purpose as the first settlers of New England, a religious establishment that gave to regenerate Christians a monopoly of political power, and a corps of ministers so abundant in intellectual genius and so notable in educational attainments beyond those of others in the population. Master John Cotton (1584-1652) and his ministerial colleagues unabashedly bore a title that emphasized their position as authoritative teacher.

"New England...was a thinking community"[3]—and every sermon was an intellectual effort of prodigious proportions, assuming the careful attention of a congregation made up of the entire population of the town. Puritans referred to the work of the pulpit as "teaching"; they knew well enough that the common Christian habit of designating the sermon as "preaching" was flawed by its misuse of the biblical term for the proclamation of the gospel to outsiders. Even so, we will defer to common contemporary usage and use the terms synonymously.

The teaching of the Word to a congregation by its pastor involved all the authority and dignity of the Roman *magisterium*. But here the fundamental authority was seen as residing in the scripture itself; the authority of the preacher derived from his knowledge of scripture and theology and his obligation to make the message plain.

The fundamental form of sermon that prevailed throughout the centuries of Puritan dominance emphasized the educational function of the pulpit. Every sermon was expected to treat responsibly *text*, *doctrine*, and *use*—that is, to do a thorough exegesis, to develop systematically the crucial principles affirmed or implicit in the passage, and to apply the lesson of the day to specific situations in the life of the people. Bringing to perfection this form of sermon, which had originated not in Protestantism but rather in the late Middle Ages, the Puritan preacher performed this threefold work overtly and explicitly in every sermon, for the edification of the saints.

Preaching, therefore, was a formidable undertaking—as was listening to a sermon. Puritan sermons normally ran well beyond an hour, and the Master in the pulpit commonly turned the glass over a second time as the sand continued to run. Moreover, it was customary to present sermons in a series, developing with precision the full range of a long theological argument on a crucial Christian problem. Most of the books written before the Revolution came from ministerial authors, and in most cases the book was made up of a series of sermons developing a common theme. The printed version, however, sometimes attenuated and disguised the homiletical form. As the thought-world of colonial New England has engaged the attention of intellectual and literary historians during the past several decades, the work of the New England Master has proved to be a gold mine for these prospectors.

The colonists established Harvard College in 1636 "to advance *Learning*, and perpetuate it to *Posterity*; dreading to leave an illiterate Ministry to the Churches, when our present Ministers shall lie in the Dust."[4] For decades its presidents and instructors were ministers, and even in the eighteenth century a third of its graduates entered the ministry. Even though the zeal of the first settlers had cooled after a hundred and fifty years and the theological certitude of the earliest ministers had softened, the preachers still exercised an important intellectual leadership and still thought of themselves as the teachers of the colony.

The preaching had important social dimensions and striking influence on the common life. A distinguished company of secular historians has worked through the sermons of the eighteenth-century ministers since Alice M. Baldwin published *The New England Clergy and the American Revolution* more than fifty years ago.[5] They conclude that it was the preachers who prepared the colonists intellectually and spiritually to assert the claims set forth in the Declaration of Independence and the principles of government laid down in the Constitution of the United States.

In their election sermons the ministers had exegeted the biblical passages about political authority in such a way as to establish in the popular mind the concept of government as validated by social contract, popularizing the notions advanced by John Locke and other major writers on political theory. Sermons on such topics circulated widely as pamphlets, and wherever the influence of the preachers extended, "these truths" had indeed become "self-evident."

In 1783 after the victorious outcome of the Revolution, Ezra Stiles, the president of Yale University delivered the annual election sermon in Connecticut. His title was "The United States Elevated to Glory and Honor." In its published form, though surely it must have been cut in delivery, it runs to 120 pages.[6] It sets forth a political and social program for the new nation ranging through concerns for public morality, education, defense, economic development, the cultivation of the arts, and the fostering of vital religion, with the scope of a contemporary party platform in a presidential election. For all its national pride, secular hope, and historically conditioned opinions, this sermon is a profoundly Christian statement rooted in biblical and theological understanding.

Yet the supreme concern of the magisterial pastors penetrated more deeply than involvement with the secular life of the commonwealth. Their supreme concern was the salvation of their people, and that required the ministerial teacher to become preeminently a spiritual director. Week after week in each of his pastorates the winsome and eloquent Thomas Hooker (1586-1647) had preached on the life of the "new creature," meticulously detailing each step along the way of spiritual progress. Long before William James launched his famous studies of the psychology of conversion the Masters of the New England pulpit, who reached their zenith in the eighteenth century with Jonathan Edwards, examined the psychology as well as the theology of the soul's awakening.[7]

Of course, the Bible Commonwealth reserved the teaching authority to males. Its rulers feared shamanic dealing with the supernatural alleged against the women they executed as witches, but also feared the presumption of Anne Hutchinson in holding theological discussion groups in her home and presuming as a female to pass judgment on the views of her proper Masters. From the perspective of the twentieth century we can see that the magisterial ministry of New England, for all its grandeur, fell short of the full Christian perfection that it advocated. Its understanding of scripture and theology was severely limited and distorted by the presupposiions of its age, as ours also surely is.

The magisterial position that the standing order in New England assigned to its ministers for 150 years should not delude us into imagining that their lot was easy, much less free from problems. The theological nitpicking that prominent members all too frequently directed against their parson was often an obvious subterfuge intended to conceal the genuine issues in a local power struggle. Particularly in the century of the American Revolution ministers suffered the slings and arrows of obstreperous opponents.[8] As often both before and since, the hard facts of communal reality failed to fit the glory of the vision. So often did the preachers cry out against the moral declension and the social ills of their times that their sermons became a distinct literary type, the jeremiad.[9]

Yet, despite adversity the Masters of the colonial pulpit embodied a model of ministry touched with greatness. It has much to teach us of moral grandeur, theological integrity, zeal to educate, social responsibility, and genuine involvement in the culture.

Other Protestant Ministries

Throughout the diversities of eighteenth-century Protestantism various traditions gave honor to the minister as teacher. The Presbyterians, the Dutch Reformed, the German Reformed, and the Lutherans in America all cherished the ideal, though their historical circumstances did not permit them to advance it to the high point in church and society occupied by the ministry in New England.

Within the narrower confines of concern for the cure of souls, two other traditions cast the minister in the role of spiritual director, even though they gave less attention than did the Puritans to the ideal of a learned ministry in the academic sense. Both the Pietists and the Methodists located the essence of ministerial leadership in the careful supervision and discipline of believers. These they gathered into small groups or "classes" for Bible study, prayer, self-examination, discipline, and instruction in spiritual growth. Even though the numbers of Pietists and Methodists were small in eighteenth-century America, their commitment to the concept of minister as spiritual director must not be overlooked.

Reflections on the Master

Certain elements in the concept of minister as Master greatly appeal to us. The significant place in the life of church and society indicated by the title *parson, the* person in the community, reminds us of a time when there was no confusion about ministry, no problem of definition or identity. In both the Catholic and the Reformed tradition it was clear that ministry was a learned profession with a publicly acknowledged mission of relevance to society and to the eternal welfare of each person.

What of the concept of learned ministry today? It is hard to answer that question with precision. The educational requirements for ordination in our mainline denominations are perhaps at least comparable with those of Spain and New England. Today's ministers spend more years in university and seminary than did the colonial Masters, taking more courses in "arts of ministry" and in some other areas than did they. Yet in comprehension of the general secular learning of the times, as well as in traditional humanistic studies, the colonial Masters surpassed us. Few pastors today can match the linguistic skills in Latin, Hebrew, Greek—even English!—that they commanded, as well as their mastery of logic, their familiarity with scripture, their knowledge of the history of Christian thought, and their theological power.

The radical difference between us and them, however, emerges in a comparison of ministerial learning with the level of education in society generally. Ministry then was one of three learned professions: law, medicine, and divinity. Today it seems that in many communities everyone has been to college, master's degrees are as common as high school diplomas a generation ago, and an earned doctorate is no longer a mark of much distinction.

Many persons today apparently do not think of ministry as a profession made significant by its level of education. Sometimes I am prompted to the cynical conclusion that the ideal of the learned ministry is esteemed chiefly in the catalogs of theological seminaries, that its most notable vestige in the life of the congregations is the ministerial affectation of the doctoral robe for pulpit wear—though increasingly that is giving way to liturgical vestments. Whereas ministers in the learned tradition once made a point of labeling their place of work THE PASTOR'S STUDY and of displaying an impressive library, they now call it an OFFICE and take pride in the rank of impressive business machines and communications equipment at their command.[10]

It is, moreover, a measure of the secularism of the times that well-read secular intellectuals, who may perhaps have heard of Tillich or

Niebuhr or possibly Martin Marty, seem not to know, for the most part, that the ministers of the mainline churches in their own communities are fellow intellectuals, nor do they commonly think of turning to a minister for information and analysis of a problem or for significant dialogue. In the news media mainline Protestant ministry is an invisible class. As a result many ministers themselves think of their profession as having little public significance.

Yet surely such a picture is overdrawn. In some parts of the country, especially in the county seat towns and small cities of the South, the Midwest, and New England, the old ideal of the minister as a "man of letters" persists, increasingly incarnated in the person of an educated woman. Members of the community with cultural aspirations have learned to depend on the men and women in the pastorate to embody and encourage the arts and the humanities. Even in secularized and increasingly paganized southern California I repeatedly met ministers pressed into the leadership of community organizations because of their informed knowledge of social and psychological problems, or even co-opted into teaching courses in the public schools because of their educational competence. Moreover, the popular mind still expects a minister to be able to explain any question about the content of the Bible or the fine points of religious doctrine most commonly discussed by the electronic evangelists—the rapture, the imminent signs of the Second Coming, the identity of the anti-Christ. (If it is no longer the Soviet Union or Iran, might it possibly be Iraq or Cuba? It never occurs to such a mind, of course, that it might be the United States!)

The persistent loyalty of some denominations in the Reformed tradition to the ideal of the learned ministry is impressive. Some of these have developed their own academic examinations for ordination, unwilling to abdicate to the seminaries the responsibility for maintaining scholarly standards. Presbyterians have continued to insist on the biblical languages even after many seminary faculties have caved in. In the Consultation on Church Union I have been at once instructed and frustrated by the Presbyterian reticence to accord the rank of presbyter to the Disciples elder lest the insistence on a learned ministry be compromised.

Perhaps we most need to emulate the eighteenth-century divines not just in insisting on high standards of theological education, not just in striving to project an image of the ministry as one of the learned professions, but rather in their perception of ministry as essentially an educative task. The colonial Master stood in constant readiness to use his learning in the instruction of the laity. I discern too great a tendency of young ministers today to lament the theological and biblical ignorance of their people, to conclude that from the pulpit they must not discuss substantive themes or untraditional views because the people have no background to understand their position, and to abandon the educational task of the minister. Such ministers engage in honest intellectual dialogue only when they meet with other ministers or graduate-school types.

From the days of Baxter and Cotton, the Reformed pastor respected the capacity of the people to learn and trembled at the heavy and constant responsibility of teaching. In the words of Jonathan Edwards,

> Ministers are set as guides and teachers, and are represented in Scripture as lights set up in the churches; and in the present state meet their people, from time to time, in order to instruct and enlighten them, to correct their mistakes, and to be a voice behind them, when they turn aside to the right hand or the left, saying, *This is the way, walk ye in it*; to evince and confirm the truth by exhibiting the proper evidences of it, and to refute errors and corrupt opinions, to convince the erroneous and establish the doubting.[11]

There was a model of ministry not soon to be forgotten!

Model 4

AWAKENER

The three concepts of ministry thus far noted—Saint, Priest, and Master, embodying Holmes's types (sacramental person, enactor of the sacramental rite, dispenser of the sacramental word)—are early American manifestations of three far more ancient figures: shaman, priest, and sage. In the eighteenth-century colonies each of these took on a form authentically rooted in Christian tradition and authentically related to the American scene. Subsequent history would involve the reshaping, diminution, even displacement of these forms by others considered more relevant to new conditions of ethnic, cultural, and religious pluralism. Dramatic changes in the historical context would make for radical revision of traditional ministerial patterns. One such transformation occurred already in the eighteenth century: the thrusting into prominence, even dominance, of a form of ministry essentially new within English-speaking Protestantism, the Awakener.[1]

As the eighteenth-century forerunner of the Revivalist, the colonial Awakener appeared at a time and place in which the uniformity of the former religious establishment had broken down.[2] Society and culture were still nourished by their Christian roots, the government of this colony or that still gave preference to the one true church long established within its jurisdiction, the clergy of that church still enjoyed the status of public officials, and people generally thought of themselves as living in a Christian society. But many of these people were unchurched. The religious institution had been unable to keep up with the rapid growth of population on the colonial frontier.

Indifference accounted for the condition of many who had never been brought to baptism or had never sought it on their own. Many others, who gave assent to notions fostered by Calvinism, longed for

50

salvation and feared the imminence of hell, but had never received the experimental—we would say "experiential"—assurance of divine grace and election. Yet the Puritan and other early American versions of the Calvinist scheme required such assurance as a condition of admission to church membership.

Then came the Awakener, declaring divine judgment and proclaiming salvation to the spiritual orphans. In the religious excitement of the Great Awakening, thousands were converted and swept into the churches.

In describing our first model, the Saint, we mentioned the Great Awakening because its model of ministry, the Awakener, showed some marks of kinship with the shaman: a preacher displaying evident signs of direct engagement with the holy. But the Awakener was neither shaman nor Saint, but something more. While they spoke out of ecstatic experience of the sacred and shared the knowledge received from the spirit-world, it was no necessary function of the shaman or Saint to attempt to induce such an experience in the people generally. The shaman-Saint was rather a mediator of the ecstatic *vision* than a general purveyor of shamanic ecstasy.

By contrast, the primary function of the Awakener was to preach the gospel of salvation with conviction and fervor, in faith that the Holy Spirit would work with power through the Word in the hearts of the hearers, moving them to repentance and confession and at last to the glad assurance of salvation. Humanly speaking, the Awakener communicated not the vision but the ecstasy itself, in a setting where that direct, inward, highly volatile encounter with the holy was considered the essential requisite of Christian experience.

The Great Awakening seized public attention throughout the colonies through the work of a few ministers whose preaching drew large numbers of hearers and resulted in many conversions. An upsurge of religious zeal at Northampton, Massachusetts, beginning in the fall of 1733, led Jonathan Edwards to see it as the work of God. Soon other ministers, praying for similar results, rejoiced in revival in the surrounding areas, while more reserved and more rational types looked on, first with alarm, then with opposition, to what they considered extreme emotionalism and dangerous "enthusiasm." Wishing to make an acceptable case for "the Awakening," Edwards entered into active correspondence, and a long letter to Benjamin Colman of Boston was published in London as "A Faithful Narrative of the Surprizing Work of God in the Conversion of Many Hundred Souls in Northampton, and the Neighboring Towns and Villages...."[3] It evoked a warm response in John Wesley, who had just begun to preach in the fields of England and who entered into eager correspondence with Edwards.

About the same time, Wesley's friend and collaborer George Whitefield, who had preceded him as a field preacher, sailed for Georgia. Soon great crowds met him wherever he went. From his base in England, Whitefield made a total of seven voyages to America, preaching to great throngs of colonists from Georgia to New England. By far the most dramatic of the Awakeners, Whitefield stirred the crowds to a high pitch of emotion. John Wesley described it:

> Incredible multitudes flocked to hear, among whom were an abundance of Negroes. In all places the greater part of the hearers were affected to an amazing degree. Many were deeply convinced of their lost state; many truly converted to God. In some places thousands cried out aloud; many as in the agonies of death; most were drowned in tears; some turned pale as death; others were wringing their hands; others lying on the ground; others sinking into the arms of their friends; almost all lifting up their eyes, and calling for mercy.[4]

These three leaders were clergymen of the established churches who looked to the power of the Holy Spirit to break through the rigidities of prevailing liturgical convention and commend the power of the gospel to the thousands of common people now largely untouched by the routine religion that then prevailed. Wesley and Whitefield were Anglican priests, educated at Oxford; Edwards was a graduate of Yale and a pulpit Master in the Puritan tradition. William Tennent, a graduate of the University of Edinburgh who came to Pennsylvania as a Presbyterian minister, established a small frontier school in 1735 to promote the revival. His detractors dubbed it the "Log College," but soon a company of his protegés, schooled far from the centers of intellectual culture, were carrying the revival throughout the middle colonies; we have already met one of these, his son Gilbert, famed for his sermon on "The Danger of an Unconverted Ministry." [5]

The colonial Awakener differed from the popular penitential preachers of the late Middle Ages despite some obvious resemblance. The Catholic penitential preachers pleaded with people already baptized and united with the *corpus christianum*. Their message was "Repent! Repent! Turn from your wicked ways! Return to God!" The message of the Awakener by contrast was "Repent and believe! Confess your sins! Put your faith in Jesus Christ your Savior!" Although the Awakener functioned as penitential preacher to persons already within the fold, seeking to arouse those whose Christianity was merely nominal or formal, a more dramatic vocation belonged to this office: Its primary and definitive task was to bring salvation to the unsaved.

The Awakener differed from the nineteenth-century Missionary in that the latter worked beyond the pale of Christendom, seeking conversions among a people who had not known the gospel. The essence of the Awakener's task was to arouse, within a society avowedly Christian, persons so sunk into spiritual torpor that they had never laid hold of the common religious heritage to appropriate it for themselves.[6] (While this description uses the cool language of the sociologist, the Awakener cast his speech in the fervid vocabulary of Calvinism, employing such words as sin and damnation, election and repentance, salvation and justification.)

In the tradition of the Great Awakening, revivalism still flourishes in the Old South more lushly than elsewhere because social patterns there more than in other parts of the country still take for granted the notion that American society is intended to be a Christian community. Similarly, the recent dramatic growth of conservative churches through the work of contemporary revivalists seems to occur among those elements of the population in whose minds the assumptions of traditional Christendom still largely prevail, whereas their message seems irrelevant if not incredible to the more thoroughly secularized types in whose minds the traditional intellectual assumptions have been repudiated. This observation is not intended as a putdown of traditional believers, contemporary Awakeners, or modern thought. It is simply an effort to say: The methods of revivalism presuppose a traditional ideological consensus in support of Christianity, even though it may be seen as threatened by "secular humanism." Where such a consensus no longer prevails, the situation calls for a Missionary, an evangelist, whose message and methods must necessarily differ from those of the Awakener (or Revivalist).[7]

Reflections on the Awakener

How did the work of this eighteenth-century model affect the American concept of ministry?

The Awakeners exalted individualism. While trading on the assumptions of the traditional cultural consensus and often relying on the forces of crowd psychology, they nevertheless elevated the individual to the dominant and determinative place in the American religious myth. They wanted to generate in their hearers a personal experience of the holy. They proclaimed Christ as Savior. They called for personal conviction. Even before the First Amendment wrote religious individualism into the fundamental charter of American law, the Awakener had unwittingly placed it at the center of American religious assumptions. Like conversion, religion became a personal matter, not an issue settled by one's distant ancestors, nor a question for group decision, nor a consideration of public policy.

The concept of ministry implicit in this individualistic assumption incredibly complicates the work of the minister and multiplies its difficulties. For now the minister must please the people one by one and convince them one by one.

Closely related to the individualism elevated by the Great Awakening is the subjectivism that has ever since characterized American religion and made life difficult for American ministers. Gilbert Tennent advised the people, as we have seen in discussing our first model, to sit in judgment on the spiritual state of their ministers: The criterion they were to use was the "experience" of "conversion." In practice this meant that ministers with the shamanic type of personality who in ecstasy entered into direct encounter with the holy and who could induce such ecstasy in their hearers were accounted converted. They could communicate the experience they celebrated as the heart of true religion. At the outset, members of the old school opposed this assumption, holding out for rational and ethical definitions of Christian faith and life. But because of the voluntarism resulting from freedom of religion, the place of individual experience has become determinative in American religion, even if that experience does not follow the pattern which the Awakener deemed essential.

The American minister is constantly being judged by church members who look back nostalgically to their most stirring or satisfying moments of religious experience. They account that minister good who can induce within them now the emotions and elation they experienced then. This prominence of subjectivism has militated increasingly against the teaching model of ministry and the priestly model as well.

Present-day subjectivism does not really demand that the minister should be a Saint or an Awakener, but it longs for the kind of personal religious experience it cherishes. The longing is hardly a desire for a biblical experience of judgment and grace. Rather, it wants a reawakening of an earlier joyful feeling that accompanied one's conversion—or stirred the community during an earlier season of revival. Too often, it seems, there is a readiness to settle for the sentimental assurance, "I'm OK," things here are nice, and Jesus is sweet.

At a less subjective level, the model of the Awakener established the statistical mode of measuring ministerial effectiveness. How large is the attendance? How many new members this Sunday or this year? Such questions are not altogether improper or irrelevant, but often they are asked and answered in a sociological and spiritual vacuum.

The minister who does not get a dramatic response is blamed for the inevitable result of forces of community change beyond anyone's control. Church members and denominational officials who look primarily to statistics as the measure of "church growth" have fallen unwittingly into a secular or "worldly" mentality that looks only to the "bottom line"—without even asking if such a figure can give a true reading of spiritual health and achievement. Unlike the great Awakeners themselves, who knew that the Spirit blows where it wills and that times of revival come and go unpredictably in the mysterious providence of God, those who measure simply in terms of numerical "results" apply an external, material standard of "success" to the concept of ministry.

And yet—do we never long for the conversion of those outside the faith? The poet John Greenleaf Whittier, living at the midpoint between the Awakeners and ourselves, celebrated the effects of their ministry:

> Through ceiled chambers of secret sin
> Sudden and strong the light shone in;
> A guilty sense of his neighbor's needs
> Startled the man of title-deeds;
> The trembling hand of the worldling shook
> The dust of years from the Holy Book;
> And the Psalms of David, forgotten long,
> Took the place of the scoffer's song.
>
> The tide of spiritual life rolled down
> From inland mountains to seaboard town.[8]

We have already mentioned in passing the considerable opposition encountered by the Awakeners, an opposition that centered in the Harvard faculty and the intellectual leaders among the Boston clergy. These critics deplored the outbreaks of "enthusiasm," that is, of unrestrained religious emotion, and the tactics used by some of the Awakeners to induce it.

Ever since then, American Christianity has been divided into two houses: the one commending reason and emotional restraint in religion; the other valuing emotion and emotional experience, even when it produces irrational behavior, as the accompaniment of conversion. Jonathan Edwards attempted to walk a fine line as defender of the Awakening in his "Treatise on Religious Affections." But many Americans look askance at emotional demonstrations in religion, and the party devoted to keeping cool has grown to include not only the rationalists such as Charles Chauncy and the old school Presbyterians in the eighteenth century, and the Unitarians, Episcopalians, and Disciples in the nineteenth cenury, but most of the mainline churches today—the very churches that have fallen under increasing criticism for their diminishing memberships and their failure to evangelize.

We struggle with a paradoxical heritage. If we resort to the emotionally charged methods of the Awakener, we invite criticism from our members and from within ourselves, for we have violated our commitment to a sane and reasonable faith. But if we fail to attract new converts, we run the risk of spiritual rigor mortis, the forerunner of congregational and denominational death. The greatest of the American Awakeners intended a holistic appeal to mind and heart. May it be that a true revival of Christian faith and life is possible in our time without the excesses and divisions of the Great Awakening in the eighteenth century?

Interlude: Mummies, Ghosts, and Haunts

One observation regarding the eighteenth century clamors for expression: Only the Saint managed to slip through the iron bars that patriarchy erected around ministry. Priest, Master, Awakener—each was indubitably male. And because these models fixed themselves so firmly in the popular religious mind, the presumption of masculinity as somehow essential works almost imperceptibly to color the expectations regarding ministry that continue to emanate from them. Nothing in this book intends to support that presumption, even though the persons chosen as examples from the colonial era are, except for shaman or Saint, necessarily men. When we come to our final assessment of the models in the closing chapter, we shall attempt to evaluate the forms with no implication that masculinity is essential to any one of them. On the contrary!

A second observation may be stated with equal brevity. Few ministers of the eighteenth century would have had to contend with a mixed bag of expectations comparable to the conflicting popular notions that complicate the work of a minister today. In nearly every case, such expectations as were encountered belonged essentially to the model a given minister had taken as normative and tried to follow. People may have considered one a failure, but they were not importing alien standards of measurement unconsciously taken from another model.

The striking exception to this observation was, of course, the model of the Awakener. A novelty on the religious scene, it took its own presuppositions as the measure for every other ministry: Had the preacher been converted? The charge that many a parson had no "experimental" knowledge of the new birth was responsible for much of the turmoil stirred up by the Awakening.

We, however, face a quite different situation. In America the earliest forms of ministry past continue to haunt the twentieth-century church. While neither shaman nor Saint commands the current scene, a cluster of extravagant expectations deriving from the model still thrust themselves rudely upon our ministry, no matter what alternative form may have commended itself to us. Descendants of the Priest still process through contemporary sanctuaries, while here and there a conscientious teacher or rabbi still functions as the Master of a congregation, if not of the community at large. No farther away than the television screen, the Awakener flickers before our eyes, reincarnated as electronic evangelist and purporting to summon the powerful Spirit of God into the lives of our contemporaries. From all these models, not just from the Saint alone, various members of our flocks continue to impose wildly diverse expectations upon us and our work.

In particular instances these old forms, masquerading as living ministries, prove in reality to be only carefully preserved mummies, decked out in contemporary garb and currently fashionable makeup so as to project an initial appearance of life. Despite their seemingly remarkable state of preservation, we can watch them actually withering before our eyes, if not already transmuted to powdery dust. Yet though death has obviously triumphed, the ghosts of these ministerial mummies from our past continue to haunt us with the expectations they aroused when they still lived and breathed.

The crucial question we must consider about the old models can be put quite bluntly: Is there a credible prospect that the life-giving Spirit of God may animate the dry bones of any of them so that it will confront us as a living option? In one instance or another that may perhaps be the case.

But we must defer our attempt to answer that question at least for a while, since the models we have considered do not offer all the choices confronting us. Neither do these mummies provide all the ghosts that haunt us. Still other forms arose in the centuries that followed.

PART

II

The American
Reshaping
of Ministry

THE NINETEENTH-CENTURY SETTING

With serene confidence the Great Seal of the United States pro-claimed a "new order of the ages." Adopted in 1782, the Latin words *Novus ordo seclorum* spoke more truly than anyone could realize at the time. The century that followed reshaped ministry in radical ways, with new forms emerging from the molds of historical circumstance, accompanied both by new concepts appropriate to them and by altered concepts of the older forms that still persisted. As to popular expectation concerning the work of any particular minister, confu-sion arose to compound the heritage of perplexity regarding voca-tional identity that the nineteenth century bequeathed to the minis-ters of our own times.

Most of the changes came unexpectedly, not as the intended result of overt choice but as the indirect outcome of decisions taken for the sake of liberty, or as the unforeseen product of other historical forces. Once again history proves to be the story of what happens to good intentions.

A New Order: Religious Liberty

In 1776, after the zealous Christians caught up in the continuing effect of the Awakening and the political liberals allergic to ecclesias-tical control had joined forces in intense agitation, the Virginia House of Burgesses adopted Thomas Jefferson's Statute of Religious Free-dom. In 1791, the First Amendment to the Constitution of the United States prohibited a federal establishment of religion or inhibition by Congress on its free exercise. While such guarantees were not man-dated on the states until the adoption of the Fourteenth Amendment (1868), only Massachusetts, Connecticut, and New Hampshire made any effort to continue the colonial system of an established church, and that effort came to an end within a generation. It has fallen to the Supreme Court of the United States, in a continuing series of decisions, to define the extent and limits of religious liberty, but to the ministers and the churches of the nineteenth century fell the task of working out the implications for the reshaping of ministry.

Everyone had foreseen that no ecclesiastical official would have any automatic claim, by reason of position in any church, to office in any branch of government. It was also clear that government could not exercise its authority in the selection of leaders for any church or in determining its teaching. Most important of all in the minds of those who agitated for the Bill of Rights, the First Amendment enjoined government from collecting taxes or tithes in behalf of any church and from diverting public funds to the use of any religious institution. In short, religion was to be free from intrusion by the state, the state was to be free of ecclesiastical entanglements, and the people were to be free to make their own choices in matters of faith.

As a result of this liberty, religion in America took on a distinctive character that in turn gave new shape to American ministry.

Voluntarism

Voluntarism in religion resulted from the new freedom. It was a new thing under the sun, previous societies having everywhere assumed that the state was obligated to maintain the true faith, with the grant of toleration to dissenters being only a recent innovation. With religion now a matter of personal choice, persuasion became the base on which the entire enterprise depended. For a time churches accustomed to wielding authority continued to exercise it over their members—but only for as long as those members were willing to have it so.

In order for religious institutions to continue, people now had to be persuaded to join them and support them: The tide of revivalism that rose and ebbed in the Great Awakening ran again in the nineteenth century, with wave after wave sweeping thousands of converts into the churches. The solicitation of voluntary gifts from the multitude of ordinary members to underwrite the work of the churches was systematized into an art that would have turned Johannes Tetzel green with envy, and the stewardship of wealth, hitherto a minor point in Christian ethics, was elevated to the dignity of a major religious doctrine.

While revivalism and stewardship gave significant new twists to the form and concept of ministry, no force on the American scene shaped it as radically as yet another product of voluntarism. That new product was laicism within the church. At least as far back as the fourth century, bishops and priests had dominated ecclesiastical life, adding to their own moral force and the plausibility of their magisterial doctrine the power of the civil magistrate. While Protestantism, especially in the Reformed-Puritan tradition and in the ethos of the Radical Reformation, had asserted the universal priesthood of believers and had elevated the power of representative laity in the councils of the church, American religious liberty produced an unforeseen emergent: the utter dependence of the ministry upon the membership of the churches, not only in matters of finance but also in the determination of policy.

For a time the Roman Catholic Church stalled the momentum of laicism by clamping down on the "Americanist" movement. Episcopalians, Presbyterians, and others devised systems of constitutional checks to outweigh the numerical superiority of the laity, but such maneuvers could gain only a little time. The people had the votes and they had the money. In the American churches "the people became the ultimate theologians" and ministers had to learn to persuade or manipulate.

Pluralism

Pluralism inevitably accrued from a situation of religious freedom, with a number of rival sects already present in every colony despite widespread legal prohibitions and disabilities before independence. Now with a more active movement of population within the new nation and a dramatic increase in immigration, diversity grew ever more complex, and the available options in religion multiplied in nearly every community.

The new state of affairs brought a striking innovation in ecclesiology: the notion of the denomination. Heretofore every Christian nation had recognized only one body, the established ecclesiastical institution, as the "one true church," relegating all others to the category of sects, whatever their claims for themselves. Adherents of a given faith might even be members of the true church in one country and sectarian dissenters in another, e.g., a member of the National Kirk in Scotland but a Presbyterian in England. Governments decided the issue: *cuius regio, eius religio*. Even so, each "church" and each "sect"—no matter how many of them—regarded itself as the "one true church" and regarded all other bodies claiming the name Christian as defective or apostate.

No "church" in the young American nation could claim to be the "one true church" with any plausibility among outsiders, though for a good while the habit persisted within given religious communities and still persists among some. Increasingly, however, Christian people recognized a large measure of validity in the life and faith of their neighbors who adhered to different "churches." The notion of denomination soon became normative in discussions of religion in America—except for the persistence of the old pretensions within a given household of faith.

In essence, a denomination is understood to be not *the* church but *a* church, existing alongside other legitimate churches. To the outsider these bodies appear remarkably similar insofar as the essential character of Christianity is concerned. While a denomination seems to impute great importance to a specific peculiarity, often incorporating reference to it into its official name, it lives and carries on its mission in dependence on and loyalty to the common Christian faith and magnifies its "distinctive witness" chiefly in occasional seizures of corporate self-consciousness—at a regional synod or general assembly, or in the current hysteria about "identity." The rest of the time it assumes that in building up a church (namely "ours") we are building up the great church, and the denomination rarely becomes an object of reflection—even to this day.[1]

The pluralistic situation means that a minister is ordinarily perceived as an officer of a particular denomination rather than as one related to an entire community. In a church where the sense of territorial responsibility has been strong (Roman or Anglican diocese or parish), or where establishment during the colonial era bestowed unique status (the Congregational "Church on the Green"), the minister may for a time carry a sense of obligation for the entire populace and for the common life of a place. But soon other denominations enter the scene, and one engages in not too genteel rivalry with other ministers in trying to maintain the strength of one's own congregation and denomination. The institutional dynamics of religious freedom have turned ministerial attention inward from concern for society to preoccupation with a particular church.

Yet pluralism also encourages ecumenism. In a situation where a number of Christian bodies exist side by side in freedom, both the mission to which they are all committed and the need for greater influence than any one denomination can command combine to draw the churches toward one another in various kinds of cooperation. So ministers of diverse churches begin to consult together, to plan common ventures that will not threaten their own congregations, and to draw strength from one another. Revivalists, social reformers, and promoters of every good cause play down their particular affiliation in a bid for the broadest Christian support, and many significant nineteenth-century ventures prospered under the label "undenominational." Out of such experiences and out of sober reflection on the doctrine of the church, a more overtly theological thrust toward ecumenism arises. But the American minister's ecumenical endeavors inevitably operate within a context of religious pluralism.

Privatism

The privatism so characteristic of much American religion, and so determinative of popular expectations concerning the minister, likewise springs from a too widely held understanding of the meaning of religious freedom. The losers in the effort to continue some kind of ecclesiastical establishment in the new nation had argued that religion is necessary to morality and the public welfare. But the opponents of establishment countered that *all* the churches—indeed, all religious faiths—were alike in inculcating belief in God, basic morality, and the doctrine of eternal punishment or reward as an incentive to the good life. These views were commonly held to be essential to the welfare of society, but the argument prevailed that all the churches, even the "natural religion" of the Enlightenment, promoted them. Accordingly there was no justification for the state to prefer one religion above another, since the differences among the churches had to do with matters of no demonstrable public consequence—the form of church government, the relation of the divine persons within the Trinity, the mode of baptism. Having no competence in such matters nor reason to consider them as pertaining in any way to the general welfare, the state would keep its hands off, leaving it up to each person to make an individual choice in religion. Government would suffer no harm if someone chose no religion at all, as long as that person lived a moral life and obeyed the law.

From the political argument that religious differences had no public consequence and that one's choice of religion was therefore a private matter, many Americans inferred a fallacious *theological* assumption: namely, that Christianity is altogether a matter of private concern, that it has no relevance to public affairs such as business or politics or international relations, and that any legitimate involvement of the church in the affairs of state should be limited to agitating for legislation to uphold Christian standards of personal morality.

A companion fallacy follows: that since all the churches (presumably) teach the basic morality essential to the general welfare, the essence of the churches' duty is to uphold the stability of the state. This means, of course, providing divine sanction for the status quo. Hence the tendency to mingle religion with "patriotism"—actually nationalism. The inclination may spring from common memories going back to the way things were under the religious establishments of the Old World. In any case it is imbedded in the popular mind by the motto, "For God and

Country." In the United States it is widely taken for granted that a congregation will display the nation's flag in its chancel, a custom that may come as a surprise, even a shock, to Christians from abroad.

The widespread notion that the church should uphold private morality and patriotism without getting involved in divisive political issues generally marches lockstep with another presumption: that the church should also support the capitalistic system. In the unexamined but fervently cherished axioms of privatism, religion is a matter of upholding the status quo, helping people to be "good Christians," and not getting "mixed up in politics."

The privatist misunderstanding of Christianity completely distorts biblical faith—the law, the prophets, and the gospel. It also misconceives the principle of separation of church and state. The intention of the founders in providing religious liberty was to bar ecclesiastical officials from authority in government and governmental officers from authority over the church, and to guarantee the freedom of all citizens—including ministers—to discuss political issues in the free forum of public opinion until a majority could be persuaded to adopt a particular course. As a voluntary association, a church has as strong a constitutional right as any other organization to express a corporate opinion on any public question. What it cannot do is to invoke the power of government to enforce its view—unless, by majority vote, such a view is enacted into law. Even then it must be justified on grounds of public policy and must not involve the state in enforcing adherence to a religious doctrine.

But the privatistic understanding of religion and of the American system prevails widely, and some ministers have promoted it as a means of gaining popular support for their ostensibly nonpolitical ministries. Ministers who believe in the public relevance of the gospel face the temptation to soft-pedal that relevance because of the popular prejudice. And because so many Americans have inferred from religious liberty a privatistic notion of religion, every minister must deal with the accompanying assumption that his or her views on any public issues are no more than a matter of personal opinion better kept to oneself, that his or her work is of no public consequence, that religion is for those who happen to like that sort of thing.

Subjectivism

Subjectivism in religion also follows from the constitutional separation of church and state. Since one's religion or lack of it is in the eyes of the government entirely a matter of personal choice, one chooses whatever happens to appeal to one on whatever grounds one finds it appealing.

Thus freedom of religion puts intense pressure on the minister to give people what they like. Since the whole venture rests on persuasion and depends on funds freely given by the people, the minister is required to develop a popular following for the church's program and, depending on the magnitude of the issues at stake (for example, a major fund-raising effort), is sometimes driven to neurotic attempts to avoid displeasing anyone. The unctuous professional manner of pouring oil on troubled waters becomes a hallmark of the "successful" religious leader. Perhaps most debilitating of all is the requirement that the minister be forever running in a popularity contest with the members of one's congregation in order to carry out one's ministry.

In popular understanding American subjectivism in religion has undercut the teaching authority of the ministerial office. People pick and choose among religious doctrines on the basis of what *appeals* to them. "Prophetic" preaching, even the quiet discussion of social issues, is discouraged—not necessarily out of opposition to the minister's views but from the fear that someone might take offense.

The people must be satisfied. The minister must be "perfect." That notion, already given the appearance of theological legitimacy in Gilbert Tennent's sermon on "The Danger of an Unconverted Ministry," now becomes an operational necessity imposed by the general understanding of the constitutional principle of religious liberty. Despite expectations of ministerial authority carried over from earlier models—shamanistic, priestly, magisterial—expectations still operative in the minds of the people as well as of the minister, the minister may encounter a roadblock around any turn. It is the rock of subjectivism. The people expect the minister to give them what they want.

Ministry at its best persuades the people to want what they believe God wills for them. But sometimes the minister fails to persuade. And ministry is not always at its best.

Developments in American Life and Their Impact on Ministry

A dramatic transformation of the nation during the first century of its life had the effect of reshaping ministry in America. Here we suggest major elements in that transformation.

The Growth of the Nation

In 1790, the date of the first federal census, 3.9 million people inhabited the states along the Atlantic seaboard, while something like 750,000 American Indians occupied the territories belonging to the new nation between the Alleghenies and the Mississippi. Spain and

France still held the vast colonial realm to the south and west, and the Oregon country lay, for the most part, still undisturbed.

By 1890 a population of 62.9 million had surged across the continental domain acquired by the United States from the European empires, the United States Army had broken the power of the Indian tribes to interfere with the incursion of more and more white settlers, and the frontier line on the national map had passed into memory. The black population of 750,000 in 1790 had grown to 7.4 million a century later, freed from slavery during the Civil War but still deprived of civil or economic equality. Much of the growth of population, both white and black, had resulted from the natural increase of a vigorous people. But the coming of eight million immigrants from Europe and more than one hundred thousand from Asia greatly added to the ethnic diversity and religious complexity of the nation.

Meanwhile, steam supplanted water and wind as the major source of power, and the rapid growth of industry introduced a revolution in labor, lifestyle, and religion. Great manufacturing cities with populations running into the millions grew out of the quiet colonial towns that had preceded them—or, in the case of Chicago, sprang up from the open countryside. Thousands of rural young people seeking their fortunes, as well as escape from the tedium of labor in the fields, thronged into the cities. A vast array of new social problems confronted the nation: housing, conditions of labor, civic corruption, and domination by new combines of economic and industrial power.

All at once the churches, their hands already full with too much work, faced a new set of unprecedented demands. The effort to serve the vastly expanded population in countryside and city, to bring it within the fold of the church, and to provide religious institutions equal to the task—all within so short a time—gave a peculiar bent to American religion. Its common traits arising from the national experience of the nineteenth century began to loom far larger than the differences among the denominations. These new developments gave further impetus to the reshaping of ministry.

Religious Activism

Activism in religion was one of the chief results of these developments. So much to do and so little time! Millions to be converted, a continent to be redeemed! Increasingly, churches came to measure their fidelity by their response to that missionary challenge, with a corresponding diminution of emphasis on contemplation, liturgy, theology, and other concerns that for so long had preoccupied the Christian community in the Old World.

This activist people projected their new expectations upon their ministers. But American ministers did not resist. On the contrary, they took the lead in prodding church people to an ever more activistic concern. And they themselves helped to shape a new concept: A good minister was someone who *got things done*!

If the ministers suffered any frustration with respect to this activist ideal, it arose not from the expectation itself but from the slow or inadequate response of those whose help the minister needed. So Jason Lee, who went out to the Oregon country in 1834, returned on horseback to the eastern seaboard in 1838 to solicit greater support for his work. In the same way Marcus Whitman, after bringing the first wagon train to the Northwest to launch the mission at Waiilatpu on the Walla Walla River in 1836, hurried back East in 1842 to plead for the cause and hastened again to the Oregon country.

Localism in Religion

In a nation so vast, a strong sense of localism soon came to dominance. The trait was paradoxical, for it combined a vociferous insistence in the new communities of the West on "deciding things for ourselves" with a clamor for assistance from government or denomination. Yet even though the pioneers looked to Washington for easy access to ownership of new land and for public improvements such as roads and canals, their fabled self-reliance was undeniable. In one situation after another, whatever the matter at hand, they dealt with it themselves—even with a crisis of life and death—for there was no one else to do so. In politics, justice, defense against Indians, disaster of fire or storm, they took what action they could and lived or died by the results. And they did not appreciate second-guessing later on from outside "authorities" who had not been there at the time.

This trait of localism operated powerfully in the realm of religion. The people moving west in prodigious numbers simply outran the power of the churches to keep up with them. If there were to be religious services in their community, the people there must often take the initiative. So they gathered in houses or barns or groves to read the Bible and sing and pray and muster what force they could to convince the people back east to send them a preacher.

A common notion held that a burial had not been completed until a minister could be found to say a few words over the grave, and sometimes that was not until weeks after a death. With such a scarcity of professional pastors, the new patterns of ministry developed from within the resources of a rural congregation by the so-called people's churches had an understandable appeal—the farmer-preacher of the Baptists, the "local preacher" of the Methodists, the elder of the

Disciples.[2] Going out on the Oregon Trail, members of a party without a preacher would designate some man among them as minister pro tem. Then the rise of the Sunday school gave laypeople an instrument for providing religious fellowship and instruction even when no preacher was at hand.

Many communities of American Christians who found the reality of God and the comfort of religion through such unconventional ministries came to like the unpretentious directness of the worship thus provided, with its strong reliance on the sacred language of Bible and hymnal. They responded with something less than cordiality later on when denominational officials "from back east" undertook to "impose" other standards on them. The notion still surges powerfully through American congregations, as long as they have strength enough to keep going, that "we are capable of managing things ourselves." Whatever the ostensible polity of the denomination, "congregationalism" flourishes, with its strengths and weaknesses, in nearly all the churches. The minister who undertakes to develop a sense of greater responsibility to and involvement in the life of the larger church sometimes faces an uphill battle.

The Nation's Place in Religious Faith

A vibrant faith in the vocation and destiny of the American nation countered the spiritual localism of believing communities who responded only feebly or negatively to overtures from denominational "headquarters" and who had little sense of the ecumenical dimensions of the church. What has been called "the religion of the republic" or "American civil religion" was a fact of nineteenth-century life in the United States.[3]

Accepted without question by most ministers, native-born or immigrant, Protestant or Catholic, rigidly orthodox or undeniably liberal, the religion of the republic gave them status as interpreters of the common faith, and they accepted it without embarrassment. The sermons and articles in the religious press, from Ezra Stiles's magnificent deliverance in 1783 right down through World War II, reveal an unquestioning faith in the unique place of the United States in the counsels of divine providence. Troubled as the moralists of the pulpit might be about the sinfulness of the people, and even of the nation itself in permitting slavery or the liquor traffic or abortion, they believed in freedom and the Constitution and the ultimate triumph of righteousness in this land.

In language steeped in the vocabulary of scripture, the preachers recounted the myths of the Pilgrims, the patriots, the framers of the national charter, the virtuous Washington, and—remarkably soon after the assassination—the righteous Lincoln. Ministers of Caucasian descent confessed uncritically the common faith in the superiority of the Anglo-Saxon peoples, manifest chiefly in their supposed innate devotion to liberty, freedom from superstition, and genius for civilization. The rapid acquisition of the national domain, especially of the California goldfields just before the discovery of gold at Sutter's Mill, they regarded as evident signs of divine favor on this nation and people.

While too many political orators and even preachers turned the common faith into a raw blend of jingoism and religion, ministers generally tempered their belief in national destiny with their biblical understanding of divine judgment and their sense of vocation to call for repentance. The paradox of the old Puritan jeremiad recurs again: a doom-filled denunciation of the people's wickedness, a call to repentance, a fervid reaffirmation of the glorious purpose of providence for this unique nation.[4]

The flurry of discussion about American civil religion a few years ago, when taken up by preachers and theologians, tended to pursue a negative line leading to wholesale rejection. No responsible Christian can condone idolatry of any kind, including idolatry of the nation. And some of the unguarded utterances of nineteenth-century ministers bordered on idolatry.

But the common faith in a divine purpose for the American nation was not necessarily an idolatrous delusion. Without an established church, and in a society obviously fractured by the competing claims of many denominations, the nation itself proved a symbol of that unity in society which in all previous experience it had been the function of religion to provide. Acknowledged to be less than ultimate, "this nation under God" was to be held accountable before the divine judgment seat, but its youthful devotion to the ideals of freedom and equality and its unprecedented achievement of material abundance for masses of its people seemed convincing evidence of its special place in God's beneficent purpose. The phrase "manifest destiny" could be used as a rationale for territorial expansion; it could also, however, express a sense of national vocation to serve the cause of freedom and human dignity.

The prevalence of the common faith gave many American ministers a position of significance in society of larger general importance than their status as ministers of particular denominations could offer. According to the credentials of office, any one of them stood up as a Presbyterian, a Methodist, a Baptist, a representative of a small minority within the community. But when a preacher spoke of the divine purpose for the nation, he or she gave voice to the common faith and assumed in the popular mind a rightful position as spiritual guide to the community as a whole. Some ministers today shame-lessly exploit this possibility in waving the flag on "I Love America" Sundays. Others with a world vision or cynicism about the present state of the nation may have fallen into too great a reticence about any expression linking patriotism and faith. In any case a readiness to affirm a common belief in one God, in the biblical understanding of God's involvement in the history of the nations, and in this nation's particular vocation and destiny profoundly occupied the ministry of the nineteenth century. And the popular mind still looks to the minister to voice this faith.

Intellectual Leadership

Intellectual leadership in nineteenth-century America under-went dramatic diversification. The number of learned professions multiplied at a time when the burgeoning of the "people's churches" on the frontier gave prominence to a ministry with limited schooling. It is customary for historians to note the surrender of intellectual leadership to secular figures.[5] Certainly few pastors or theologians commanded an acknowledged place at the cutting edge of theory and discovery or instructed the mind of the nation as the preachers had directed that of New England in the colonial era. But many ministers, even an impressive number from the "people's churches," consti-tuted a sizable part of the "educated class" and provided significant cultural leadership in their own communities, while the more cel-ebrated preachers and editors of religious papers drew attention to new issues and continued to help form the popular mind.

What did change radically in the nineteenth century was the general level of education. Public schools developed rapidly in the new nation in hope of assuring an enlightened citizenry, and Protes-tant ministers led the movement for their support, moved both by their confidence in the triumph of truth and right if only the people could be taught to read for themselves, and by their fear at the growth of Roman Catholic parochial schools. Even at the end of the century, however, only a minority of young people were privileged to attend public high schools. The religious "academy" or "young ladies semi-nary" conducted under denominational auspices, or the private proprietorship of a minister, still held an important place on the educational scene, and the church-related college—its administra-tion and faculty still largely made up of ministers in 1890—domi-nated higher education numerically.

The growth of tax-supported universities and normal schools proceeded throughout the century and leaped forward with the passage of the Morrill Act in 1862. First the "natural sciences" and then psychology and sociology detached themselves from departments of philosophy to become the domain of specialists in empirical research, and by century's end workers in these fields had raised new issues that were troubling to the traditional religious mind. The trek of young graduate students to the German universities had barely begun, and the spectacular growth of American graduate schools was yet to come. But the giants of American thought whom the historian of ideas now identifies on the national scene in the generation following the Civil War were "men of letters" and university professors rather than ministers.

For all that, the "humanities" still dominated American education, as did a tone of high idealism, commitment to service, and a spirit that can best be described as practical-Christian even if not identified with theological orthodoxy. Ministers on the "cutting edge" who were prominent in the world of culture moved from pulpit to classroom to lecture platform and back to pulpit again. They planted the dream of an education in the mind of many a young person. They discussed intellectual and social issues that were beginning to attract popular attention; the "topical" sermon provided a great deal of excitement in the latter half of the century.

If ministers of limited education and rigid minds locked into traditional notions of cosmology too often linked religion with the forces of anti-intellectualism, their influence must not blind us to the total scene. Even on the frontier, the farmer-preacher or circuit-rider without academic pretensions exerted a positive intellectual influence. Such a minister read the Bible, dealt with sizable ideas, and sought to point young people to a "larger world." If that minister had managed to learn Latin and Greek, as was frequently the case, the way was open into the heritage of the classics.

Although a style of religion flourished in the "people's churches" that willingly identified with the poor and the ignorant—the cultural outsiders—that religion commonly worked to broaden the vision, enlarge the opportunity, and improve the lot of those to whom it came. Since the 1830s, these churches had undertaken to raise the education of their preachers considerably above the level of the masses.[6] Much of the religiously inspired philanthropy of the years after the Civil War sought to provide colleges that could supply religious leadership for the black churches.

For a time Roman Catholic parishes took on a strong ethnic character, intensified by the high proportion of immigrant priests—French, Italian, and especially Irish. They enjoyed the confidence of the newcomers and possessed both the education and the "know-how" to help these bewildered and courageous strangers find a place in American society.

The vulgar impression of nineteenth-century ministers as igno-rant, narrow-minded, and reactionary stems from only part of the frontier religious tradition. The life and work of ministers in that tradition as well as in the settled communities also gave rise to the common expectation of the minister as interpreter of high culture and current issues, not theology and biblical history alone.

Nineteenth-Century Forms and Concepts of Ministry

In the land of new beginnings, the radically new situation of religion and the overwhelming changes in society functioned as molds for casting new forms of ministry and reshaping the old. A distinctive set of patterns emerged in the nineteenth century to supplant the traditional forms that had held sway in the colonial era.

Four models of ministry again dominated the scene: *Pulpiteer, Revivalist, Builder,* and *Missionary*. None was without precedent in Christian history. Indeed, Pulpiteer, Revivalist, Builder, and Mission-ary might be said to have been the nineteenth-century adaptations, respectively, of Master, Awakener, Priest, and Saint. But emphasis, expectations, and function were so radically revised that we must give them new titles. While social context, popular demand, and models of ministry have changed yet again in the twentieth century, these nineteenth-century forms and concepts still exert a powerful force on current definitions of ministry.

PULPITEER

Magisterium had departed. The power of any pastor to speak with binding authority to ruler or citizen—a theoretical power that, even at the medieval apogee of churchly dominance, had always been tempered by the facts of *Realpolitik*—ended with the separation of church and state. Gone was the legal right of any preacher to teach officially in the name of a Christian government, as the Master had done in New England. From now on, the authority of the pulpit was its power to persuade. The mantle of the colonial Master was traded in for the frock coat of the Pulpiteer.

This Christian orator embodied the form that set the public image of ministry in nineteenth-century America, while secular counterparts in courtroom and legislative hall dominated law and politics.[1] The generation of the Revolution had thrust the public speaker to the center of popular attention and affection—the person gifted with words, who could command a hearing, help the audience understand and analyze issues, then move them to action. As "the People's Voice"[2] the orator enjoyed the kind of extravagant adulation that this generation heaps upon its rock stars. The golden-tongued speaker continued as a culture-hero through the decades when the nation hung on the eloquence of Daniel Webster and Henry Clay, when the Lincoln-Douglas debates caused a sensation across the land, when William Jennings Bryan emerged as the "boy orator from the Platte." Women with a cause proved their mettle on the platform—Lucretia Mott as champion of women's rights, Frances E. Willard as crusader for temperance.[3] The orator was the molder of public opinion, the mover to action, the celebrity of the hour.

The orator incarnated the highest ideals of nineteenth-century education. Its goal, as in the days of classical antiquity from which the liberal arts derived, was, in the words of Cato, to produce "the good man skilled in speaking."[4] In the American republic, which like Cato's Rome gave a notable place to the orator and in which the curriculum of the schools majored in the cultivation of eloquence, the church, expectedly, gave prominence to its preachers.

At least twice before in history, great eras of oratory had reached their culmination in magnificent Pulpiteers who equaled or surpassed their contemporaries on the secular rostrum—namely, the patristic bishops of the fourth century, whose sermons won for them abiding influence as "Doctors of the Church," and the Catholic court-preachers of eighteenth-century France. Now once more, both in Britain and in America, society prized and heeded eloquence in every part of public life, and the church provided a setting in which the most accomplished practicians of the art could flourish. Everywhere they were acclaimed as "princes of the pulpit."

The art of preaching deliberately appropriated classical models, putting the eloquence of antiquity to the service of the Christian message. The most influential textbook of homiletics ever written by an American, a work still in print a century after publication, came from the pen of a Southern Baptist professor, John A. Broadus, in 1870. Aside from its counsel on exegesis, *The Preparation and Delivery of Sermons* is a forthright Christian restatement of the principles of classical rhetoric.[5]

The most eloquent of all the Romans had summarized the duties of the orator: to teach, to please, to persuade.[6] In the new setting of religious liberty, these duties taught by Cicero became the responsibility and opportunity of the Pulpiteer. And, increasingly, persuasion became the heart of the matter.

Part of the basis for the preacher's authority had collapsed. The Masters of the colonial pulpit had instructed their hearers in the meaning of the biblical text, handing down their impressive word with the dual authority of scripture and magisterial office. Where the popular mind still accepted biblical authority, the nineteenth-century preacher had only to convince the hearers of the correctness of his or her interpretation, as opposed to that of some other preacher representing a different denomination. But all audiences were not like that. Rather, the Pulpiteer now had to contend with doubts in the popular mind concerning the Bible itself, stemming from the skepticism of Tom Paine at the outset of the period and the theatrical infidelity of Bob Ingersoll toward its end. With the two solid piers of scriptural and magisterial authority undercut, only two of the four bulwarks that once had upheld the solid structure of Puritanism now remained, namely the authority of experience, which became the special province of the Revivalist, and the authority of reason, to which the Pulpiteer especially appealed.

In the young republic, despite the still limited extent of education and a popular tendency to be swept along by tides of emotion, the folk prided themselves on their powers of logical thought. To that much prized "common sense" the orators unfailingly appealed—or pretended to appeal. In their effort to persuade their hearers, attorneys at the bar, statesmen in the marble halls of the capitol, candidates atop a rude platform on the hustings, and preachers in the churches addressed the intelligence of the people. In order to persuade, the orator must convince.

In the latter part of the century, interest shifted from doctrinal hairsplitting to new issues of public policy and religious thought. Henry Ward Beecher established the topical sermon as a popular genre, and it was essentially a mode of teaching. A little later the advocates of the Social Gospel undertook to help people understand the problems of the new urban-industrial society and to respond as Christians.

The typical Pulpiteer preached in his own church on Sunday morning and evening and one other night during the week. Dismissing the Puritan distinction between preaching to outsiders and teaching in the church, nineteenth-century Americans tended to use *preaching* for both kinds of work.[7] Perhaps the broader designation was now appropriate, since the overwhelming majority of the population was still unchurched and the typical "audience" would contain a high proportion of "outsiders." The Pulpiteer remained alert to the situation and, in a manner appropriate to the tradition of his church, undertook to persuade the unconverted to decision. Since teaching was his essential mode, the two distinct functions coalesced in practice.

The Pulpiteer's teaching intent led from the pulpit to the debate platform—a highly popular source of amusement and education at the time—and to the lecture hall. The celebrated preacher Russell Conwell delivered his sermon "Acres of Diamonds" thousands of times. The Chautauqua circuit gave the accomplished orator enthusiastic audiences of hundreds, even thousands, in town after town, and noted Pulpiteers were rated among the most surefire drawing cards. People expected to "learn a lot" from hearing them. Many a famous preacher also carried on a venture in religious journalism, with articles didactic in content and rhetorical in style.

Teaching went on throughout the life of the churches. One measure of its effectiveness is the strong sense of denominational tradition as centered in certain crucial elements, "our distinctive witness," which persists with such power even yet in churches where no formal indoctrination has gone on for half a century.

Many of the teachers would hardly strike us as orators: unschooled farmer-preachers, elders elected out of rural congregations, zealous volunteers in the Sunday school movement that swept across the continent just ahead of the properly organized churches, young people improving their skills at public speaking in meetings of the Society of Christian Endeavor or the Epworth League. But these teachers knew and loved the scriptures, they believed in the saving power of the gospel, and they wanted their relatives and friends and neighbors to understand the word of life that had come to them.

So they spoke as best they were able, relying on their familiarity with the Bible and such other helps as they could lay their hands on. Though some lacked any inherent talent for speaking—we must not overly romanticize the situation—the natural eloquence of a people still living in a largely oral culture sometimes gave wings to their words. Their models were preachers they had heard, perhaps Peter Cartwright or Alexander Campbell or Henry Ward Beecher himself, and remembered arguments, illustrations, and phrases recurred in their own efforts. Moreover, in the face-to-face contact of rural life where much of the "news" had to do with the behavior of one's neighbors, these local "preachers" got no hearing unless they backed up their talk with their daily living. As the classical rhetoricians had known, the ethos of the orator was a crucial element in the power to persuade.

The black preachers stand among the most effective teachers of the nineteenth century. In the years before emancipation they maintained the distinctive style of preaching initiated by their predecessors in colonial times. That style tells and retells the great biblical story from creation to redemption to consummation.[8] It recounts again and again the many well-loved narratives making up that story. It charges every sermon with illumination and emotional power by appealing to the example of biblical characters. It elaborates the central images of the Bible. It involves the hearers through call-and-response.

In the face of overwhelming odds, notable black preachers emerged. Richard Allen gained freedom early in the century and gave his life to ministry on behalf of his people.[9] Many of his colleagues, however, did not receive emancipation until Lincoln's proclamation and the victory of the Union armies. Restrictions on teaching slaves to read and the difficulty of acquiring books and materials for writing resulted in few transcripts of antebellum black preaching. Nevertheless, the eloquence of speakers brought up in the oral culture of the slave community and given opportunity for enough education to read the Bible and a few basic books, rose to notable power in a preacher like John Jasper.[10] Some of his sermons survive, warranting a place for him among the great Pulpiteers.

In his famous *Lectures on Preaching* (1877) Phillips Brooks characterized the art as the communication of "truth through personality."[11] He devoted more attention to truth than to the unique person of the preacher, thus making clear his commitment to the task of teaching. But he also demonstrated that the unique individuality of the preacher's person is an essential element in the transmission of Christian faith, and he incorporated that insight into a "theology of preaching." The phrase "truth through personality" outran Brooks's careful use of it and became a catchword among preachers who ventured to trade on their personal magnetism. The peril of their approach for the integrity of ministry points up the dangers implicit in persuasion. For according to Cicero, the orator must "please."

By *pleasing*, the rhetorician meant gaining the goodwill of the audience and holding their interest by the use of narrative, ornamentation of style, manner of delivery, change of pace, and—if their eyes began to glaze over—a lively digression, perhaps even irrelevant to the argument but designed to recapture their attention. Nearly every good speaker does these things naturally, if not by design, realizing the futility of making a speech if people do not listen.

A great part of the nineteenth-century art of rhetoric was given over to the cultivating of the various devices calculated to delight the hearer. The Puritan Master had spurned all such tricks on principle, even while using some in spite of everything. In the Bible Commonwealth the saints needed no such distractions from the plain style in an effort to make the truth palatable, for sometimes it must necessarily offend; the unregenerate could be converted only by the working of the Holy Spirit, accompanying the preaching of the Word and not dependent on any human devices. In the nineteenth century the Revivalist struggled overtly with the theological problem of employing rhetorical art and decided it was proper to use the measures of persuasion to the full extent of their power. The Pulpiteer did so with less reflection on the theological issues involved and with a more relaxed frame of mind. At ease with audiences, enjoying the mutual interaction, the Pulpiteer knew what they liked and gave them enough of it to keep them coming back.

In the best of the preachers, such readiness to please their following in the form and manner of presentation involved no compromise of substance. With integrity it followed the wisdom of Jesus in couching some of the most difficult, even offensive, elements of his teaching in thoroughly delightful parables. But it was only a short step from the authentic drama of the gospel to the theatrics of striking a pose, from a contest over great issues to the mock heroics of "taking a stand" on behalf of a prejudice held by the majority. More than one orator who offered himself as the "man of the people" turned out in fact to be the people's man and not God's.[12] It proved perilously easy for a gifted speaker to please people sufficiently to persuade them to support a religious enterprise that would continue to please.

Some of the most celebrated Pulpiteers built up huge personal followings, preached to hundreds every time they entered the pulpit, and filled their hearers with inspiration, but failed to engage serious issues of thought and public policy, thus leaving the church unprepared to deal with a rapidly changing world. T. De Witt Talmadge (1832-1902), for example, preached to adoring throngs, deploring new urban problems and cheering his hearers with potshots at Darwin and Marx, but "left little lasting impression....Like a falling star which blazes and then is forgotten, Talmadge shot across the American pulpit scene."[13] Celebrity for the moment did not assure every Pulpiteer of abiding significance.

The new "sciences" of sociology and psychology were in their infancy in the 1870s. The preachers seized eagerly on psychology, and the people were pleased to have their interior problems talked about. But comparatively few Pulpiteers passed on to their people the facts and insights of sociology that would have helped them grapple with problems of modern society. Some of these problems were soon to bring to an end the supremacy of the great downtown church over which the "prince of the pulpit" held sway. This neglect is all the more striking in view of the important part a few ministers played in pioneering the study of sociology.[14] An important exception must be noted in the serious efforts to engage the new problems by the early champions of the Social Gospel. Walter Rauschenbusch was an impressive preacher, and Washington Gladden and Frank S. Gunsalus clearly deserved the title of Pulpiteer. Though they preached to great crowds, their message did not universally please.

Reflections on the Pulpiteer

What impact did the Pulpiteer have on the concept of ministry in America? Our heritage from this model is once again a mixed bag. Preaching was established as so obviously the primary function of a minister that, in large parts of the nation, "Preacher" came to be the most commonly used title for the pastor of a church, and in some places still endures as an informal term of address. The noblest practicians of the art raised their work to a level of almost unprecedented excellence on every count. They succeeded in placing a number of religious questions high on the agenda of popular interest. In these eloquent voices the church made full use of the most effective mode of public communication then available, the mode that enjoyed greatest prestige, and offered orators of its own who equaled in skill and influence the most notable celebrities on secular platforms.

In a culture that prized oratory and hailed the eloquent speaker as an important public figure, the accomplished Pulpiteer was a big name, not only in churchgoing circles but in society at large. Toward the end of the century and for some time after, the great cities all had their famous preachers. Even smaller cities such as Buffalo, New York, and Independence, Missouri, boasted of preachers who were nationally known, as did the towns of Strasburg, Virginia, and Columbus, Indiana. Within a state, members of every denomination knew the names and personalities of their leading speakers and lamented that their fame had not gone as far as it ought. The people of any place knowledgeably compared the oratory of the ministers in the chief churches of the different denominations and heard them all at various public events.

The minister's most important professional function was the work of the pulpit. A massive piece of furniture, the pulpit claimed the center of the platform in an imposing church building located at a major intersection served by streetcar lines converging from every part of town. What a leading preacher said on Sunday was commonly reported in Monday's newspapers, even when it dealt chiefly with the religious life and offered no suggestion of anything sensational; not uncommonly the full text of a sermon was printed for the readers. In the age of the orator the minister was a public figure whose spirit and influence were felt throughout the community. From such a lofty eminence, the "prince of the pulpit" held sway.

The nineteenth-century preachers effected a shift of focus from the abstractions of doctrine to the reality of life as it is lived. Hundreds of sermons from this period possess even now a vitality, a freshness, a strain of human interest, an insight into the way the gospel touches life and experience, that may be found only rarely in texts from earlier centuries. And although the age of the Pulpiteer passed so long ago and many congregations rarely hear a sermon that is genuinely significant or even interesting, even yet an air of expectancy sometimes sweeps perceptibly over the people when a minister stands up to preach. This enterprise remains so close to the heart of the American religious tradition that a person who has been stirred by a sermon may still be heard to say, "Today I've really been to church!"

The popular mind, however, also retains some memories that make our work difficult for us. It entertains a stereotype of the pulpit virtuoso as one who can occupy a considerable space of time playing with verbal effects while saying nothing of consequence and making no change in a bad situation. The negative expectation of the would-be Pulpiteer as windbag is projected on us. So is the notion of the small-town Pulpiteer as moralistic nag: "Don't preach at me!"

The cult of personality that in the nineteenth century exalted the orator to the pinnacle of popular acclaim now reserved for professional athletes and rock musicians survives here and there in the well-cultivated adulation of the local religious celebrity who has succeeded in building up a large personal following with all the earmarks of presumed ministerial success: a massive, predictably garish temple declared to be nondenominational; a fleet of buses; weekly attendance running into the thousands; a regular television program; recurring displays of advertising in the press; well-publicized ventures into charity or education; an occasional foray into politics; a continuous procession of guest stars at the temple; and constant attention from the media.

As if all this were not enough to turn the old Adam within us a shade of electric green, what with the knowledge that such "success" has typically been bought by giving the customers what they want, by frequent flag-waving and unabashed appeals to sentiment and a constant bath of nostalgia, by confirming the ugliest of popular prejudices under the guise of an unctuous piety, by attacking outright or through innuendo the kind of honest, relevant, prophetic religion with which we strain so hard to keep faith—as if all this were not enough, every week or so some member of our congregation innocently, or not so innocently, asks, "How is it that our church just doesn't grow, and they have those thousands of people every Sunday over at the temple?" The preacher at the temple does no honor to the memory of the Pulpiteer, but that memory makes this phenomenon possible.

As for our own ministry, the influence of the Pulpiteer means that, whatever our other strengths, the people wish we would do a better job of preaching than we usually do. To a surprising extent, search committees looking for a new pastor still list strength in the pulpit high among their priorities, even though in practice the congregation often pushes other demands much harder.

Most of us really like to preach, despite our frequent need to confess insufficient preparation and to rid ourselves of guilt for not honoring our pulpit obligation with a larger measure of responsibility and devotion than we sometimes bring to it. When we do preach well, we know inwardly that we are fulfilling the work central to our calling—holding up the vision of God's glorious purpose for each of our hearers and for our common life, announcing God's forgivenenss and constant readiness to make all things new, and doing it all with love for the people and the conviction that rises from a heart truly committed. Even so, we are sometimes haunted by nostalgia for a day when the pastor of a church was *somebody* in this town, and we long for our voice to win a larger hearing for the good news.

Model 6

REVIVALIST

An even higher pitch of excitement surrounded the Revivalist than that which attended the Pulpiteer. Obvious similarities linked these two forms of ministry, for both made preaching their central work, and both appealed to the popular fascination with the spoken word. But the Revivalist concentrated all the forces of a powerful personality upon a single objective, the "winning of souls," and developed that process into such an effective mechanism in American religion, for a time, that this model requires a place of its own in any consideration of nineteenth-century ministry.[1]

The activity that goes under the name of revivalism today offers only a pale and distorted imitation of the powerful movement that surged through the life of this nation more than a hundred years ago. What we see on television or catch occasionally in an anachronistic tent meeting conveys little sense of the power or the ambiguity of that movement. And the historical context has radically changed.

Recall the observation in the chapter on the Awakener, that revivalism was a mode of offering the gospel to a population brought up within the common assumptions of a Christian culture but nevertheless unchurched. Whether a sufficient residue of Christian assumption remains in our secularized, increasingly materialistic society for revivalism in the nineteenth-century mode ever to work again is open to question. The places where it still seems to achieve occasional results are the cultural backwaters of our time—which may, however, cover much more territory and run far deeper than the liberal mind can realize.

The Revivalist is the nineteenth-century incarnation of the model of ministry that appeared in late colonial times as the Awakener. In the early decades of national life, revivalism reached such heights of influence that almost anyone engaged in the practice of ministry in any form—certainly any Protestant minister—felt its effects and either imitated or resisted the Revivalist.

The Great Western Revival, which broke out in Tennessee and Kentucky at the turn of the nineteenth century, brought the Revivalist to the center of popular attention that the Awakener had briefly held, then lost thirty years before as political concerns displaced religious anxiety in the excitement of the struggle for independence and the establishment of a new nation. Already a "Second Great Awakening" had stirred the seaboard states when a meeting at Cane Ridge, Kentucky, in 1801 seized the interest of the nation.[2]

Religious fervor ran so high that newspapers in the eastern cities carried full accounts of the meetings and the strange behavior manifested there.[3] Thousands of frontier folk came to camp on the open ground around a rural Presbyterian church. In preparation for a "sacramental celebration," perhaps a score of preachers—Presbyterian, Baptist, and Methodist—addressed the people in different parts of the encampment, calling for repentance and offering forgiveness to those who were truly converted.

Indescribable excitement attended the preaching. "Seized by the Spirit," people fell to the ground weeping or laughing, leaped or barked uncontrollably, or engaged in other bizarre "spiritual exercises." When the seemingly irresistible seizure had passed, these people felt a great sense of peace with God and, taking the experience as a sign of their election, professed conversion. Hundreds of converts were made in this way, many from among the curiosity-seekers and scoffers who came to laugh at the strange goings-on and found themselves caught up in them in spite of everything.

Out of the Great Western Revival came the new institution of the camp meeting, designed to replicate the marvelous happenings at Cane Ridge. It became an annual occasion for the ingathering of souls in the rural areas of the newly opened West and, particularly with Methodists, a primary instrument for winning conversions. The preachers who now and again participated in such an event carried on in their regular charges during the year, recalling the victories of that great occasion and looking forward to others yet to come. So the urgency, the threatening, the pleading, the shouting, the expectation that characterized the preaching of the Revivalist in the camp meeting came to mark the work of many a minister the year around. Rarely outside those great gatherings was such a pitch of spiritual excitement reached, but the style was firmly established.

Such demonstrations of religious excitement offended some Christians and troubled many more. Ministers with a strong sense of liturgical propriety—Roman Catholics, Episcopalians, Lutherans—looked on in horror. Rational types—Congregationalists, Unitarians, Disciples—repudiated the emotionalism with batteries of argument. Presbyterians split into factions, Old Lights opposing revivalism and New Lights advocating it, much as they had done in the colonial Awakening. But Methodists and Baptists and Cumberland Presbyterians and New Light Christians continued to pray for revivals and to rejoice in periodic "seasons of refreshing."

In the first decades of the nineteenth century, the form of Revivalist consequently asserted itself as a major model of ministry on the American scene. Strangely enough, however, at the outset no exemplar of this model attained wide recognition as a celebrity. James McGready, Barton W. Stone, and the other preachers who conducted the meeting at Cane Ridge were simple frontier pastors who never achieved a place in the national limelight except among those settlers of the back country whom their ministry reached in person. Yet they gave life to a pattern of ministry destined to affect virtually every minister in America.

Then revivalism came to the cities and moved into the urban East. When Charles G. Finney began to preach in western New York in the 1820s, an imposing Revivalist captured national attention.[4] Finney was tall and gaunt and dynamic, with piercing eyes that no squirming sinner could evade, and an air of total command. Having read law and practiced at the bar before his call to ministry, he brought the withering manner of a prosecuting attorney to his indictment of the sinner and a battery of well-tested techniques for moving the accused to almost unbearable discomfort and then to the psychic release of conversion.

Finney's highly publicized "New Measures" excited intense controversy. Critics attacked them as manipulative, which they surely were. Objectors moved by humane concern were outraged at the violation of personal integrity, while the theologically inclined believed that Finney's measures usurped the prerogative of the Holy Spirit in conversion. The Revivalist had a simple answer. The New Measures worked. They won converts. The pragmatic mood of young America accepted the argument.

The full story of revivalism is too long and complex to be detailed here. But appearing at a time when the churches felt with increasing intensity the burden of the unsaved in such overwhelming numbers all about them, as well as the pressure to bring in new members in order to build up their institutional strength, the nineteenth-century Revivalist effectively broke the iron grip of the old Calvinist doctrine of election. Ministers wanted to see the multitudes saved. Now they had the means to bring about conversions. They could no longer believe that God willed the death of those who might be moved by the New Measures to a profession of repentance and faith. What generations of theologians arguing for free will had been unable to achieve by disputation, the Revivalists accomplished. Their pragmatism ended the sway of the old Calvinism within the churches of the Calvinist tradition (Presbyterian, Congregationalist, and Baptist).[5]

Many continued to preach the old doctrines of total depravity, human helplessness, and divine election, but they preached them while making full use of the New Measures in the sure confidence that in the kindly Providence of God the measures would work. They did. Thus the Revivalist launched American religion on a course toward that increasing preoccupation with technique and statistical results that ultimately robbed revivalism of integrity and at last caused the mainline churches to abandon it.

But we cannot lightly dismiss Finney and his colleagues. They proclaimed redeeming love in the high faith that the God they preached would provide a way for the penitent sinner to claim the salvation purchased by Jesus Christ. They were reaching for a theology of conversion in accordance with that message, for they could no longer reconcile with the gospel the old Calvinist understanding of foreordination, election, and reprobation. No matter what estimate we place upon their theological formulation or their New Measures, these preachers served as ministers of grace.

The urban Revivalist also preached a gospel of broad relevance. Believing that Christians should enter the social struggle in opposition to slavery, intemperance, and other evils in the body politic, Finney and others preached for conversion. They made explicit the demand for a change in social attitudes and practices and not in private habits alone. The urban revivals of the 1830s and 1840s gave major impetus to the movements for abolition, temperance, civic reform, Christian higher education, and foreign missions. The narrowing of the Revivalistic focus to interior personal concerns did not develop until later in the century.

Preeminent among the Revivalists was Dwight L. Moody, whose work as a young Sunday school teacher won such overwhelming response that he gave up his position in a shoe store to devote his life to preaching. Though he lacked a college education, Moody had remarkable insight into the fears and longings of his generation, as well as evident zeal and a unique facility for telling simple, moving stories that entranced his hearers. Teaming up with gospel singer Ira D. Sankey, he attracted audiences of thousands, won many conversions, and generated excitement here and abroad.

In Moody and his contemporaries the raw power of the camp meeting and the blatant manipulativeness of the New Measures gave way to a more genteel mode of persuasion. The title Evangelist gradually became more common than Revivalist, but the function was still the same: to bring the unchurched people of a Christian cultural tradition to claim for themselves the grace of Jesus Christ and the responsibilities of discipleship.

It was an age of sentiment. Most of the population still lived on farms, isolated by the lack of good roads or other means of communication. Growing up in large families, their total experience of human companionship centered in the old home and in contacts with a few neighbors. When that circle was broken—as young couples married and went west, as the men were called to the colors in the Civil War, as young people left home to seek their fortune in the rapidly growing cities—many suffered intense loneliness and heartache. The songs of the war years and of the Gilded Age were unabashedly sentimental, as was the popular drama. One of the chief concerns of the preachers was the plight of such uprooted young people alone in the city and subject to temptation.

The Revivalist now turned the force of all this sentiment into the effort to save souls. The gospel songs, with their vivid, moving lyrics, and with their stirring, heart-melting tunes by Sankey and others like him, used powerful imagery of home and friendship and love and longing, as well as of Bible stories known since childhood. Consider Sankey's "There Were Ninety and Nine," "For You I Am Praying," "Under His Wings," "Hiding in Thee," or "Faith Is the Victory."

Preachers filled their sermons with one story after another containing touching accounts of a mother's careworn face, a godly and hardworking father, the old home, a rebellious youth, the old country church, a sinner's untimely death, an orphaned child with memories of a drunken father, the death angel's coming for an aged saint, a humble working girl who remains faithful, a rich man who comes to Jesus and is saved.

The cumulative effect of such music and preaching, continuing night after night, with vast audiences of persons who admired the evangelist—and who, let us remember, had never heard a radio, looked at a moving picture or television screen, or heard a lecture on psychology—the effect was overwhelming. On any given night scores would come to Jesus.

Conversion was still associated with an overpowering inner experience, however this wringing-out of sentiment might differ from the old Puritan's experimental knowledge of grace and election or the raw spiritual exercises of the camp meeting. And subjective emotion established itself as the sure criterion of religious experience in America. At the same time, Christian theology was reduced to an oversimplified explanation of atonement. Life in the church came to emphasize the seasons of revival above all else. Except for the old liturgical churches, Protestant worship took over the informal manner of the great revival meeting, and gospel songs soon claimed a large place in the standard hymnals. The focus of Christian concern narrowed from the broad social involvement of the earlier Revivalists to a total preoccupation with the salvation of the individual sinner.

Yet for all the reliance on sentiment and a total lack of interest in intellectual problems—evolution and biblical inspiration excepted!—the Revivalist did not necessarily preach an overtly anti-intellectual message. Moody made an impressive impact on Harvard, Yale, Oxford, Cambridge, and Edinburgh. He greatly influenced the development of the YMCA, the Student Christian Movement, and the Student Volunteer Movement for Foreign Missions. The church-related college was still a major force in shaping the ethos of higher education, and even in the universities not tied to any denomination, a significant proportion of ministers served on the faculties. Until after the end of the century, a college president was more likely than not a preacher and champion of revivals, assuming in surprising numbers the task of Revivalist in the school chapel or on the road, as time permitted.[6] Out of the revivalism of the Gilded Age came a great stream of idealistic young people who committed their lives to the cause of religion and who moved increasingly in the direction of humanitarian service. Their motivation sprang from the revivals.

Parallel to the mainline of revivalism, extending from the Great Awakening to Moody, Sam Jones, and Billy Sunday, ran some other tracks which, though comparable, were nevertheless distinctive.

Roman Catholicism in America developed its own patterns of revival, featuring celebrated priestly orators with a gift for rallying the faithful and for calling back to the fold sons and daughters of the church who on moving to a new city had failed to find their place in it, or in the confusion of their family's immigration had never received baptism. Episcopal and Lutheran ministers, with a liturgy that did not lend itself to the folksy informality of the revival meeting, from time to time conducted "missions" designed to attract persons to church membership. The preacher Phillips Brooks, in his regular services, drew young people to seek him out and ask for instruction leading to baptism, even without turning his sermonic conclusion into an altar call.

Earnest Congregationalists who avoided the raw emotionalism of the camp meeting and the anxious bench, or even the buildup of high-pressure excitement in the manner of Moody, kept alive a more restrained tradition of revivalism that from time to time produced an ingathering of souls. Disciples of Christ, following the rational bent of Alexander Campbell and his colleague Walter Scott, taught the "steps of salvation" that the latter had deduced from the book of Acts, and made a point of contrasting their biblical "commonsense" approach to evangelism with the emotionalism of the revivalists. Despite the distinctiveness of these and other movements, they all flourished in the same cultural context as revivalism itself.

Despite prevailing patterns of patriarchy, the model of the Revivalist opened a pathway to public ministry for at least a few women. As in our own century, most of the openings for them led to subordinate roles: leader of singing or the women's meetings or the children's programs. Some writers of songs and hymns, notably Fannie J. Crosby ("Pass Me Not, O Gentle Savior") and Elizabeth C. Clephane ("Beneath the Cross of Jesus"), left a lasting contribution. From such a start, some women went on to make it as Revivalist proper. Sarah Catherine McCoy, an Illinois schoolteacher, was conducting a Sunday school institute for a pastorless rural church. One night during the closing hymn a person came forward. In surprise she received the confession of faith in Jesus Christ, and the institute turned into an unplanned revival; before it ended she had received 96 persons. Sadie sent for a preacher to baptize them and was subsequently ordained in 1892. During a long ministry she baptized more than 5,000 persons.[7] Black women also made their contribution, in white churches as well as those of their own people. We have the stories of Amanda Smith and of Harriet Baker, famed in church circles as "the colored lady evangelist."[8]

Foremost among the female Revivalists was Phoebe Palmer, who gave impetus to the spread of "holiness" and initiated impressive Christian programs addressed to social problems. As revivalism lingered into the early part of the twentieth century, one of the most dramatic representatives of the model was Aimee Semple McPherson. Not a few now-forgotten women held meetings in small towns and rural churches that left an influence for good that lingered long afterwards. Both Jesse M. Bader, who headed the Department of Evangelism for the Federal Council of Churches during and after World War II, and Harold E. Fey, an editor of *The Christian Century* from 1940 to 1964, used to tell of their conversions in meetings conducted by a "lady preacher."[9]

About the end of the century the Revivalists began to run out of steam. The metaphor is apt, for the glory days of revivalism were the horse-and-buggy days, the days of the trolley car and the iron horse, when most Americans still lived on the farm or, having moved to the city, remembered the little red schoolhouse and the little brown church in the vale. That rural culture with its simple folk piety and value system that had so long set the nation's moral standards and spiritual tone appeared to prevail until World War I, but with the eye of hindsight we can see the omens of its passing before the end of the century.

Reflections on the Revivalist

Moody died in 1899. Two years earlier William James had published his epochal Gifford Lectures on *The Varieties of Religious Experience*, in which he treated the phenomena of conversion under the mode of the new science of psychology. The universities in America had become a more potent force in the life of the nation as a whole, and a new generation of intellectuals—Charles Sanders Peirce, James himself, Josiah Royce—turned ethical, philosophical, and even religious thought from the preoccupation with salvation that had commanded its primary attention since the days of the Puritans. The Gay Nineties asserted the new mood of a nation coming into recognition as a world power, its unbounded confidence in human possibilities assured by the country's economic growth and the new marvels issuing from the workshops of its inventors and the laboratories of its scientists.

The long-held view of human nature that despaired of it as utterly lost except for the intervention of a divine Savior began to lose the grip it had held on the American psyche. The old Calvinism that the Revivalist had effectively undercut now seemed to be finished off by the promise of science, and fewer people worried about their salvation, which was the Revivalist's stock in trade. The inclination of most Revivalists to deplore the new developments in urban society and to oppose the new worldview of science caused many to identify them with a past that was gone. Where the old way of life lingered and the old view of things persisted, notably in the rural South, revivalism hung on yet a while. But as a major force in church and society and as a model for ministry, the Revivalist belongs to the nineteenth century.

The legacy of revivalism was another thing. Institutionalized in the hymnody, architecture, and worship patterns of the churches, established in the religious memories and pious sentiments of the people, transported overseas in the generation when the patterns of life were being set in the new churches resulting from the missionary movement, revivalism affected popular expectations of ministry here and abroad for a long time to come. Not the least of these is the assertion expressed in unexamined aphorisms that are still frequently repeated as self-evident: "The primary business of the church is evangelism," or "The number one goal of the congregation is growth."

People who have heard preachers say that across the years cling to expectations not always easy for a minister to fulfill.

On the model of the Revivalist, people came to expect a good minister to infuse excitement into every undertaking, to awaken new hopes of great victories for their church, and then to deliver. The minister is supposed to get results, and statistics provide the most obvious yardstick for measuring them. The numbers claimed by some of the Revivalists in reporting attendance at their meetings or decisions secured proved in the long run to be about as relevant to the spiritual health of the nation as the daily body count did later to the outcome of the war in Vietnam.

The Revivalist came and went. The work did not require a large barrel of sermons—just a new place in which to unpack it. So after two weeks or six or eight, the show took to the road again. For a long time, the pastoral ministry followed a similar pattern among Baptists, Methodists, Presbyterians, and Disciples. A year or two was as long as most ministers stayed. Each would have a measure of success with a certain type of prospect, then slow down and decide it was time to move on. As long as revivalism prevailed, it was easy for a minister to leave a church quickly and honorably. One lined up a meeting or two with the help of friends, resigned one's pastorate "to enter the field of evangelism," and departed in search of greener pastures. In the course of a few meetings one had a chance to make an impression on a church that was open and "received a call," and it was time to return to the pastorate at least for a while.

The revivalism of the nineteenth century heightened the tendency toward subjectivism in American religion that began in the Great Awakening. People expect the minister to touch their hearts and to make them feel good. Unless the "great move toward propriety" in the churches of suburbia after World War II has totally obliterated the memory of the Revivalist, they even expect the minister to make them laugh on occasion.

But here a paradox confronts today's minister. The nineteenth century was sentimental, as we have said. It was also psychologically unsophisticated, its people readily subject to emotional manipulation—as dramatized in Meredith Willson's *The Music Man*. Every preacher worth his salt in those days had a line of stories that were guaranteed tearjerkers. The people wept, and soon the minister had them coming down the aisle. But our people are streetwise when it comes to psychology. They are leery of being manipulated. They are "cool." So many preachers have found the old tearjerkers counterproductive that they have quit using illustrations altogether.

Another problem was the object of the emotion being evoked. As the focus of revivalism narrowed more and more to purely private concerns and behavior, people were left weeping only about their own interior state and not about the woes of the world. One keen observer of the nineteenth century noted that each successive revival was a revival of less and less. Christian theology was reduced to the power in the blood of the Lamb, the great biblical themes were privatized and double-dipped in sentiment, emotionalism turned inward, and people measured the genuineness of religion by the intensity of feeling it evoked. "In contrast to eighteenth-century hymns like those in the influential collection of Isaac Watts, the focus of revivalist songs shifted from praise of the awful majesty of God and the magnitude of his grace revealed in Christ's atoning work, to the emotions of those who encounter the Gospel."[10]

Yet revivalism brought thousands to a personal profession of Christian faith and built up the strength of the churches. The laity stubbornly maintain the notion that the church ought to be growing, and all our talk about more honest statistics or being stronger after the uncommitted have dropped out has not succeeded in changing that notion—nor in giving an accurate analysis of our decline. The appeal of the church growth movement to many members and ministers arises from concern at this point. I confess an uneasiness about "church growth." Too much of it is obviously self-serving and falls into patterns of activism and exploitation that caused our churches to repudiate revivalism two and three generations ago. But not everything can be put in that class. We who believe the Christian message want to see outsiders confronted by it. And we who love the church want to see it grow in strength—with Christian integrity.

One thing the Revivalist knew how to do that most of us do not know was how to get the ear of the outsider. Something interesting and exciting was promised at the meeting—a popular singer from the city, someone playing a musical saw, a magician. The Revivalist was commonly a colorful personality with a platform presence larger than life, a "ball of fire," a "real stemwinder," whose gifts of humor and courage and ingenuity had considerable popular appeal before the days of the mass media. A news dispatch datelined from a mountain town in Kentucky in 1890 recounted a story that another journalist rewrote more than half a century later:

> An evangelist conducting a revival service in the hill town was annoyed by a local badman who stood in the rear of the tent and interrupted the religious proceedings. He reprimanded the badman and the badman challenged him to a duel. The parson accepted the challenge on condition that

he could choose his own weapons. When the fatal day came the parson chose potatoes at 50 feet.

The parson, it seems, had been a baseball pitcher in his time. Both men backed off and wound up. The parson's first throw caught the gunman squarely in his rather ample midriff; the second grazed an ear and the third caught him on the button and laid him low. When the badman came to, he took to the woods and was seen no more.[11]

Even when the excitement failed to reach such a peak of irrelevance, the Revivalist offered something in the name of religion at the big tent or in the tabernacle that was interesting enough and vital enough to draw hundreds of the unchurched to attend. They came, even though they knew they were likely to be made uncomfortable and to be pressed for a decision. Still, they came. In a day when the people idolized orators, the Revivalist could hold a place with the best of them.

It should not surprise us that this model of ministry attracted preachers good at promoting themselves and preoccupied with success, understood as the ability to prompt large numbers of hearers to "come forward" or make decisions" or "hit the sawdust trail." It was not at all uncommon for a celebrated Revivalist to be detached from the church, hoping to exercise a broader appeal when not identified with a particular denomination, or perhaps chafing under ministerial discipline. Professional revivalism became unabashed free enterprise in religion, and in the second quarter of the twentieth century fell into widespread disrepute in many of the churches and even among the general public.

The waning of revivalism leaves the mainline churches puzzled: How do we attract the attention of persons not now involved in the Christian enterprise? People don't turn out for oratory anymore. Though TV evangelists raise millions of dollars by questionable means in an effort to reach the unchurched, studies indicate that their listeners almost entirely are church members of long standing. We really don't know how to gain notice from the outsiders. Martin Luther King got it. Mother Teresa has it. Pope John Paul II has it. Most of us don't even try to get it. We might take a leaf from the Revivalist's book and ask ourselves what we can do to awaken interest in our church's presentation and living of the gospel. Maybe we could do some things less boring and more deserving of attention.

The dramatic focus of the Revivalist's work was the altar call or the appeal for decisions on the part of the unconverted. But in addition to its evangelistic appeal, the meeting held in a church building or public hall or tent or campground helped to reawaken the interest of many church members whose religion had fallen to the level of grim routine or cold neglect. Resorting to the only show in town, they found their religious interest reawakened and, for a time at least, took their Christian commitment seriously. The resurgence of life as converts and backsliders alike "stood up for Jesus" gave the worn-out workers in the church, both ministers and members, a great boost in morale.

The Revivalist stirred up excitement by preaching for decisions, by asking people to change their ways, by expecting people to start on a new course. How long has it been since most of us have seen adults professing faith and taking their stand with the church? In a society becoming more and more secular, less and less influenced by the gospel, thousands of miserable persons await the strange good news of divine love past all deserving, made known in Jesus Christ, of forgiveness and new birth and the possibility of a wholly different way of life offered by One who brings deliverance from all that enslaves and promises true happiness in the love of God and neighbor. For millions of people today, to come into that kind of life would require drastic and dramatic change. And that would restore excitement to our ministry. So would directing a new generation of youth to a life of humanitarian and idealistic service in the name of Christ.

When revivalism was at its best, that is what the Revivalist expected. Can we be satisfied with a concept of ministry that expects any less?

BUILDER

The most common, most necessary, and most typical form of ministry in nineteenth-century America can too readily escape our notice: that of the minister as Builder. Less theatrical than the Pulpiteer, less swashbuckling than the Revivalist, the Builder nevertheless furnishes the model after which the majority of ministers thought, somewhat deprecatingly, of themselves.

Not everyone had the gifts of creativity, imagination, dramatic presence, impressive voice, and persuasive ethos to gain much more than a passing grade as an orator. Only a few attained celebrity as evangelists. But literally thousands of unsung and forgotten ministers, toiling amid poverty and discouragement and often too little self-esteem, succeeded at a task more impressive by far than the building of the pyramids.[1] In the space of a hundred years they transformed the religious situation in America. Where churches had gathered into the fold only about one person in twenty when the young nation began, these workaday ministers brought in, instructed, motivated, organized, and equipped such numbers of people that by 1910 church members made up more than 40 percent of the vastly expanded population. From one in twenty to eight out of twenty! No wonder that at the turn of the century Christians were speaking confidently of "the evangelization of the world in this generation"!

The tremendous work of bringing in, holding, and organizing all these people—an achievement that gives some substance to the notion that America was a Christian nation—cannot all be credited to the Revivalists any more than the musicality of a population can be attributed to the few prima donnas who are pelted with flowers and huzzahed with cries of "Brava!" after the curtain falls. Much of the work of revivalism itself was accomplished not by the big names but by ordinary pastors. In their own communities they did their best with the methods they copied from the stars, too often held up to them by insensitive members as examples of ministers who could really get the job done. Not only in winning disciples, either during the excitement of a summer revival or more commonly in the quiet witness of ordinary Sunday preaching and personal conversation, but even more in holding these new converts firmly in the life of the church, these ministers built up the body of Christ, both as community and as institution.[2] In Pauline language, each of them did the work of a wise master builder (1 Cor. 3:10).

For the minister as Builder, nineteenth-century America shaped the model as surely as the ideal of the orator inspired the Pulpiteer. On the edge of the wilderness, again and again, a young couple arrived, felled trees, raised a cabin, made it livable, filled it with children, put up barn and sheds, gradually cleared the forest, worked up a fruitful farm, then crowned their achievements by erecting a stately white-framed house they had dreamed of all along—so well crafted of solid oak beams and floors, of maple siding and walnut or hickory panels that many such residences still stand as beautiful landmarks after more than a hundred years.

All over the country shrewd and lucky entrepreneurs built new communities to perpetuate names from their families until the nation surrenders unconditionally to zipcodes: Lynchburg, Jonesboro, Smithtown, Susanville, Gary, Sedalia, Baldwin, Eugene. Merchants and mechanics built thriving establishments. The robber barons built railroads and oil companies and fortunes running into millions, then erected universities and theological seminaries to atone for their sins. Meanwhile the underpaid, overlooked ministers were building the church.

The figure of the Builder is embodied in the circuit-rider, the slave preacher, the home missionary, the pastor, the bishop, the secretary of the voluntary society for Christian action, the ministerial worker in whatever capacity who labored to gather the Lord's people and unite them into a company prepared to carry on the task. Of the traditional forms of ministry inherited from the long Christian past and familiar to us from colonial days, the Priest comes closest to providing the prototype for the model of the Builder. But when we say "Priest," we tend to think "liturgy," "sacraments," "altar," "vestments," or "clerical collar," rather than the total pastoral task of building up the church.

The many practical chores that the Builder must necessarily do or arrange to have done involved the minister more and more in attention to organizational matters as the decades went by, inclining toward the model of the Manager that has achieved such dominance in our time. (Early in the nineteenth century, Jedidiah Morse was one of the first ministers in America to achieve widespread authority through his skills as an organizer.[3]) But as a model, the Builder was one who kept an eye to the totality of ministry, to the educational task, to the quality of life envisioned for church and community. The nineteenth-century Builder derived little aesthetic pleasure from contemplating organizational flow charts, a form of art that had not yet come into its own. The Builder's chief concerns were the people and the task. The Builder loved the church.

The building of a congregation came first, even though many times over, at the outset, it seemed an impossible dream. The enterprise typically began with an initial stage of rounding up a few Christians to serve as nucleus for a community of faith—work generally done by the farmer-preacher, the circuit-rider, or the itinerant evangelist, though commonly a Macedonian call came from a lonely family or two on the frontier asking for a minister to come and preach and help get something started.

The Sunday school was a device well suited to pioneer conditions. One or two devoted Christians who loved the Lord gathered a little band about them to meet regularly for the study of the scriptures and in due time handed a preacher an audience. Once such a rural congregation had been stabilized and then "set in order" by the appointment of elders or other local leaders, the evangelist could go on his way. At this stage a monthly visit from a traveling preacher provided inspiration and pastoral guidance, while the annual revival meeting rallied the members whose zeal had cooled and brought in new believers to augment the little church's strength.

Voluntary leadership on the part of laypersons was essential to the working of the process, and the successful Builder inspired it. We marvel at the quantity of time given and the work accomplished by women and men of limited education and little leisure. Two factors were important:

1) There was no one else to do it. In other times and places the church had been conducted primarily as an enterprise of the clergy. In rebelling in 1794 against the ministerial system being developed for American Methodists by Bishop Asbury, James O'Kelly had charged that there was nothing left for the laity to do but to "pray, pay, and obey."[4] If such an accusation was ever true, it did not apply to the frontier in the nineteenth century. Little flocks of Christian believers were scattered thinly over the raw countryside like sheep without a shepherd. Again and again it was devout Christians lonely for worship and fellowship who, by taking matters into their own hands,

laid the foundations, both spiritual and literal, for a new church.

2) Most of the pioneers in new areas were young.[5] They did not have to defer to older heads who knew how things used to be done, but could move into challenging tasks while their zeal was still hot. (The leadership of the laity was, however, a notable feature of nineteenth-century religious life throughout the United States, not only on the geographical frontier.)[6] For all that, the guidance and inspiration from periodic visits from or consultations with the minister were crucial ingredients.

A congregation had obviously reached maturity when it could call a pastor full time. This happened more commonly in the cities and towns than in the countryside, though many strong rural churches flourished, especially where a sizable band of immigrants had settled a neighborhood. The pastor of a church commonly preached a revival for it every year, in addition to two sermons on Sunday, a meditation for the midweek prayer meeting, a lesson for a Bible class, and addresses for special occasions. No wonder that ministers moved on to new fields every year or so!

In congregations that had reached this stage, American Christians began to experience, many for the first time, what it meant to have a shepherd of the flock living among the people. (The situation had, of course, prevailed in the towns of Puritan New England and at other settlements in the colonies.) If we think of the office of pastor in its full sense of offering care for the members of a congregation and community in the crises and the joys of life and of guiding their Christian growth, as well as of strengthening the institutional base, it began to find expression across the continent in the work of the Builder. But pastorates were brief by contemporary standards, and the sense of shepherding, in contrast with the thrill of bringing in the lost sheep one by one, came slowly.[7]

The developing relationship between pastor and people gradually altered the tone of American religion. People grew in their understanding that faith involves a great deal beyond the crisis of "getting saved."[8] Preaching came down to earth, slowly untangling itself from its involvement with abstract doctrinal quarrels among Christians to deal more directly with the practical problems of everyday living and the certainty of dying. Ministers of diverse denominations living in the same town established personal friendships, formed alliances to press common concerns, and inched toward an ecumenical future. Denominational polemics slowly abated. The term of pastorates gradually lengthened.

The crowning work of many a minister, fulfilling the dream of a lifetime, was the erecting of a church building. On the frontier and in new towns, a congregation frequently passed through two or three simple log or frame structures, hastily put up by the labor of the members themselves, and useful chiefly in providing a space shielded from the elements where the people could meet. But vital congregations soon outgrew these rude houses and dreamed of possessing at last a "permanent" structure. In the last generation of the nineteenth century, as in the first generation of the twentieth, hundreds of substantial church buildings, designed by architects and built by professional contractors, raised the cross above a new tower of stone or brick to dominate the commercial establishments or private residences in the surrounding blocks. The sentimental climax of the old film *One Foot in Heaven* pictures the aging minister with a light of triumph on his face, standing in his splendid new brick church on the day of its dedication, while the pipe organ sounds out "The Church's One Foundation."[9]

The Builder—who had for so long envisioned a splendid church, who had inspired the people to give larger sums than ever before, who had spent hours with architect and committees, who had doggedly seen the project through to dedication, could rejoice in the thought that the congregation, equipped at last with sanctuary and classrooms and fellowship hall—was now free for a greater mission of service. (Few Americans then understood the terrible dynamics of the city, which in a few years can engulf block after block in an uninhabited sea of office buildings or factories, or overwhelm a once serene boulevard with the deafening noise of heavy traffic, while streetcars give way to buses that do not run on Sunday. Within a short time urban change has rendered the "permanent" building obsolete and it soon becomes prohibitively expensive to maintain.)

In all the work of building up congregations, the service of women in ministry has been largely overlooked. Usually by the time a church was coming into its own, it could afford to call one of the "big men" of the denomination to its pulpit. But in reading of pioneer days one comes again and again across the names of forgotten women preachers—tough, determined, tireless, self-effacing—who kept isolated congregations alive in the desperate early times when they "couldn't really afford a preacher." These were women who traveled by stage or rail from one discouraging post to another, who left no more than their obscure names in the record—and the young congregations nurtured through a hard childhood for a promising future.

In a denominational history of Oklahoma, for example, occurs the name of Lura V. Thompson, a home missionary, who in 1900 shepherded churches at El Reno and Norman until they could get "the right kind of man."[10] Both grew into strong congregations of the

Disciples of Christ. In their Northern Texas and New Mexico conferences the United Brethren had eight women, licensed and ordained, serving before 1920. Church historians still have their work cut out for them as they continue the research necessary to give us a proper account of the ministry of such women and then to integrate this information into the general histories of religion in America. Along with the brethren who later came to serve the congregations that these heroic sisters had stubbornly refused to let die, they did the work of the Builder.

The few female ministers who managed to secure ordination and then to carry on effective work in the face of opposition were made of strong, stern stuff. When Clara Hale Babcock was challenged by a man who said women lacked the physical strength for the work of a pastor, she provided a memorable response:

> I have fully demonstrated woman's power, physically, as in over three years I have baptized [by immersion] all candidates presenting themselves. I have stood in ice water and baptized many at once, in and out, any time the occasion demanded, mid summer's heat and winter's cold, both in the baptistry and rivers. Have never taken cold or been hoarse in the work; am forty-three years old, the mother of six children, and every living relative of mine has been brought to faith and obedience. I have a happy home; each member is willing to sacrifice some, if need be, for the salvation of souls and the glory of God.[11]

In one annual report she listed 96 additions, 240 sermons, 470 visits, and 1,500 miles traveled.[12] Sadie Crank organized 15 churches, reopened 16 that had closed down, and helped 18 in their building program.[13] Angie Debo served as a Methodist pastor in the early years of the twentieth century.[14]

But the educational and philanthropic ministry of the churches offered more openings for women than the pastorate. In 1888 the Methodist General Conference gave approval to the deaconess movement after the European model; this servant order enrolled hundreds of women in teaching, nursing, and other helping vocations in church-sponsored institutions.[15]

The building up of a denomination was likewise a major task. It is hard now to imagine the vision and strength of leadership required to draw the scattered people of a new land into a sense of mutual obligation and the readiness to band together for the cause of Christ. Just managing to meet the technical requirements for securing canonically ordained bishops demanded the best efforts of those who built the Episcopal Church. John Ireland of Baltimore, the first Roman

Catholic bishop in the United States, and Jean-Baptiste Lamy, the missionary from France assigned to the diocese of Santa Fe after Mexico ceded its northern provinces to the United States, faced difficulties such as few American ministers have encountered. The genius of Bishop Francis Asbury conceived and brought into being the Methodist system so superbly adapted to the evangelizing and churching of the frontier and now so fearful and wonderful an administrative machine.

Meanwhile congregational types of Christians rallied around the work of voluntary societies organized to promote missions or religious education or temperance. Some of these in time coalesced into the nucleus of denominational organization, a development their proponents sincerely denied would ever take place. But as Sidney E. Mead has observed, the denomination was essentially purposive; it emerged on the American landscape as an instrument of mission.[16]

By 1890 the crucial infrastructure of the major American denominations had been set in place, enabling them to discharge their internal responsibilities for building up the congregations and for providing necessary services to their people, as well as to carry on the work of the worldwide mission. We may observe the magnitude of the achievement in the life of a single minister:

> A man named John Engle died in 1881 at the age of ninety-five. He had been confirmed by [Roman Catholic Bishop] Carroll in 1796 and lived to see the original diocese divided and subdivided "till the hierarchy numbered fourteen archbishops and fifty-six bishops and holy mass was said throughout the land in more than six thousand churches and chapels by as many priests."[17]

On a comparable scale, given the varying sizes of total membership and the diversities of polity, the process went on in each of the mainline denominations.

The figure of the Builder includes not just the pastor but the Sunday school missionary as well, who was often first on the ground, laboring to establish beachheads for the Christian faith. It includes the state secretary of the denominational society for church extension or the women's board of missions, and the national secretary of each such comparable body in the various denominations, as well as the official in each region called bishop or president or some other general title.

The field of "general work"—serving organizations promoting Sunday schools, Christian Endeavor, temperance, schools for freed blacks, missions, and the like—offered both challenge and opportunity for women, and here we find some of the most gifted and influential examples of the Builder. The Women's Christian Temperance Union, working across denominational lines, proved to be the most powerful organization of the nineteenth century run solely by women.[18] And the boards of missions established and administered by women conducted a significant part of the worldwide enterprise; within any given denomination the executives of these boards earned an acknowledged place among its outstanding leaders.[19]

All these workers tended to be tireless and colorful women—not then numbered among the bishops!—and men, able to inject the excitement of high purpose into the life of the churches and possessing in many cases the oratorical gifts of the Pulpiteer. The nineteenth-century denomination was a kind of extended family, often held together by its loyalty to and love for these "secretaries" and other leaders.

When a reporter pressed C. C. McCabe of the Methodist Board of Church Extension about the charge by "infidel" Robert Ingersoll that the church was dying, McCabe countered quickly: Methodists were building new churches across the land at a rate faster than one a day and would soon make it two. Before long his people were triumphantly singing, "All hail the power of Jesus' name! We're building two a day."[20]

The dream of the Builder included the vision of a Christian society. Influential Christian leaders of the nineteenth century, postmillennialists in conviction, commonly held that once the churches had won a majority of the population to membership, their dream of a Christian America would be realized. But even while trying to make disciples, ministers also led in the formation of voluntary organizations to propagandize for temperance, sabbath observance, abolition, and other social reforms. Winthrop S. Hudson has noted that in the early days of the republic, when Christians knew themselves to be in the minority and made the most of the voluntary principle in seeking to alter public opinion by persuasion, they exercised a more powerful influence on national thought and action than in later years, when they had a majority of the people and no longer held a distinctive point of view.[21] Most of the voluntary organizations for social reform included ministers as key leaders or advisers.

Ministers also provided constructive leadership in the communities they served, from the days of John Chapman, frontier preacher in the Old Northwest, who came across the mountains in the earliest days of the republic with seedlings and packages of unsprouted seeds that would blossom in time into the abundant apple orchards of the Ohio Valley—celebrated in popular legend as Johnny Appleseed.

Hundreds of less colorful ministers rendered service of comparable importance outside the narrow field called religion as they worked to establish schools, libraries, hospitals, and other useful services. After Jane Addams opened Hull House, a "settlement house" to serve immigrants and other homeless persons in Chicago, ministers in other cities copied her example. With a similar intention of serving the total needs of the people in its community, the "institutional church" came to the fore in the 1880s to provide needed activities for city-dwellers seven days a week. These included classes in the elemental skills of urban living and facilities for wholesome recreation. Ministers promoted the growth of such programs, and the variety of services offered opened opportunities for women as well as men in new forms of ministry.

About the same time, Walter Rauschenbusch and his associates launched the Brotherhood of the Kingdom to agitate for public righteousness and to proclaim the Social Gospel. Ministers and religious leaders more concerned for a great cause than for denominational differences increased the thrust toward ecumenism, forming Sunday school associations, the Young Women's Christian Association, the Young Men's Christian Association, and other organizations working for a Christian world. Washington Gladden labored for the coming of the kingdom of God in the faith that "People will be living in heaven right here in the Scioto Valley."[22] Sustained by a similar vision, thousands of ministers fulfilled the ministry of the Builder.

Reflections on the Builder

The heroic activism of these workers achieved impressive results in the nineteenth century. How did the model of the Builder affect our concept of ministry?

On the negative side it left American Christianity with an edifice complex. When a congregation or denomination is growing, religious euphoria runs high and ministers take satisfaction in their work. Such growth inevitably calls for major building enterprises, and almost total attention is commonly diverted into these projects in the conviction that, once they are completed, resources can then be directed to more significant aspects of mission. But often by the time the building is paid for, or even sooner, the congregation is left stranded by the rapidity of urban change and sometimes cannot even afford to pay for lights and heat. Once the building is done, moreover, the minister is frequently at loose ends. The project has required total time and attention and resources for so long that one asks, "What do I do now?" What one does, in many cases, is to find another congregation that wants to put up a new building, without ever stopping to ask, "What does Paul's 'master builder' do besides stack up bricks and mortar?"

A heritage of institutional*ism* derives from the legacy of the Builder. Not that the busy minister of the nineteenth century intended it that way. But from his or her work, contemporary American Christians have derived a devotion to the institution that tends to elevate its preservation above every other value, even the cause it was formed to serve.

Since the 1980s, American churches have seemed to be wallowing in a trough of congregational*ism* (recall the earlier discussion of localism[23]), while interest in the larger mission of the church and devotion to the ecumenical cause languish. Too many congregational leaders grow nervous over prophetic preaching by the pastor or declarations by the denominational assembly, fearing they will lose the financial support they need to keep going. Going where?

The contemporary minister often carries so heavy a responsibility for maintaining the institution as to think of Sisyphus—forever doomed to roll the great stone up the hill one more time, only to have it careen down again—as the figure of ministry today. At such times one is tempted to see the activism of the Builder not as apostolic but as Promethean.

But the Builder has much to contribute to our concept of ministry, and it is an essential ingredient. The Builder takes seriously the historical existence of the church. The Builder's faith is an incarnational faith: The purposes of God are to be worked out among communities of women and men living in the real world and struggling with life in society. Our task is to form the believers into effective companies of faithful disciples and to help them develop the necessary institutions as instruments for mission and service.

It is not up to us as ministers to do all the work or even to run the show. Far more important is clarity of vision in seeking to understand God's purpose for our times and the sharing of that vision in motivating God's people to serve the divine intention. In order to do this in the late twentieth century, the minister needs a more profound knowledge of society than most of us possess and a greater effectiveness in helping church people understand the world to which we are all called to minister. An equal need is a fuller comprehension of the gospel itself. That achieved, in love for God and for people, we can proceed with the commission entrusted to us as a skilled master Builder.

MISSIONARY

The nineteenth-century form of Saint was the Missionary. The concept arose in a world of perception and sentiment so radically different from our own that anyone born after 1940 can scarcely conceive its energizing power and emotional pull on the life of the churches while it flourished during "The Great Century" of foreign missions.[1]

The marks of holiness showed as clearly upon the Missionary as ever upon any Saint. The great commission to go into all the world had come as a divine call personally addressed to each young woman or man who volunteered for this ministry, whether the voice of God was heard in ecstasy actually sounding out one's name and guiding to Burma or China or Africa, or, as was more often the case (just as it had been with many of the medieval saints from St. Anthony to St. Francis), the reading of a particular scripture seized one as unmistakably as if a letter with one's name on it had just fallen from heaven.

The sacrifice necessitated by the Missionary's spending years on end among an alien people of strange speech and custom—exposed to diseases and hostility and danger to life, cut off from home and family and one's own kind, tested by endless months of fruitless witness before one convert could be claimed and by the outspoken doubts of critics at home—marked this minister with a holiness as patently genuine as that bestowed by any shaman's ecstatic vision.

Especially touching to the Age of Romanticism was the recurring departure of the Missionary, after a brief furlough in the homeland to recruit one's strength and spirits and to inform the churches of the work. The evident eagerness to return to the task, the firm renunciation of enticements and attachments so dear to the sentimental heart

105

of the time, the resolute faithfulness to the divine call, the willingness to be separated even from one's children—all gave evidence of a level of devotion at which ordinary pastors and church members could only marvel.[2]

To Protestants all this was new, even though it was an old, familiar story to Roman Catholics. A stylized manner of reporting the work soon established itself, as did a popular hagiography recounting the adventures and sacrifices of these new Saints and martyrs. The accounts read so much alike that it is sometimes difficult to discern the unique motives and private opinions of particular Missionaries. If Protestantism had heretofore had no need for Saints and no acquaintance with them, it had them now.[3]

The dramatic surge of missionary zeal and activity in the nineteenth century provides a stirring chapter in the history of the church. Before 1800 Protestants had had their hands full, what with the religious wars of Europe and with internal dissensions. Except for late eighteenth-century ventures in India by the German Moravians and then by English Baptist William Carey, other missionary efforts largely centered on attempts to provide ministers for the European settlers in the New World. Only a few pastors among the English in New England and the Dutch in New York had conscientiously undertaken to preach to the Native Americans who had occupied the land before the colonists arrived. The first missionaries of the Society for the Propagation of the Gospel in Foreign Parts, organized in London in 1801, braved the wrath of slaveholders by preaching to blacks in the South.

In the young American nation knowledge of the great world elsewhere, brought chiefly by the Yankee sailors engaged in the China trade, heightened awareness of strange peoples in "heathen" nations. The thought of millions living and dying in darkness, without the light of the gospel, stirred Christian hearts. In 1806 a group of students at Williams College, on taking shelter under a haystack during a thunder shower, put the time to religious use by praying together for the conversion of the heathen. From that haystack prayer meeting, long to be celebrated in inspirational lore, they returned to their lodgings with the firm purpose of going out as missionaries. Only six years later five of the students sailed with their wives for India.

Soon a dozen others followed, then scores, then hundreds. By the end of the century Christian graduates streamed from the campuses every year to offer themselves for service, as the student volunteer movement gained momentum. Congregations began to measure their vitality by their giving for the cause, but more especially by the number of their own young people who had answered the call.[4] The tide continued to rise until the Great Depression of the 1930s, and only after World War II did it dramatically slacken in the mainline churches as the Christian movement in the far fields came to maturity and indigenous leaders assumed the leadership in evangelization and teaching.

When the great migration of missionaries was at its peak, few other Americans had even crossed the Atlantic, much less the Pacific, and sea mail was the most rapid form of communication with home. Every denomination had its missionary society or board, with a remarkably well organized root-system reaching into the congregations for nourishment by their gifts and prayers.

Scores of hymns written and sung in those times catch up the excitement, the fervid hopes, and the dedication exemplified by the Missionary, but expected in every good Christian:

> If you cannot cross the ocean,
>   And the heathen lands explore,
> You can find the heathen nearer,
>   You can help them at your door;
> If you cannot give your thousands,
>   You can give the widow's mite,
> And the least you give for Jesus
>   Will be precious in his sight.[5]

Alongside foreign missions, the movement for home missions grew apace. In response to a widely circulated story about a party of Flathead and Nez Percé Indians who had made their way from the headwaters of the Missouri down to St. Louis to ask for "the white man's Book of Heaven," Methodist Jason Lee set out for the Northwest in 1834, to be followed the next year by Congregationalists Marcus and Narcissa Whitman and in 1840 by Jesuit father Peter De Smet.

The most notable result of their labors was to direct the attention of people in the East to the Oregon country, and soon so many pioneers were heading for the Far West that the churches were expending all their efforts in trying to plant congregations among the settlers. The dispossessing of the Indians by land-hungry Americans and the wars that put an end to all resistance wiped out much of the native population and made missionary work difficult among those who remained. Under the circumstances, it is surprising that any conversions took place and that congregations of Baptists, Methodists, Roman Catholics, and other brands of Christians continue to flourish even yet among American Indians.

The work in home missions broadened to launch Protestant efforts among the Hispanics in the newly acquired Southwest. These people were of course already Christians, but the institutions of Catholicism were weak and Protestants deemed that faith inadequate for freedom-loving Americans. These Missionaries enjoyed some early successes which proved for the most part transitory. Spanish-speaking congregations continue, however, in a few of the mainline denominations and in a number of evangelical bodies that entered the scene in the twentieth century.

Home missions boards sponsored educational efforts among the newly freed blacks after the Civil War, but it was hardly necessary to establish churches, given the effectiveness of the black preachers already on the scene.

As the flood of immigration mounted, effort turned toward the evangelization and Americanization of the millions of newcomers. For many their entry into a strange pattern of life was eased a bit, and some found their way into Protestant churches.

The home missionary enterprise was much broader in scope than can be suggested here. Less exotic than the overseas venture, it arose from the same impulses, flourished in the same environment, and appealed, if with slightly less emotional power, to the same sense of the romantic. The sacrificial image of the Missionary overshadowed the total effort. Yet most people, when they heard the term, thought of a "soldier of the cross" on some far foreign field.

The ministry of the Missionary was monopolized less by white males than any other nineteenth-century form of ministry. Young African Americans of unusual ability returned to the lands of their ancestors in the service of the gospel. Several Indian American preachers received tiny allowances from boards of home missions to support their ministry among the tribal peoples, as did a few Hispanic Protestant preachers to labor among their own in the Southwest. When work was undertaken among Asian immigrants on the Pacific coast, a preacher of Chinese or Japanese or Filipino descent was occasionally found.

Most notable was the service of women in the vocation of Missionary. Under leading Protestant boards, both husband and wife received an appointment and stipend, both had responsibilities, and both were set apart for the task in moving services of dedication that, in churches not maintaining a priesthood, had few if any marks to distinguish them from ordination.[6] In addition to wives, numbers of unmarried women also entered this ministry. Bible-quoting adherents of patriarchy in the churches at home seemed untroubled about sending women to teach the heathen. While a woman Missionary might not administer the sacraments in the nineteenth century, except in those rare churches willing to ordain women as ministers, presiding at the eucharistic table was a relatively infrequent function for most men in the Protestant work overseas, with the result that the differentiation of roles by gender was minimized.

The women served primarily as teachers, nurses, and supervisors of the manifold operations of a mission station during the frequent absence of the men on preaching tours. When they returned to the United States on furlough, the women were often more effective than the men as speakers and writers for the missionary cause.

Women took a similar part in the work of home missions and also in Christian higher education as teachers in the church-related academies and colleges where the philanthropic and sacrificial ethos of the world enterprise pervaded the common life. Here, as we have noted, the churches offered them far more openings than it did in pastorates.

Of the teachers who went South to conduct schools for the "Freedmen" in the years after the Civil War, two thirds were women. Later in life, one who had been a student of theirs offered a tribute that rings with the zealous spirit of the missionary venture:

> These noble women left homes, their friends, their social ties, and all that they held dear...to labor among the recently emancipated slaves. Their courage, their self-sacrificing devotion, sincerity of purpose, purity of motive, and their unshaken faith in God were their pass keys to the hearts of those for whom they came to labor....Their monument is builded in the hopes of a race struggling upward from ignorance....As long as the human heart beats in grateful response to benefits received, these women shall not want a monument of living ebony and bronze.[7]

Likewise, teachers in the Congregationalist, Methodist, and Presbyterian schools in the Southwest, the most effective point of contact for Protestant missions to the Hispanic people, were nearly all women. A correspondent observed that "The lady teacher is welcomed at homes where the Protestant minister is regarded with suspicion."[8] In ministry according to the model of Missionary, women in significant numbers took a larger part than with any other pattern.

Impressive leadership in the American churches also arose within the great women's missionary societies, which provided much of the motivation and funding for worldwide evangelization. In several denominations these organizations had full-time "secretaries" (administrators) at the national and state levels. They led the boards that formulated policy, chose missionaries (men as well as women) to go to the fields, raised the finances, administered budgets, and directed the program. They delivered missionary addresses at denominational conventions and in the churches, published successful magazines, wrote articles, organized auxiliaries in the congregations, and traveled to the foreign fields to inspect the work and report on progress. In every functional respect their activity precisely paralleled that of the men who, holding similar positions in the general boards of the denominations, were universally perceived as ministers. If the women were not so perceived, it was because of gender, not because of any difference in the nature or quality of their ministry.

The assumptions that motivated the ministry of the Missionary and the support from the churches belonged to the thought-world of nineteenth-century Christianity: To a creation lost in sin, its people justly condemned to everlasting torment for their wickedness, the all-loving God has sent his Son to take their guilt upon himself and make atonement by his death on the cross, thus satisfying the divine righteousness. In his name the good news of salvation is now freely preached throughout the world. Whoever repents and is baptized will be saved. But those who refuse the message will be damned, and those who have never heard go down to death and hell without hope.

The Missionary believed wholeheartedly in the power of the gospel to save and in the obligation to make that gospel known. All this had been revealed by God in Holy Scripture. One of the chief tasks of the missionary pioneers, therefore, was to translate the Bible into the languages of the many peoples to whom they had come. The innate truth of the gospel would soon bring down idolatry, freeing the multitudes now living in superstition and moral depravity to a life of joy in the Lord and to the blessings of Christian civilization.

With rare exceptions, the early Missionaries saw their faith and their culture as of a piece: To offer one was to offer the other. Those who went from the United States also assumed that their nation, committed to the holy cause of freedom, represented the fullest flower of Christian civilization. Thus they commended along with the gospel the political concepts and the heroes of their people. The nation was young and hopeful. Cynicism was not yet a conditioned reflex. And many Americans, including the Missionaries, loved this land with a pure and simple devotion. That affection makes all the more striking their sacrifice in order to share the good they knew. It was a case of *noblesse oblige.*

The encounter with strange cultures and religions worked transformation not only among faraway peoples but also in the Missionaries themselves and, at length, in the churches that sent them. The compassion of the Missionaries, along with their belief that modern knowledge could reduce the miseries they saw on every hand, moved them to address a broad range of human need. They preached the gospel in every way they could. They also started hospitals, clinics, orphanages, schools, colleges, printing establishments, projects in translation, agricultural experimental stations, light industries, and every other constructive venture they could imagine and manage. Some did so to win the confidence and gratitude of the people; some acted in pure responsiveness to desperate needs. Some, actuated by both motivations, could never decide which concern was or ought to be uppermost. In any case, the conviction grew that all this was an essential part of the Christian presence and witness.

The Missionary soon came to love with deep personal affection some of the strange people to whom she or he had come, especially those who responded to Jesus Christ with faith and devotion. Nevertheless, the habit persisted of thinking of all non-Westerners as simple and childlike. Whatever the denomination, the Missionary tended to deal with the new Christians with the parental autocracy of an early Christian bishop.

Yet as skill with the language and understanding of the culture increased, some sensitive spirits among the Missionaries soon found themselves moved to a high regard for the cultural tradition and even the religious heritage of their adopted land. To a few the new awareness came with such force as to undercut their sense of missionary vocation, and they put their new knowledge to work in the diplomatic service or in the university. Commonly, however, the Missionary found the new insights wholly compatible with the commission to preach and to serve. They pressed on in the work with a greater spirit of tolerance than before, sharing the faith in less condescending fashion and beginning to bring to the supporters at home an attitude of greater understanding toward other cultures and religions.[9]

The fruition of the missionary venture came in the emergence of indigenous leadership and the independence of the "younger churches." This development had scarcely begun by the end of the nineteenth century. Many converts had been made, from whom evangelists and teachers had been enlisted. But the "episcopal" tendency both of the Missionaries themselves and of their sending boards prevented the rapid rise of these new Christians to significant positions of leadership. At the great World Missionary Conference at Edinburgh in 1910, only two of the speakers were natives of lands where the Missionaries were at work.

In the twentieth century indigenous leaders have assumed increasing responsibility for ministry in congregational and general church life and for administration of hospitals, schools, and other institutions, the ownership of which has passed to the new churches themselves. Among many so-called evangelical and conservative bodies, however, older paternalistic patterns persist with force unabated, as do the cultural and theological assumptions from which they derived. But in the life of the mainline Protestant churches the Missionary has all but vanished, except as a specialist with a rare and needed skill invited by the church overseas for a term as a fraternal worker. Yet the church continues to prosper. The church in China has literally multiplied in numbers since foreign missionaries were forced to withdraw by the victory of Mao-Tse tung's Red Army at the end of World War II. By the close of the twentieth century, if present trends continue, Africa will have a larger number of Christians than any other continent.

Reflections on the Missionary

The Missionary had greater influence on the concept of ministry in America than might at first be imagined. As key interpreter of the worldwide enterprise to the congregation, the pastor promulgated the prevailing rationale for it, as well as pastoral understanding could keep pace. Stories about the Missionary and soon about the "fine native convert" provided telling sermon illustrations. The emotions and commitment associated with the missionary cause sustained more than overseas ministries; they sustained in many at home a powerful zeal for the work of their own congregation and for the total program of their denomination. The recent decline (in terms of constant dollar value) in giving to the general work of the church beyond the local community, which afflicts most religious bodies today, has followed relatively quickly after the passing of the missionary era and the emotions it sustained.

When a nineteenth-century pastor or board secretary spoke persistently and with conviction about the world mission, something of the aura of the Missionary began to attach itself to popular concepts of ministry, so that this image too entered into the complex of expectations and emotions that complicate a minister's work. From the thought-world of that century some popular notions about missions still linger. In many congregations, there remains a good deal of the old racial arrogance, cultural imperialism, and religious snobbery, untempered by the lessons taught by the experience of more than a hundred years. Even where these attitudes have passed, the old emotions have faded but gradually, emotions associated with sacrifice, giving on behalf of the ignorant and unfortunate, and the expectation of speedy and universal triumph by the gospel.

The image of the Missionary as Saint was readily assimilated into popular expectations regarding the minister and the minister's wife (sic). Though considerably eroded by the pressure on all women to bring home a paycheck if not to aspire to an independent career, these expectations persisted well past the midpoint of the twentieth century.

Outside the churches the negative caricature of the Missionary as a narrow-minded, tight-collared, joyless embodiment of moralistic propriety still remains, perpetuated in films, cartoons, and novels.[10] These impressions are sometimes projected on a minister by persons whose personal contacts with religious leaders are limited.

For the minister—aside from being regarded as a bluenose by outsiders—the hardest aspect of the Missionary's legacy to live with in a materialistic age has been the expectation, held by not a few church members and outsiders, that the minister should sacrifice to an extent they would never consider for themselves. Even today many persons have difficulty in adjusting to the idea of a minister nattily attired in voguish sportswear, tooling off to the country club in a late-model sports car, and hobnobbing with the "beautiful people." The image of success projected through the media and lived out by the celebrity-evangelists of the "electronic church" may have tempered somewhat the idea that the minister's life, like the Missionary's, should be one that sacrifices all such symbols of wealth and creaturely comfort.

But the notion of ministry as self-denying has not died. It clings to the conscience of many a minister, so that we feel downright uneasy about the display of obvious luxury (even though we resent the attempt of some in the church to keep us poor). To such an extent, the model of the Missionary has preserved the memory of the apostolic ministry which, though weak and impoverished, enriched the life of the world.

The avenue into ministry that this model opened to women requires a significant place in any assessment of its influence. A respected historian of the world mission calls it "the first feminist movement in North America."[11] A more recent scholar, in language and concepts clearly belonging to the late twentieth century rather than to the nineteenth, observes that the missionary movement

offered the independence, status, and opportunity for achievement associated with the professions, but it was not a profession. As a calling it was characterized by a rhetoric of self-denial rather than of personal ambition....Missionary women...share many of the needs that led women into the professions; but they had one unique need—to clothe their ambition in a garb which did no violence to their sense of feminine Christian virtue.[12]

True as that insight may be, as far as it goes, it overlooks an important insight expressed by another observer, who emphasizes "the vitality and joy that so clearly marked many of these women's lives" and who maintains:

In contrast to the anxiety and stress that mark the lives of many women today, the[se] women...found their arena in an environment that allowed them to combine "feminine" characteristics with "masculine" scope.[13]

The Missionary conferred on American ministry generally a sense of informed commitment to serving human need of whatever sort. With that dedication came status as a representative of a far-flung, ecumenical faith and officer of a worldwide body who has a significant involvement in global ministry and a knowledgeable awareness of world problems.[14] Some even see in the minister what some ministers see in themselves—the advocate of a dynamic faith for which no sacrifice is too great and which one would gladly carry to the ends of the earth.

In 1925 a young American minister brought up on the Atlantic seaboard was called to a pastorate in Walla Walla, Washington. On arriving in the Northwest, he was driven out the six miles to the great grave of Marcus and Narcissa Whitman and their children, slain nearly eighty years before by the people they had sought to help. "I wished to rededicate my life at his grave. I had come to serve in the land he had helped save."[15] Such was the aura of the Missionary and its effects on American ministry generally.

Interlude: Confused Expectations

As the nineteenth century drew to its close, the confusion of expectations regarding ministry increased in American church life. The old colonial models from the eighteenth century still trailed nostalgically through the dreams of good people, coloring their desires for the kind of minister they would like to have.

The pattern of the Saint continued, however, to dissolve, no longer able to maintain the once distinct form so well known in the Middle Ages. Its primeval pattern in the shape of the shaman persisted among Native Americans, whose hope of staving off the advance of the white settlers vanished in the blood and smoke of

Wounded Knee in 1890. A stirring revival of shamanic excitement had swept the tribal communities for some months before that massacre, which broke the resistance.[1]Afterwards charismatic holy women and holy men continued to appear, bearing the spiritual burdens of their oppressed people, keeping faith with the vision that conveyed their call, doing their best to sustain hope in a situation all but hopeless.[2]

Among the victors, who did not have the insight to see themselves as oppressors, some ministers continued to bear the marks of personal holiness so evident in the Saint.

More than one well-known Pulpiteer manifested the essential traits—the gift of "vision" so conspicuous in John Jasper, or the winsomeness of a personality like Phillips Brooks, aglow with the sense of the divine presence. But many celebrated preachers attained eminence primarily through the gift of eloquence or the power of an agile mind or even a voice "like an organ." Though patently sincere, they did not aspire primarily to sainthood, nor did their admirers think of them primarily in terms of that model.

A similar phenomenon prevailed with respect to the Builder: The essence of some ministers' ability to build up the church was their evident saintliness of life, but it would have been insufficient without the gift for getting along with people or for helping them develop workable plans, or for persistent application to the task, or for inspiring others to work.

Through the Awakener and then the Revivalist the "blessed assurance" of direct encounter with the Spirit of God was conveyed to the people. The self-denial and total love for God so evident in the Saint shone with equal brightness in the Missionary, but again other elements and concerns gave distinctive shape to the new form.

The form of Priest persisted in apparent continuity with the colonial model, but appearances can deceive. For priesthood, as known in biblical Israel and in Christendom from the fourth century on, had been a public office with liturgical responsibility for an entire people under a covenant made by their leaders with God.

Since the adoption of the Bill of Rights, however, the United States had made clear its purpose to have no national church or establishment of religion. As a consequence, even though Roman Catholics and Episcopalians and Orthodox continued the form *within* the life of the church and quickly developed an effective episcopate, one of the central concepts of priesthood had no possibility for proper expression, namely, its relationship to a total population rather than just to the members of a congregation (and a bishop) standing alongside several other congregations (and bishops) serving the same territory.

This reduction of a church of all the people to a denominational chapel serving some of the people put a radical crimp in the model.

Not a few bishops and priests carried a fond memory, sometimes avowed, from the days of establishment, and some might dream of a coming victory for the true faith, but in actuality theirs was now an internal ministry to a congregation culled from a much larger populace. Within a given church of the "catholic" tradition the ministry of the Priest continued to function as it had in the past, but it was a ministry drastically curtailed. Some of the work of the Builder continued part of the former service of the Priest, but the models are clearly distinct.

So with the Master of the Bible Commonwealth. The social and political context of his ministry had altered so radically that, though the Pulpiteer clearly adapted a primary function of the Master, namely preaching, to the new situation of religious freedom, both form and content had changed. Master and Pulpiteer are related but demonstrably distinct models of ministry.

The most obvious kinship prevailed between the Awakener and the Revivalist. We might justifiably call the latter Son—or in a few cases Daughter—of Awakener. But there were differences. The Great Awakening happened within a limited, though not insignificant, geographical area, namely the eastern seaboard. At the turn of the nineteenth century the second Great Awakening crossed the mountains, and the Revivalists carried it from sea to shining sea. The earlier movement had taken its rise within the meetinghouse, though it soon spread to the open fields, but the nineteenth-century Revivalist established the camp-meeting, the tent, and the "tabernacle" as temporary loci for the work. Furthermore, the repudiation of the Calvinistic doctrine of election, sometimes implicit in the work of the Awakener, was generally made explicit by the Revivalist, first in practice, then in overt argument. Theology accommodated to democracy.

Despite the change from the old order of the eighteenth century and the disappearance or radical transformation of the colonial models, expectations related to them persisted in the new era and still endure today. Without repeating those expectations at this point, we simply reiterate that they did not vanish with the passing of the older forms, but were projected onto ministers of quite another type, or even taken over in the new models. The Revivalist and, in many cases, the Pulpiteer, for example, gave large place to the emotions of their hearers, taking into account the subjective "experience" so prized by the Awakener.

As for the dominant nineteenth-century models, they appear to have emerged naturally in interaction between the heritage of ministry and the new situation in which the church found itself. Each of them developed its own peculiar shape and dynamic as a result of new conditions of the times. It is obvious that intelligent, sincere creativity went into the process (consider Finney's handbook on *Revivals of Religion*), but it will not do to look on any one person as sole inventor of one or another of the new forms. All four of them were so clearly adapted to the needs of the times that they seem to have been the products of corporate intuition within the church. Perhaps new models for our time will come in the same way.

As the twentieth century dawned, the models of ministry that had emerged in the hundred years just prior seemed firmly fixed for the future.

The Pulpiteer was embodied in well-known preachers in every city in America, and the ideal remained a force as late as World War II.

The Revivalist seemed equally well entrenched and lasted virtually as long—though more rational, less emotional religion continued its vigorous criticism of the model and the methods, as did a cynical secular press. Still the big tents went up summer after summer along the sawdust trail across the South and the Southwest to the Northwest, while the style of music and of conducting religious services yielded with glacial slowness to the new liturgical emphasis in the churches. In an effort to retain the evangelistic power of the old revivalism in a mode with less of the backwoods about it, the Federal Council of Churches as late as the 1940s was conducting preaching missions in major cities across the United States, with well-known ministers delivering sermons to thousands.

As urbanization brought increasing problems for the churches, success came with ever greater difficulty for those who followed the ideal of the Builder, and the more glamorous, up-to-date model of the Manager tended to replace it, bringing a different style and ethos and set of goals.

The Missionary seemed surely ensconced among the ideal figures of Christian heroes as the century dawned. But the pedestal erected for this model of ministry weakened during the Great Depression and received heavy blows during World War II and after. The emergence of indigenous leadership in the new churches of Asia and Africa, the revolt against colonialism, uneasiness in the Western churches about cultural imperialism, as well as the increasing ease of travel and communication, all reduced the idealization of the Missionary in the mainline churches.

From the mid-twentieth century on, religion in America found itself increasingly overwhelmed by secularism and social change that undercut the old sense of triumphalism in the churches and destroyed Christian assurance as to the older models, which only a short time before had seemed so secure.

In a desperate bid for relevance after World War II, the religious community eagerly embraced the notion of new forms of ministry. With increasing clarity we can now see that the churches of this century put their faith in four primary models. Three of them are strikingly characteristic of the times — the Manager, the Counselor, the Impresario. Surprisingly, the fourth is the Teacher. Around these four clustered the faith and hope of twentieth-century ministers and members. And tangled with those hopes, in grand confusion, lingered many of the expectations associated with the older forms we have examined.

PART

III

Perplexity over Form and Concept

THE TWENTIETH-CENTURY SETTING

The twentieth century has brought mounting uncertainty about ministry, a decline in its public visibility, and confusion for those who practice it. The grand old forms, once so majestic, no longer dominate the skyline. The bold talk about "new forms" that lilted through the conversations of seminarians and the ministerial avant-garde a generation ago died upon the smoggy air. With it vanished the dogmatism of those who asserted the irrelevance of congregation and pastorate, and church work has gone on amid less of an uproar than in the turbulent sixties. But mainline denominations decline in membership, and congregations wither on the vine, despite the fretful solicitude of faithful pastors and the continuing loyalty of devoted members. Ministers keep up a brave front. But sometimes when they gather in informal groups and open themselves to one another, it becomes clear that hearts are troubled.

A Shattering of Traditional Forms

Our fundamental problem in ministry, this book contends, is confusion as to its form and concept. This problem is, of course, related to a larger crisis of faith, a theme too large to engage here. We shall, however, address a major aspect of the confusion that is central to our argument, namely, a consideration of the forces in twentieth-century life that have undercut the relevance of once imposing models and have begun to shape new ones, some of which are problematic.[1]

Dissolution of Community

Our sense of ministry's declining significance in society has its roots in the breakdown of community. Metropolis dominates twentieth-century life. It crushes human relationships, along with the institutions

121

that once sustained them, under the relentless advance of high-rise buildings, freeways, new parking garages. and expanding airports.

For almost a hundred years, people have fled the central city, moving farther and farther into the suburbs and beyond. There they "live." That is, there they sleep and bring up the children and mow the lawn. But their work scatters them throughout metropolis, as do their play, their schooling, their church life, and other voluntary activities. Appointments with doctor or dentist or hairdresser may well take them to locales otherwise unvisited. In this bleak, impersonal setting the sense of community that once characterized life in the village, the small town, or the county seat has no chance. Even in the city, back at the turn of the century, one could "manage." In megalopolis we speak rather of "coping" and try to convince ourselves we are doing so.

Urban magnitudes and complexities have overwhelmed the institutions that once made for community by enabling people to relate to one another on the basis of common experience and shared values. But the marvelous multiplicity of options for work and leisure that initially seems so attractive in the great city palls after a time. Everywhere we go we encounter different persons in such numbers that we are surprised when we come across someone we already know. Demands on time and energy compel us to restrict our pursuit of varied interests, and we settle into a routine of cheering the Dodgers or the Dolphins from an anonymous seat in the stands or near the television set. It is doubtful that people in today's cities enjoy such diversity of firsthand involvement in "live" activities—athletic, cultural, religious—as was common in a small city with a liberal arts college a generation or two ago.

Our scattered and separate involvements fracture the life of even the most "favored" families. In many a suburban driveway the early morning jogger can see four cars parked, signifying the separated lives of the four members of that home who gather under the same roof chiefly to sleep. Public schools no longer serve as centers of community. The corner grocery has given way to the supermarket on the mall, too far away to walk. The franchised hamburger restaurants on the strip all look alike; they stand where Joe's Place or Bessie's Diner used to be, gathering places for a neighborhood that has been taken out to make way for the new office complex and the used car lot. The afternoon newspapers have folded, and the surviving daily centers its attention on the big scene, worldwide and regional, a landscape in which an ordinary mainline congregation and its pastor seldom receive notice.

The dissolution of community has left church and ministry without the arena in which they once knew how to work with effectiveness. From the beginning of Christianity, its structures for ministry (diocese, parish, presbytery, congregation) have related themselves to geographical communities and their needs—even when the meetinghouses of competing denominations stared balefully at one another across a busy street. But community is no more.

Year after year the magnificent downtown churches where the Pulpiteer once had the ear of the city have decayed in melancholy isolation from the people they formerly served, often from any people at all. Hundreds of such buildings, at one time the pride of their communities, have fallen to the wrecker's ball. Here and there a new ethnic population has provided the human base for a vital new congregation in an abandoned sanctuary, but its people are powerless, its minister rarely a public figure in the great city.

Meanwhile the pastor of the suburban church that grew so dramatically at mid-century deals with people not in the totality of their lives, but far from their vocational involvements and from the desperate problems of the city—often a separate municipality where the pastor has no influence whatever. The nice people who come to church want help with their families and guidance for their personal problems, but the church no longer stands at the center of the common life, for the common life itself has largely dissipated.

As interests and involvements fractionalize, some ministers have developed specialized chaplaincies—to hospitals, to campuses, to prisons, to the military, to the carnival and the circus. Their services often engage persons in crisis and must therefore be valued, but they are directed to transients.

The form of Christian ministry that in earlier centuries had profound territorial integrity and influence, that of bishop, has been rendered ineffective by the church itself through the folly of denominationalism. Instead of one bishop for all the Christians of a city—or even for most mainline Protestants, as would be possible in a united church on the model proposed by the Consultation on Church Union—today's metropolis provides the base for half a dozen to a score of "bishops" and "bishop-types," each responsible for an area embracing half a state, or even two or three states. Occasionally a Roman Catholic or Methodist bishop has a large enough constituency to retain standing as a public person, but most of these officials dash harried and hurried from one meeting to the next, so burdened with the minutiae of ecclesiastical administration as to have little opportunity for involvement in the life of their city, much less the half-dozen other cities illogically included in their overstretched dioceses.

Yet another factor in reducing the influence of the minister in the community has been the rapid increase of specialization in higher education, accompanied by the multiplication of fields of knowledge and a corresponding expansion in the number of professions and of persons working in them. Until late in the nineteenth century, divinity, law, and medicine had constituted the "learned professions," bestowing on those who qualified to practice them a store of specialized knowledge, a reputation for disciplined thought, and a local eminence that readily translated into respect for their office and deference to their opinions in matters lying outside their field of certified competence. It naturally followed that ministers readily exercised no little influence in their communities. This was especially true of the Pulpiteer, whose oratorical gifts attracted a large popular following.

But as the twentieth century wore on, the mushrooming of the social sciences and of specialized professions in every aspect of community well-being meant that in addressing almost any local problem people could turn to acknowledged authorities with more expertise on it than that possessed by the minister. Because local organizations committed to the common good rely so heavily on volunteers, ministers still have many opportunities to serve outside the life of their congregation. But the boards or committees with which they work commonly have other members with greater expertise on the issue being addressed than that possessed by the pastor. The tendency is for community leaders to honor the minister for goodwill, dedication, and general intelligence, but to assume that her or his specialty has to do with the inwardness of the spiritual life, not with public affairs. An unintended privatism is thus forced upon religion, following as an unplanned and frequently unnoted result of the increase in general and professional education. Thus the minister's sphere of influence is pushed back within the circle of a particular congregation.

It is not for glory that a minister aspires to visibility for her or his office. It is for ministry to the human family in a particular place, engaged with the totality of its needs and involvements. Today's minister works to the point of weariness in dealing with personal crises of individuals, in serving on boards and committees concerned for various local needs and problems, and in trying to keep a congregation afloat. But all this effort, no matter how dedicated and intelligent, makes little discernible impact on Los Angeles or Chicago, even on Bakersfield or Peoria. Most members of a congregation rarely see their minister except in the chancel or beside a hospital bed. Here and there a minister of unusual insight, courage, and good luck may get the ear of a city. But such instances are rare because the city is no longer a community. Its channels of "communication" are broken down or inaccessible.

Loss of Human Scale

Not only ministry has been diminished. The changes in society accompanying metropolitan dominance have issued in massive complexes in almost every area of endeavor. Our way of life has lost human scale. Multinational corporations control the world of business. Government rests in the hands of vast entrenched bureaucracies. Candidates for national office must raise such staggering sums to pay for a campaign as to fall under obligation to faceless "committees," unions, and corporations. Administrative offices, layer on layer, operate the public schools. Hospitals and universities have become cities in themselves. Publicized by breathless, meaningless "hype," sullied by unprincipled devotion to the big buck as their driving concern, professionals dominate the world of sports. Farming has given way to corporate agribusiness.

The major decisions in all these enterprises are made by high-salaried executives separated by a great abyss from the people those decisions touch most closely. Concerned not so much with serving the real needs of the public as with pushing a product and even more with quick profits, they manifest an arrogant cynicism toward consumers, employees, and government regulators alike. The obsession of boards of directors with the "bottom line" on quarterly financial reports terrorizes even the most sensitive and humane of executives. Less and less does the gigantic machine serve human beings in their needs, less and less does it leave a place for response to human concerns within or outside the corporation, less and less does it allow the possibility for any human being to divert the "abominable thing" from its inhuman course. Many agree with E. F. Schumacher that *Small Is Beautiful,* but *small* is not the order of the day.

"Communication" is now the province of the mass media. In its early days radio had a humane quality, not yet entirely lost from local stations but diminished by the heavy reliance on the recording industry for programming. Film and television are now so expensive as to require the financial resources of great corporations, which run them with an eye only to the bottom line. The same is true of publishing, its houses of distinguished name swallowed up into conglomerates, its finest magazines caught in the same fate or worse—termination. In the first half of the century some remarkable individuals still exercised significant influence on the nation's cultural life, their personal standards and sensitivity setting the tone for thousands of discriminating readers. No more. The press is still "free" from governmental control, but too costly for even the most gifted individual to have continuing access or significance. It remains to be seen whether the new economies of scale made possible by desktop publishing and video cameras can open the way to influence for persons more preoccupied with principle than with profit.

Meanwhile, the mass media control the flow of information that gives us our notions of reality. The debasing of the public taste or the constant appeal to the baser levels of popular interest—the continuing target of religious critics and reformers—is only one aspect of this dominance. On most issues people are limited, both in knowledge and interpretation, to impressions gathered from the monopolistic media. One article in *Reader's Digest* with a distorted picture of the World Council of Churches produces a public image that all the religious periodicals in the country and all the preachers too can scarcely alter. When the media themselves slant their reporting or misrepresent fact, as they did a few years ago when Billy Graham participated in a Moscow rally promoting nuclear disarmament,[2] an individual or institution has no effective way of countering. On this score even the President of the United States feels the limitations of "the most powerful office in the world."

Even though ministers may have at their fingertips amazing devices for "communication"—typewriters, duplicators, copy machines, word processors, modems, video cameras—their access to the public is limited for the most part to the small circle of their congregation's constituents and friends. Hence their newsletters deal for the most part with announcements of meetings and the personal concerns of members or an "in-group." If the minister-editor addresses a community problem or public issue, the comment is not likely to reach far. Who reads a piece of second-class mail unless it obviously promotes a favorite hobby or, better yet, bears the signature of a current celebrity?

The celebrity is the insubstantial creation of the mass media.[3] Whimsically defined as "someone who is famous for being well known," the celebrity most commonly attains that envied status by way of sports, entertainment, or politics—and increasingly the big names in the third activity get there by switching from one of the other two. The celebrity serves a function similar to that of royalty: the living icon who personally embodies the professed values of a people, the distant but observable individual who by accident of birth or chance, quite apart from intrinsic merit as a person, lives out the drama of romance, marriage, separation, reconciliation, parenthood, anniversaries, new successes, failure, grandparenthood, nostalgic return to scenes of remembered glory, and death—not only as one making one's own particular journey through life, but as a representative pilgrim on life's journey whose experience radiates a golden touch to the thousands of commoners making essentially the same trip without ever attracting much notice.

The perquisites surpass those of royalty. Not only does the celebrity "live well" by the standards of a materialistic culture, but by making constant guest appearances on talk shows is asked to express a personal opinion on every topic of the day. This person, basking in the adulation of millions on account of an ability to outrun eleven other athletes on the gridiron or to fill most provocatively their sexual fantasies, is thus given an access to the means of shaping public opinion that is unavailable to the most knowledgeable authorities on an issue, much less to a local minister. Whereas the Master of the New England pulpit spoke with authority on every issue of life and death and social policy, the president of the National Council of Churches rates barely a line in the paper or a passing phrase on the evening news, not even being mentioned by name. Yet every adolescent in metropolis, and in the boondocks too, has constant opportunity to know what the current rock star or centerfold model thinks on every issue from ERA to nuclear disarmament to the ethics of informing one's date that one has been exposed to AIDS.

The tyranny of the celebrity presents ministry with a problem far more serious than the personal peevishness of a minister upset over having little chance for even local fame. Lesser folk have always envied royalty, and a dash of pastoral bitterness toward each new crop of teenage millionaires is understandable if not of much consequence.

What is devastating is the widespread assumption that no one is really very significant except the celebrity, certainly no one in our town, no one that we know. The media constantly peddle that impression, both by indirection and by intent. Nothing really happens except in metropolis, and no one there is anyone except the celebrity—not the president of the American Medical Association or the nation's best informed scholar on the contemporary Middle East or a resident authority in child development. The popularity of such a feature as Charles Kuralt's "On the Road," with its attention to interesting persons in out-of-the-way places, does little to counteract that impression; its popularity is doubtless its appeal to nostalgia. In my youth we could honestly believe that the teachers in our high school were significant persons in society, that some ministers we knew as friends were honored around the world for the importance of their contribution, that our local editor exerted nationwide influence. All this was in fact true. It might well be true in many communities today, but because of the tyranny of the celebrity and the dominance of the media it would be hard to get any young person to believe it.

The bishop of a Protestant denomination may rate a notice in the metropolitan press on being elected to office, and again on retirement, but will be virtually ignored in between except in case of scandal, major controversy in the denomination, or an outspoken utterance on a public issue that strikes the media as bizarre. As for the local pastor, nothing. Even the neighborhood throwaways limit their congregational notices to "hiring and firing," Christmas and Easter programs, and an occasional tradition such as the annual strawberrry festival, which hardly presents the minister with a significant platform. The ten major news stories in religion featured annually at year's end rarely have to do with a local pastor, except in the case of a particularly lurid scandal.

The diminution of the individual in a society that has lost personal scale is my point. I do not want to make a whippingboy of the media, though they may deserve a few licks. But editors and directors have a pretty good idea of what attracts public attention, and the ordinary person rarely rates it. Throughout the course of the eighteenth and nineteenth centuries, ministry relied primarily on the public exercise of personal influence—on other persons, on a congregation, on a community, on society at large. In our mass society few ministers have access to the general public; their influence is sharply curtailed.

The Dehumanizing of Higher Education

In the revolutionary developments since World War II, a dehumanizing of higher education has intensified the loss of human scale. Gigantism has taken over the campus. This phenomenon has compounded the difficulties of ministry.

Until mid-century the traditional liberal arts colleges established under denominational auspices still stood high in public esteem for academic excellence and their long record of service. The unprecedented expansion of the college-age population and of the proportion of young people enrolling for higher education totally transformed the academic scene. Tax-supported universities reached enrollments exceeding fifty thousand. State colleges that a generation earlier had been called normal schools took on an even larger complement of students. Community colleges sprang up in every town with traffic lights. While most church-related colleges have survived, they now serve only a small minority of the nation's students and they draw their faculties largely from the big graduate schools where the new secular ethos prevails.

These developments have necessarily made for the depersonalization of higher education and for the dominance of secular assumptions and values. "The community of scholars" has become a ritual incantation, which enchants academic orators but refers to nothing discernible in the real world. In most of the major universities a single department now occupies its own building with a faculty that would outnumber the entire teaching force of many a traditional liberal arts college. With the growth in the number of commuting students and part-time adjunct professors, the old context for learning—the intimate association of teacher and student living in a closely related community with common commitments—has been destroyed. The prominent place that the minister had in higher education, as an influence on the campus of the nearby church school or as an acknowledgedly qualified candidate for appointment as a professor or administrator, has been undercut. The loss of human scale in higher education has diminished ministry.

Higher education has also been dehumanized in a more subtle way. The understandable emphasis on scientific and mathematical studies in a technological society and on vocational ends—"You have to go to college to get a job!"—has diminished the place and significance of "the more humane letters" that once furnished our culture with a common center. Literature (and not just the classics), languages, history, philosophy, ethics, the arts—now disparaged as "frill courses"—have been leeched from college and high school curricula in favor of "more relevant" subjects. As a result, students and teachers rarely confront together questions of truth or meaning or value, questions that since antiquity have formed the heart of education and of the cultural heritage.

Great moral issues raised by reflection on *Macbeth* or *King Lear* formed, even earlier in this century, the basis of serious conversation and of telling illustrations in sermons. Every high school graduate had read and discussed the stories in English class, and the aspiring person who had not had a chance to finish a formal education struggled through the classics with an eye to self-improvement and admission to the world of cultivated persons.

The shift in the focus of education has intensified the secular orientation of the culture. A minister who has been personally exposed to the great heritage can still use it with effectiveness in preaching or teaching if there is time to explain each allusion, but for the immediate recognition of a fictional character one must refer to a recent film, thus leaving older members of the congregation in the dark, or a current television series, and relatively few of these enactments show much artistic or ethical sensitivity. The dissolution of community has occurred not only in a geographical context, but also at the heart of the culture.

The accelerating specialization of scholarship has not only muffled interdisciplinary dialogue for most run-of-the-mill scholars; it has limited meaningful substantive discourse even between members of a department. It leaves even the most brilliant and erudite authority regarding some thin slice of human knowledge, often quite ignorant about the rest of the loaf. It permits a tendency to downgrade the significance of knowledge in fields that one knows little about, and to assume of a field like religion that anyone working there must be ignorant of other areas or even unbalanced. Whereas the minister in colonial New England and throughout nineteenth-century America was an acknowledged intellectual leader, the scholarly credentials of today's seminary graduates go widely unrecognized, particularly by those who should take them most seriously. It is not evident that the shift of nomenclature for professional degrees to Master of Divinity and Doctor of Ministry has materially altered this situation.

Once again a change in social structure over which no minister has any control has radically diminished the image of ministry and removed a cultural platform on which the minister once stood.

A Post-Christian Era

The dissolution of community—geographical, interpersonal, cultural—has subjected society in our time to shocks as severe as the barbarian invasions, the wars of religion, or the early phases of the industrial revolution. The old order has passed and will never return.

We knew how to do the work of ministry in the old order, and we did it reasonably well, even though that work was hard and often discouraging. We still profess our faith in the God known to us supremely through Jesus Christ. We still believe the world needs the ministry of the church that lives by that faith. But we have not yet learned how to do the work of ministry in this kind of world.

It is a post-Christian era. That is a phrase we have often heard and do not like. It describes our society. It does not mean that there are no Christians any more, that the people of our time no longer need the Christian gospel, that the decision makers of former times were more virtuous, that ministers were wiser, more dedicated, or harder-working. The phrase accurately names the kind of world we have been describing, a scene where vast impersonal agglomerations of power diminish not only the significance of the individual but also the individual's capacity to have much effect on the course of events.

It is a landscape without landmarks. The old structures of communal and ethical stability have collapsed, weighed down by the snows of intellectual uncertainty, battered by the winds of relativism, their foundations undercut by the swirling floods of subjectivism. Ours is what a political scientist calls "a loosely-bounded culture"; the ending of established religion has resulted in the decline of an ethical consensus, what Durkheim called *conscience collective.*[4] The mass media have usurped the place once occupied by home and church and school in the inculcation of standards and values. "Traditional channels of authority and respect for the same—[in particular,] the spiritual role of the local minister, priest, or rabbi—have been eroding for some time[5]" Since the counterculture of the 1960s brashly challenged them, they have not succeeded in recovering the respect they once claimed. The parson has "been moved from a central position to the private sector of life" and now "has diminishing authority with which to speak effectively to either."[6] The Christian faith is no longer generally acknowledged as the source of *ultimate* meaning.

It is a time dominated by the values of the marketplace. Athletics, once the arena for sportsmanship, are conducted primarily with an eye to the gate. The university, once the guardian of the cultural tradition and of humane values, now justifies its existence as the source of ever more incredible technology and pays its way by devising ever more lethal weapons of mass annihilation. Art, which was once the source of reflection, serene enjoyment, and the cultivation of sensitivity, is prized primarily as a hot field for investment. Even in religion, people flock to the guru who promises personal attractiveness, prosperity, and freedom from inward disturbance. They measure the success of the church by statistical norms. Their sense of values is so distorted, even when they emotionally profess their love of the old-time religion, that the minister who impresses them as the supreme contemporary apostle of the faith is the huckster of pious nostrums appearing on their TV screens in the image of a celebrity.

A crisis in ministry confronts us. The low state of ministerial morale is thoroughly understandable. Ministers are not to be blamed as personally responsible for the ineffectiveness of the churches, though they are commonly made the scapegoats both by the members of their congregations who may not know any better and by pundits from theological faculties who ought to. If blame is to be fixed in this crisis, it must be shared by the seminaries for not providing their graduates with a keener insight into the dynamics of the contemporary world, along with the ministers themselves for not more conscientiously passing on to their people the measure of understanding that they do have.

Knowing what the world is like does not solve our problem. Neither does it give us an immediate answer as to the form that ministry must take in order to serve people in this kind of world and to help make it a different kind of world. But our analysis should enable us to see why the development of ministry has taken the turns it has in our century. It should help us to evaluate emerging forms with a judgment both critical and charitable. And it may stimulate creative reflection regarding forms that can at the same time sustain the high tradition of Christian ministry at its best and grapple effectively with the realities of power in our post-Christian era.

Before moving to twentieth-century forms, however, it is necessary to comment on two developments within the church that have unwittingly weakened the effectiveness of ministry and given it unintended shape in our time.

Distortions from Within the Church

Denominations Recast as Religious Bureaucracies

Responding with the automatic reflexes of an organism threatened by change in its environment, the church has undertaken to adapt in order to survive. In behavior consistent with its past, it has begun to conform its institutions once again to the prevailing pattern in the secular order. A sound principle within limits, this course nevertheless has its dangers, not so great when the church seriously thinks through the theological meaning of the adaptation, but perilous when it just assumes that "worldlier is wiser." Largely on the basis of that assumption, however, the major denominations in America have recast their mode of operation to conform with the dominant contemporary mode in business and government, the bureaucracy.

In earlier days the denomination was channel of salvation or bearer of divine truth, and not at all hesitant to insert the adjective *sole* just ahead of each of those phrases. Even in the twentieth century one could commonly hear the participants in a denominational rally or convention exhorted to stand fast on the distinctive doctrinal ground marked out by our heroic forebears in the faith. While the overt appeal was to the theological vocation of the denomination and while many of us assumed that our chief rationale for separate existence in the Christian world was our calling to contribute our distinctive witness, such words really served as tribal battle cries to rally the troops.

The true function of the denomination, however, as we saw in our discussion of the Builder,[7] was as an agency of mission. The people who responded to our witness did so, for the most part, because beneath this jargon of particularity they heard the transforming gospel of Jesus Christ. Or if they came to us for less sublime reasons, it was because they enjoyed the music of our choir or liked our minister or found our Sunday school conveniently located for their children, but seldom because they had become convinced of the essentiality of episcopacy in the historic succession or of believer's baptism by immersion. They came in spite of our peculiarities, not because of them.

In the twentieth century the agency of mission turned into a bureaucratically structured marketing organization in the field of religion.[8] Its boards and general units assumed the prerogatives of top management in business, announcing objectives, assigning quotas, flogging their representatives in the field to increase production. This state of affairs was disguised by whatever rhetoric came most naturally, whether of theological propriety or political acceptability: "This great crusade affirmed overwhelmingly by the vote of our elected representatives!" In episcopal churches the bishops increasingly patterned their activities and schedules after the model of executives in business.

As a result, the sacral character of church and ministry has all but disappeared from the general life of the denomination except for a few tokens—a communion service at the national assembly and perhaps a sermon each evening, if that is not replaced by a new promotional film, a drama of compelling relevance, or a concert of music and dance. The big wheels in the denomination whirl from one airport hotel to the next, for one committee meeting after another. The up-and-coming minister, the leading woman, and the big layman rate inclusion in these denominational sales meetings. And the smart young pastor soon learns what one has to do to earn a promotion.

In developing this mode of procedure, denominational officials have been neither wicked nor stupid. As great and good persons devoted to the Christian cause, they did not set out deliberately to diminish the sacral character of the church or to recast the pastor in the role of branch manager or executive secretary. But that is what they have done. The irony is that the development has proved counterproductive. For all the groaning of the denominational machine, it is losing members and, when allowance is made for inflation, bringing in less money. Most devastating of all from the standpoint of this study, it has come up with an unintended definition of minister as Manager. That form and concept we shall take up as Model 9.

"Theological" Undercutting of Ordained Ministry

A strange new theological axiom, meanwhile, has gained wide currency in the church. Its pious and constant repetition has resulted in unintended downplaying of the significance of the minister, with no corresponding gain to offset the loss. The axiom is the now all-too-familiar assertion, "Every member is a minister." In thousands of congregational newsletters and worship bulletins this strange doctrine is given the appearance of official standing by straight-faced displays that read something like this:

FIRST RELEVANT CHURCH
The Rev. Earnest Workman, D.Min., Senior Pastor
The Rev. Ima Friendly Sort, M.Div., Parish Visitor
The Rev. Jack B. Nimble, Assistant Pastor
The Rev. Johann Sebastian Holtkamp, Mus. D., Chorister
Angie Ten-Speed, B.S. (Seminarian in Training), Youth Worker
MINISTERIAL STAFF = The 562 Members of First Church

Again and again moralistic homilies sound from the pulpit:

Don't think of me as the minister. I am a Christian like any of you. We all are ministers. The work of old First is done—or not done!—by all of you. I am not essential to the process. I cannot do anything you cannot do. I just happen to have studied what some of you have not yet learned. But when you have learned it you will be every bit as much a minister as I am—or Ima or Jack or Dr. Holtkamp, or as Angie will be once she finishes seminary and passes her ordination exams. But of course she is a minister now. And so are you. So get in there and raise this budget and prove what a good minister you are!

If the logic of such preaching sounds confused and likely to derogate from the office of ministry, it *is* confused, and it *does* derogate. In a well-intentioned effort to affirm a theology of the laity, to reassert for our time the Reformation doctrine of the universal priesthood of believers, and to goad average church members into a greater sense of obligation, this kind of imprecise and sentimental talk has taken over. It strips the ordained servant of the church of the grand old title of *minister* honored by apostles and Protestant Reformers alike.[9]

By the doctrine of the universal priesthood the Reformers affirmed the right of every Christian to approach God directly in prayer, to receive God's forgiveness without having to go through a priest, and to pray for one's friend without having to pay for special masses. They also meant to assert that the whole church is involved, as one body, in every ministry rendered in its name, and that the ordained minister does what ministers do in preaching, teaching, administering the sacraments, caring for the church, and serving the larger community, not as an expression of private piety or superior standing before God, but as a representative ministry of the entire company of believers. Only in the Radical Reformation was there a repudiation of the need for a special ordained ministry. The most glorious initials Thomas Campbell could dream of writing after his signature were D.V.M.: *Dei verbi minister*, minister of the Word of God.[10]

Granted the complete sincerity and good intentions of all those who have given currency to the sentiment, "Every member is a minister," and the fervor with which preachers have urged it upon the people this past generation, I have not observed as a result any significant increase of zeal or participation by the laity. As Luther stated so eloquently and Hendrik Kraemer affirmed so clearly, the ministry of the laity is their involvement in the life of the world, their service to God and humanity through their vocation.[11] But that is not to say that everyone has the same vocation as the minister.

What this whole junket into pop theology amounted to was an unintended pillaging of the dignity of the ordained ministry even within the church. The twentieth-century minister, already robbed of status in society by sweeping changes in the secular order, has found that even in the sanctuary of God among those who call themselves God's people, ministry has no status either. The irony is that this aberration in theology of ministry was not brought forward and promoted by laypersons jealous of ministerial pretensions. It was foisted upon the church by naive and starry-eyed ministers who, in an ill-considered effort to get the members to work harder and give more, passed the sentiment along without thinking it through. The misguided effort has failed all around.

Suddenly ministers have found themselves floundering without a sense of vocational definition. Metropolis has deprived them of one-time status as recognized leaders of the community. The multiplication of advanced degrees and scholarly specialization has diminished appreciation of their credentials as intellectual leaders. The bureaucratization of the denomination has eroded their significance as spiritual leaders. Now this aberration of doctrine propagated by the preachers themselves has told everyone that ministers are no kind of leader at all, that the minister is nothing in the church except what every member is. What then *is* a minister?

A Frantic Search for Status

No one can long survive in any significant public role without a sense of the importance of what one is doing. Nor will church or society honor an office that cannot affirm its own significance. No wonder ministers clamor for support groups! That is not all. They have seized on two terms this past quarter-century in an effort to assert their vocational dignity. One is *clergy*. The other is *professional*.

It is a significant measure of the secularity of our age that both of these favored terms are sociological in connotation. They do have origins in religious thought, it is true. But in the typical seminarian who gushes pompously of being a clergyperson I discern no awareness of the theological rootage of the term to designate belonging completely to God. Nor in the pastor who emphasizes her or his standing as a professional do I detect at all times the image of a believer standing up for a deeply held personal faith.[12]

On the contrary, ministers and seminary faculties seem to like these terms precisely because of their secular ring. They seem to say, "Hey, everybody! You've got to take us clergypersons seriously. We are members of a recognized profession charged with responsibility in an important area of life, namely the recognition of the transcendent. We have as much education as a doctor or lawyer and we have a set of skills learned in supervised field education and internship. Even in this secular, post-Christian age we deserve public recogniton on secular grounds." To such a pass the frantic search for status has led us.

No surer sign could be given of the collapse of traditional patterns than the animated quest for new forms of ministry that took over the seminary campuses in the 1960s. The great models of our long Christian past, even of the recent past, no longer seemed relevant. Everyone talked the line for a while. The few of us who tried to plead that some of the old forms might perhaps be infused with new power were speedily and finally rebutted by reference to new wine. A few creative spirits experimented boldly with one "new form" or another. But the more effective it was, the more it looked like one of the old forms; and the newer it looked, the less effective it proved. Gradually the talk subsided. New forms went the way of other fads in the world of theological education, perhaps before the work was done.

Despite all that, and without portentous beating of drums, significant new forms of ministry characteristic of our time and responsive to its needs have come forth. They are not really what the idealists back then had in mind. But they belong to this moment in history as surely as the forms we delineated earlier belonged to the centuries past. It may be doubted whether anyone can clearly read the signs of one's own times, but in reflecting on ministry in the twentieth century, I see four characteristic forms as dominant. They are *Manager, Counselor, Impresario,* and *Teacher.*[13]

Let us now consider these forms and concepts of ministry that have served to focus the labors of the church's leaders in our century.

MANAGER

The model of the minister as Manager obviously emphasizes professional expertise and lays claim to indisputable relevance in our bureaucratic society. What we have already noted about the tenor of our times and the reordering of the denominations on the bureaucratic pattern indicates some of the major pressures that have recast ministry in the managerial mold. But these forces are not alone responsible.

The minister as Manager is the model that the congregation most insistently demands. And it is the model with which an increasing number of ministers themselves feel comfortable or in which they find a sense of importance. This is not to say that most ministers are good managers or that they ought to be. Nor is it to deny that many would fill the role of Manager more effectively if they gave greater attention to the strengths of some of the earlier forms of ministry. But it is to note that increasingly our society, our denominations, our congregations, and our ministers themselves see the office under the managerial image.

The trend had already begun toward the end of the nineteenth century, when Dwight L. Moody overtly applied the methods of business to the organization and conduct of revivals. "He not only was a businessman, he looked like a businessman, talked like a businessman, took things in hand like a businessman," and he numbered businessmen Cyrus McCormick, Marshall Field, and John Wanamaker among his friends and supporters.[1]

As early as 1890 John D. Rockefeller was calling for the introduction of business methods into the churches. It became increasingly fashionable to lament the otherworldliness of ministers, their alleged ineptitude in financial affairs, their presumed incapacity to deal with reality.[2] "After all, he never had to meet a payroll!" it was commonly

said when I was young. That stung even more than the current charge:
"How can she run a church? I'll bet she doesn't even know how to
read a balance sheet!"

Ministers fought back with a new image and began to spend more
time in the church office.[3] In 1924 a new journal for ministers began
publication. Its title: *Church Management*.[4] Following with a book on
The Art of Church Management, a pastor named Clarence E. Lemmon
won wide recognition.[5] Given the mood of the 1930s, the title was
inspired. The book established the principles of functional organization and of involving everyone—"every member on a committee."
People in those days of the Great Depression needed something to do,
needed to feel needed. A new style of church life took over, and a new
model of ministry. Manuals and "how-to" books poured from the
presses of the denominational publishing houses, and "workshops"
succeeded classes at religious conventions.

Good ministers, of course, were not as helpless and ineffective as
the popular image would have it. The tremendous work of the
Builder in the nineteenth century indicates not a little knowledge of
the ways of the world and finds some continuity in the new ideal of
Manager. Other terms, varying from decade to decade, have designated the same essential ideal. In my youth every dynamic minister
was a gifted leader. We all aspired to such a role until the neoorthodox
generation began to inform us that *leadership* was not to be found in
the vocabulary of the New Testament. We searched for other terms,
but the concept died hard.

Getting with the growing emphasis on management the seminaries promoted courses in church administration, largely eliminating
for a time the venerable term *pastoral theology*.[6] Following the example
of the schools of business, they began to use case studies. A minister
took pride in being known as a solid administrator; the secular
executive was really the model, but the term sounded too pretentious,
given expectations of ministerial humility and the realities of congregational life. The term frequently appeared, however, in "literature"
prepared for pastors.

In reporting on the study of theological education conducted in
the 1950s, H. Richard Niebuhr proposed the term *pastoral director* as
descriptive of the actual function of the twentieth-century minister.
He argued impressively both for the legitimacy of the concept and for
the fullness that it ought to have in guiding all the activities of a
congregation to serve the increase of love for God and neighbor.[7] But
the title has not caught on. Church members are understandably
skittish about conceding to their minister the autocratic image they
infer from that word *director*.

To suit the populist prejudices of congregations and to go with the more lyrical expectations concerning the ministry of the laity, the term *enabler* was bruited about.[8] It quickly achieved orthodox standing in the seminaries, hardly anyone pausing to note that it is a title that might more appropriately be reserved for the Holy Spirit. Pastors used it for some years in explaining to their congregations their understanding of their function, but one rarely heard it in the talk of church members, perhaps because they discerned little pragmatic evidence to justify its use. The same may be said for *facilitator*—a strangely unrealistic notion of ministry that can scarcely have grown out of much actual experience in the life of the church or observation as to how it operates. The term has the authentic ring of a technological vocabulary, but scarcely suggests a religious institution.

Even less appealing to the laity was the title *change agent,*[9] a particularly threatening expression of the managerial concept. It inflated the ministerial self-image that many idealistic seminarians carefully cultivated during the 1960s and '70s as they dreamed of a ministry that would transform the evil structures of society. But on leaving the campus they found few job openings for young ministers with this ideal.

Given the overtones of the term *change agent*, it is not surprising that conservative church members feared the concept or that an influential minority of ministers throughout the twentieth century has moved forthrightly into politics, either by overt campaigning for specific measures and candidates or by throwing their hats into the ring and running for office. Such a move has not been unusual at the level of local school board or town council, generally part-time offices, but a few pastors have also served as mayors, state legislators, and members of Congress.

Early in the century ministers gave leadership to the Prohibition Party and a number stood for high office on its ticket. After World War I a surprising number of them joined the Ku Klux Klan, though probably more of them resisted, sometimes heroically, its effort to maintain WASP supremacy by terror and coercion.[10] Before Pearl Harbor, Kirby Page and others launched the Emergency Peace Campaign to Keep America Out of War.[11] During the war, the Federal Council of Churches sparked a nationwide movement to support the establishment of the United Nations and American entrance into it.

In six presidential campaigns beginning in 1928, Presbyterian minister Norman Thomas headed the ticket of the Socialist Party. For decades Adam Clayton Powell served concurrently as pastor of Harlem's Abyssinian Baptist Church and as an influential member of Congress. The civil rights campaign of the 1960s followed the leadership of black preachers Martin Luther King, Jr., and his young colleagues Ralph Abernathy, Andy Young, Jesse Jackson, and Hosea Williams. After King's assassination his lieutenants became significant forces in local, state, and national politics. In the 1980s fundamentalists and other conservatives developed clout under Jerry Falwell's banner of the Moral Majority, and television preacher Pat Robertson made a run for the presidency.[12]

We have to acknowledge the ordained politician as an obvious model of ministry in the twentieth century, but its relatively limited electoral success has prevented its becoming a dominant form. The preachers seem to have made greater impact in providing leadership for campaigns over moral issues than in running for office themselves. Because the model should not be overlooked, I mention it here in connection with the change agent as a subcategory in our consideration of the Manager. In this case the minister aspires to manage the state rather than the church.

The term *community organizer* appears less frightening to parishioners than *change agent* or *politician*, though the notion of *agitator* that often accompanies it could bring on apoplexy in some congregations. Actually, in giving expression to the quieter, less hostile possibilities within this title, many ministers spend much effort and, in at least a small way, succeed in reducing the inhumanity of our time. But in light of the realities of the job market and the fact that, in employing a pastor, concern tends to center on the obvious institutional needs of the congregation, it rarely functions as controlling concept in ministry.

Our excursion through variables has led us back to Manager. The ideal, not the term, is the crux of the matter. I know of few ministers who apply it to themselves in interpreting their work to their congregations. But they commonly use the noun *management* to describe what they do, and the people give assent. A wave of interest in management by objectives washed over the churches in the 1970s.

So Manager it is. I propose it as the dominant form and concept of ministry in twentieth-century America up to the present moment. It conjures up the image of the quintessential person-who-makes-our-society-go—cool, suave, understated, but incredibly efficient, with a sensitive finger on the pulse of the operation, able to detect the slightest suggestion of trouble before it gets out of hand, decisive in action, and, of course, successful.

This managerial ideal incarnates the myth of the executive—the glamorous and overpaid darling of our corporate life who, except during our frequent recessions, receives too much credit as the source of the nation's prosperity. The *modus operandi* of the episcopate, which through the centuries has modeled society's expectations of its gar-

den-variety ministers, reproduces the executive pattern: A group of
Roman Catholic businessmen in southern California recently raised
$400,000 to provide their archbishop with a jet-powered helicopter in
which he can zip around the archdiocese at 160 miles per hour.[13] A
contemporary historian of Methodism notes that "Increasingly, the
bishop's lieutenants, the district superintendents...continued inexo-
rably to depart from the old pastoral idea of presiding elder to become
willy-nilly administrative associates of the bishop."[14]

The denominations, the congregations (especially their official
boards), and the ministers themselves have bought that myth for their
concept of ministry. The minister as Manager deftly deploys the
resources of the congregation—human and material—so as to facili-
tate most readily the attainment of its goals. A good Manager is of
course skilled in interpersonal relations and conflict resolution, so
that if any sign of trouble appears it is quickly dealt with and the
church can get on with the job.

A good deal can be said for such a concept of ministry in our kind
of society. The basic question however tends to be overlooked. What
is the job we are to get on with? What are the goals we are out to attain?
The fatal flaw in the model is that it leaves the church obsessed with
managerial goals. These take priority on everyone's agenda.

The congregational agenda for the minister is heavily managerial. The people do not always say so. The pastoral search committee,
with which we began our discussion, frequently tells a prospective
minister that the church wants someone strong in the pulpit, a good
pastor who will call on the people and see them through life's crises,
an active leader in the community, someone good with this age-
group or that, a diplomat who can reconcile the two parties if
contention should break out (the committee does not divulge that
civil war has been going on for some time in the church board or the
staff or the choir), a minister who can put First Relevant Church back
on the map. Only when one's predecessor has been particularly inept
at administration is the committee likely to specify the need for sound
management. But the plea for a reconciler and the plaint about
putting the church back on the map ought to give the secret away.

The congregation is concerned about survival. With little reflection on the social forces we have described in the previous chapter as
causes of the particular problems in their church, the members simply
note that people aren't as interested in religion as they used to be, or
that somehow they don't find our church as attractive as the
nondenominational temple with its five choirs and its fleet of buses.
"We need a minister who can get people out. Someone who will bring
in new members to help with the budget. Who can persuade the

young parents to teach a Sunday school class. And talk with Angie Ten-Speed about all those far-out ideas she keeps bringing up in youth meeting. Some of the parents don't like that."

The more the people talk about old First, no matter what they may say to their preferred candidate about their ideal minister, the clearer it becomes that they see the real problems of the congregation as problems of management. They look for managerial solutions. Obsessed with survival, they hold the minister accountable to managerial criteria.[15]

There in essence lies the issue for twentieth-century ministry. Both one's immediate employer (the congregation) and the system on which one depends for professional advancement (the denomination) use statistics to measure a minister's effectiveness. And statistics measure only external data that can be quantified. Such a criterion for a religious community is inappropriate and cruel. But we ministers helped establish it. During the long boom in the growth of the churches, stretching from 1790 to 1960 with only occasional interruptions, our characteristic state was one of expansion. We taught the people to reward us for it. The figures clearly showed what an effective minister they had! When conditions changed and membership declined, we asked for different criteria. We were right in that, at least in part, but the people concluded that we were just making excuses.

We ministers have clearly adopted the managerial ideal. Let us confess it. We like for the people to think of us as head honcho. But how could it be otherwise? Brought up in a society that measures its values numerically and bestows its highest rewards in monetary form, we would have to be really "out of it" to achieve total freedom from such assumptions. Only the counter culture of the 1960s protested them with sufficient force to cause any trembling, and by now most of the rebels have slipped back into the mainstream.

We ministers, of course, are supposed to condemn materialism, and we do so from time to time, but our real objection is that we don't get what we consider our share of the goodies. Ministers who "make it" in even a modest way wind up with a more prestigious new car than before or a boat or a condominium. Our society has taught us that if we can do good work as a Manager we shall have our reward. And we have taken in this ideal with our mother's milk, our mother in this case being the American church. The notion of success, of achieving results, pervades the concepts of ministry imparted to us through all our Christian life.

Even the seminaries quietly inculcate a managerial idea of success. Why else do contemporary students struggle through the strange requirements in the curriculum for a "professional" degree and active pastors return from the parish to jump through more academic hoops leading to the "professional" doctorate? We who work in the schools want good statistics too—a balanced budget, an increased enrollment, a larger endowment, and (oh, yes!) a substantial increase in faculty salaries. For all our commitment to a prophetic stance—and it is sincere—few courses in church administration or even church history include a session on How to Get Arrested Like Jeremiah and Paul and Cyprian and Latimer, How to Get Run Out of Town Like John Chrysostom or Jonathan Edwards, or even How to Live Among the Poor and Lowly Like St. Francis or Mother Teresa. But then none of them understood successful church management.

In any case, most of us ministers seem comfortable with a model that society understands. To sit in a tastefully appointed office with an intercom at our fingertips, to relish a battery of phones ringing at the secretaries' desks while insistent lights flash on ours, to regard fondly the gleaming new copy machine and word processor we've had to rivet down because of past burglaries, to glance over the new annual report with all the neat graphs—all this gives us a sense of importance. Or it would if the graphs reported something more encouraging.

Ministerial adherence to the model of Manager is more than a matter of uncritical acculturation or an unregenerate fondness for symbols of prestige. It is a professional necessity. Once we get it through our heads that this is what the church is paying us for—to get results—then we try our best, even if we don't honor the model and even profess to dislike administration! We take charge. That is exactly what the settled pastors, the successors of the nineteenth-century Builders, did early in our century. Though not without a hard struggle, they took charge![16]

If ever a church in history embodied the ideal of the ministry of the laity, it was the church of the nineteenth century. The great forward movements were mainly lay ventures: abolition, temperance, the Sunday school, Christian Endeavor and its various denominational counterparts, YMCA, YWCA. Ministers sometimes contributed to the achievement, particularly at the point of motivation, but to a surprising degree they stood back and let things happen. They had their hands full as it was. A few ministers with nothing better to do opposed one movement or another, or even all of them together. But the laity kept on working, providing zeal, voluntary staffing for the many organizations, and remarkably effective leadership. In all this women were prominent. Persons without theological education or professional standing organized churches and served as pastors and preachers, sometimes for years. We would call these people lay persons, though not a few with impressive records answered calls to larger churches and spent a lifetime in ministry wihout ever receiving ordination.

It was the age of the big layman, the millionaire who wrote checks in eye-popping amounts for the congregation and the "causes" of the denomination. Such men helped establish new churches, preached on the side while they piled up huge fortunes, made things happen in their congregations and state conventions, gave generously to missions and benevolences and higher education, repeatedly stood up at the psychological moment to announce a dramatic pledge if only the others would do their part. And the big layman called the shots! It is clear why we haven't many heroic givers in the old mold anymore. The professional ministry of the twentieth century broke the mold. They would not allow themselves to be pushed around by the fat cats. The minister took charge and the big giver, with rare exceptions, disappeared.

In a somewhat similar way soon after 1900, ministers took over the movements that the laity had so effectively led in the nineteenth century, and that soon began to decline. In the takeover, pastors linked arms with their colleagues in the expanding denominational bureaucracies to argue for relating the movements to "the responsible structures of our church." That meant breaking up the older nondenominational pattern.

The most obvious candidate for this treatment was the Sunday school movement. The great new enthusiasm of ministers and theological faculties at the turn of the century was religious education. Scores of bright young seminarians, women and men alike, majored in this promising new field and went out to take staff positions as directors of religious education with the larger congregations. Some of these persons had remarkably creative and significant ministries, but as their numbers grew two things happened: The DREs, congregational and denominational, wrested control of the Sunday school movement out of the hands of the laity—it was a responsibility for "professionals" with proper training—and senior pastors asserted their own top position in the chain of command, making the DRE clearly subordinate. Then another thing also happened: The Sunday schools began to decline.

A simple cause-and-effect pattern can hardly be imposed on such a complex situation, but the same general development occurred in the movements for Christian youth. Professional ministers took over. Lay leadership was reduced to a symbolic and financial role, in which there was no reward at all comparable with the previous satisfaction in public influence and notable accomplishments.

Almost the only arena left largely to lay initiative in the churches was the so-called women's program. The male pastor generally stayed aloof, while Christian Women's Fellowship and comparable groups in the various denominations prospered, their volunteer officers administering programs of education, service, fund-raising, and pastoral care impressive far beyond the capacity of those not closely involved to imagine, and raising a sizable portion of the denominational budgets in the process.

Why did the pastor insist on taking charge? Because if the minister is going to be held accountable to managerial criteria, the minister must be the Manager. It is as simple as that. A recently published "reference for busy, active, enterprising pastors" begins "with the concept of the pastor as manager and leader of the congregation."[17]

Reflections on the Manager

How shall we assess the notion of minister as Manager? Several problems with the concept have now become clear.

Goals implied by the model of Manager tend to be uncritically appropriated from the culture without reflection on proper objectives implied by the mission of the church. Instead of "extending the knowledge of God" or "the spread of scriptural holiness throughout the land" or "the increase of love for God and neighbor" or "the broader sway of the kingdom of God," goals more readily measured in numbers are taken for granted. When the numbers look good, the minister is accounted a success, and vice versa.[18] Additions to the church and increases in membership and giving *ought* to make for clearly Christian goals of the kind just stated in traditional phrases, but do not always do so. That is the flaw in many "programs of evangelism," including the common understanding of the church growth movement.

The mark of the holy—so evident in shaman, Saint, Priest, Master, Awakener, Revivalist, Missionary—tends to evaporate from the brow of the Manager, except as transcendent symbols and rhetoric are co-opted to serve programmatic ends. The minister's style imitates the well-known manner, dress, and vocabulary of the secular executive, and nothing about it necessarily points toward God.

On coming to church, the most active and devoted layworkers are occupied in activities in no sense distinctively religious, in striking contrast to the original Methodist "classes," for example. Rather, "church work" after the managerial model duplicates down to the last staple the workaday experience from which the people have come—office routine, committee meetings, task forces, production goals, go-go-go admonitions to get more done. Committed Christians find themselves forced into the frenetic activism of Martha and no longer allowed the "better part" of Mary; little wonder that such "good workers" suffer burnout and quit altogether.

The managerial concept of ministry tends not to reckon sufficiently with the character of the church as a voluntary organization in a voluntaristic society. The models unconsciously followed and explicitly imitated are the successful Executives with authority in business corporations, not the "executive secretaries" of voluntary organizations. A minister might well ponder the difficulties of Cabinet officers and of elected officials in government confronted by an entrenched bureaucracy; putting one's title in a neat box at the top of the organizational chart does not automatically move the program through the ranks. A minister can learn more from a good Scoutmaster than from a Marine drill sergeant.

In any organization, especially if it is voluntary, the *sine qua non* is motivation. This hard reality the common understanding of the managerial model tends to overlook, even though studies of the most successful companies show that it is a primary ingredient in their outstanding performance.[19] Secular and governmental bureaucracies have their own effective systems of motivation, chiefly financial, but a congregation is a voluntary organization and its members will work only if they want to, and in the long run they will want to work only if they understand the reason for the task.

Yet the motivations we make explicit are commonly those associated with the secular goals already noted; often they are incompatible with our witness to the gospel of Jesus Christ. We hold out the promise of greater things or the prospect of doom for "dear old First." The minister as Manager becomes preacher as nag, constantly giving vent to personal frustrations over the job in sermons and meditations on Christian duty: "You seem to forget that *all of you* are the ministers here!" Ironically, we measure the success of the church by the kind of works-righteousness against which Luther rebelled. Sometimes it seems that our managerial ministers have never heard of the Protestant Reformation.

Without the motivation that springs from willing hearts rejoicing in what God has done for us and in what God offers to the world, that is, without the motivation of love and an understanding of mission as response by those caught up in divine grace, the managerial model must rely on manipulation to get things done. Increasingly the Manager depends on appeals to pride, fear, personal popularity, patriotism, or some other irrelevant emotion, without taking time to deepen Christian commitment and to increase Christian understanding. The process is inconsistent with the genius of Christian ministry.[20] One of our generation's wisest guides regarding management has neatly pinpointed the danger in this model as a pattern for ministry:

> In business your goal is not to change the customer; it's not to educate the customer; it's to satisfy the customer. The church's aim is to make a difference in the way the parishioner lives, to change the parishioner's values—into God's values.[21]

As members think back over their life in a congregation and recall the ministers who have meant the most to them, how many ever voice a grateful memory: "He was such a magnificent organizer!"

Nevertheless, the model of Manager confronts us with realities that any minister today must take into account. It is validated as an essential element in ministry, if not as controlling model, by at least four considerations:

1) The model calls for initiative by the minister in holding before the people both long-range objectives and more immediate goals, as well as for proposing programs by which progress may be made toward them. Without the exercise of such leadership, the minister compromises both the nature of ministerial responsibility itself and the principles of sound management.

2) A minister who cannot lead and manage the administration of the congregation acceptably is likely to blunder into trouble, even to be asked to leave. An observer wisely commented, "A minister rarely gets fired for poor preaching, or even for not doing enough calling. But one who doesn't know how to work with people in running the affairs of the church will not last long."[22]

3) Conceiving the minister as Manager requires neither that the pastor try to run the whole show nor pose as supreme expert in every phase of congregational life. Rather, it means involving the members at those points where their particular gifts contribute most in the corporate ministry of the church. If someone can do a task well and is willing to do it, no purpose is served by the minister's trying to prove that he or she can do it better. The primary task that the church has assigned to pastors is the ministry of Word, sacrament, and care. By doing that distinctive work in such a way as to enlarge the vision and devotion of the members, the minister's unique contribution in management is made. (If this is what the proponents of the enabler model meant, they were right.)

4) To repeat, the most important contribution of the minister as Manager is not "calling the shots," but motivation. This points the Manager back to the fundamental importance of two continuing

tasks, whatever the prevailing model. In traditional language these are preaching and teaching.

Here *preaching* does not necessarily refer to speaking from the pulpit; it means *bringing the gospel* with power to people in such a way that gratitude and love become the driving forces in their lives. *Teaching* includes the whole task of enlarging Christian knowledge and understanding—of God, the Bible, the church, self and human nature, human need near at hand and far away, the nature of our contemporary world, and the problems that confront humanity.

A young minister told of her experience in coming out of seminary all fired up to play her role as enabler. But nothing seemed to happen in her church. "It didn't take me long to discover that they weren't wanting to be enabled. They didn't want to do anything at all!" Instead of management, her church needed motivation. An earlier generation called it inspiration. The apostle called it preaching the gospel.

All this adds up to saying that the prevailing concepts of minister as Manager require considerable refinement if we are to appropriate them with integrity.[23]

Because of initial distaste for this model as popularly conceived or unsatisfying experience in trying to work under the expectations it imposes,[24] many a contemporary minister has turned to another secular model that also implies professionalism. Instead of Manager, the minister chooses the model of Counselor.

COUNSELOR

In comparison with times past, the twentieth century brought to the industrialized nations not only dramatic relief from physical drudgery but a vast increase in consumer products, and—as a result of ever more frantic advertising that offered happiness through the possession of the latest thing—a widespread search for prestige through conspicuous consumption. New freedoms in urban society granted release from the constraints of rigid mores that had earlier prevailed. As cultural disestablishment followed the earlier legal disestablishment of religion, many Americans asserted their independence from the churches, from any regimen of biblical or doctrinal instruction, from the disciplines of worship, and from former patterns of clerical influence.

Yet the anonymity of the city, the dissolution of community, the high pressure imposed by careerism, the demands of life in the fast lane, the stress resulting from overspending, the heightened dependence on liquor and drugs, the shattering effects of recurring wars, the repeated recessions with loss of jobs and self-esteem, the breakdown of marriages and the decline of the two-parent family, and the common separation of young adults from the homes and friendships of their childhood—a separation often imposed by geography, but in other cases by demands of employment and differences in lifestyle—have resulted in a high level of anxiety and depression. These trends, which were already evident in the 1920s, have been accentuated ever since World War II, rising to an unprecedented peak in the 1980s.

Not surprisingly, ours has been called the age of anxiety. Many people have lost their zest for living, their sense of meaning in life. Many have seen their hopes and expectations shattered. Many carry deep inner wounds. Numbers of workers in the helping professions,

149

including ministers, have suffered "burnout" or come close to it. (At the 1981 assembly of the National Council of Churches, more seminar-goers turned up for the sessions on "Coping with Burnout" than for those on "Human Rights."[1])

All these harried spirits cry out, consciously or unconsciously, for help. And people who take pride in their technological sophistication often act like spiritual primitives. As pluralism reduces the assumption that any particular church or even religion is "normative," people have turned to cults, old and new, religious and psychological, in a longing for satisfaction. Large numbers of Americans have dabbled in Eastern religions. To deal with widespread uncertainty and anxiety, secular wisdom has produced the certified Counselor, schooled in psychology and psychotherapy.

With the Counselor in such high demand throughout our century, it is not surprising that ministry has been attracted to this image, or that the form, with its accompanying concepts, has emerged as a dominant model of ministry in our time. For the church the readiness to serve persons one by one in the exploration of their deepest personal problems and the prescription of a regimen designed to provide release from their inner misery is nothing new.

The model of Counselor is a far older pattern of ministry than the collective image of the current secular experts who practice under that title. Shaman, Priest, Sage, and Prophet all contributed to establishing it as a central concept in the religion of the archaic world. Jesus of Nazareth drew people to himself and so to God, not only by the power of his personality and the winsomeness of his words, but especially by his evident love for all, most particularly for persons who felt rejected on account of lifestyle, handicap, disease, race, or poverty. Jesus left no more beloved image of himself than that of the Good Shepherd.

That image soon attached itself also to the ministers of the church, whose common title became Shepherd, disguised for us in the persistent Latin term *pastor*, which has been a title since the early days of the church in Rome. The term *bishop* originally had a similar meaning, with emphasis on the community as a whole: The bishop (sometimes translated *overseer*) "watches over" all who compose the household of Christian faith, and even over "outsiders" living within its precincts. The model took on additional power because of Jesus' designation of the Holy Spirit as Counselor or Advocate or Comforter. Such work, it was believed, the Spirit continued to do through the church and especially through its ministers.

In early Christian times the work of ministry came to be known by another Latin term, *cura animarum*, which persists in the archaic

English phrase, "the cure of souls." There the word *cure* has a double meaning, suggested by the Latin original: It implies both care and healing.[2]

Through most of the Christian centuries, the ministry of psychic healing has centered on concern with sin and guilt. The ancient church developed an elaborate discipline of public confession, penance, and absolution. Penance involved a long disciplinary ordeal of mourning for one's sins, enduring the humiliation of public exclusion from the sacraments, and performing good works as demonstration of a change of heart. When the prescribed period had been completed, the priest announced forgiveness. The vast institution of monasticism grew up in medieval Christianity to provide communities in which those who would be perfect might lament their sins and struggle for victory over them.

While the Protestant Reformers repudiated works-righteousness, as they characterized this whole medieval scheme, and called instead for complete trust in the forgiving grace of God made known in Jesus Christ, they still thought of pastoral care predominantly in terms of dealing with sin and guilt. Richard Baxter's epochal work on *The Reformed Pastor* commended an ideal that prevailed for generations: the Protestant minister as conscientious shepherd of souls, keeping careful track of every person in the community down to the smallest child, visiting regularly in homes or places of work, inquiring systematically as to the spiritual condition of each one, admonishing, and praying.[3]

The Puritan Master on this side of the Atlantic also cherished the ideal of the cure of souls, a phase of the minister's work in eighteenth-century New England passed over too lightly in our discussion of the Master. This relation between minister and people set the mood in which they heard the sermons of the Awakener and the early nineteenth-century Revivalist. An overwhelming preoccupation with sin and guilt has possessed the mind of ministers and community as a whole through most of Christian history.

The nineteenth century, however, gradually brought a mellower mood to the understanding of human nature and thus of the pastor's work. Criticism by the skeptics of the Enlightenment began to soften the sternness that dominated the popular idea of God. The confidence of the young American nation, including many of its preachers with their vision of the coming millennium, diminished the emphasis on human depravity and divine displeasure toward our fallen race. People talked more and more of the love of God—always an essential element in the gospel, but too often subordinated to the threats of divine judgment. The sentimental Revivalists of the latter part of the century assumed the fear of hell but emphasized the love of the forgiving heart of God if the sinner would only come to Jesus now. The liberal theologians at the end of the century made the love of God the keystone of their whole system.

Meanwhile, the peculiar situation of ministers in pioneer America required involvement in all the ordeals of daily life—on the farm or along the trail or in the mining camp. That involvement produced a companionship rarely found in previous times between minister and people, the kind of comradeship desired by the French worker-priests a generation ago.

By the dawn of the twentieth century an ideal of pastoral ministry prevailed, tinged by the spirit of romanticism, in which the pastor was idealized as good friend, loving advocate, and wise counselor in all the affairs of life. The pastor would naturally be on hand for weddings and funerals, but also would support the people in life's small disappointments and rejoice with them in its smaller joys such as birthdays, getting in a good crop of oats, or finding a position that promised advancement. Particularly was the pastor the friend and adviser of youth, encouraging them to make something of their lives and, in many communities, providing them with their only opportunity to talk with a person of education and broader vision than the narrow circumstances of farm or village. A genial pastor was a welcome visitor to the homes, farms, and shops of the people, and demonstrated a particular fondness for country dinners.

Out of such shared experience a relationship developed in which pastoral care meant a genuine concern for persons throughout the whole range of their experience, a loving involvement without intrusiveness, an authentic friendship rising out of continuous cultivation. A perceptible spiritual tone pervaded the relationship, which rested on an awareness of God's love. But a tacit understanding obtained that the language of piety need not dominate every conversation, and that the minister would talk religion chiefly when asked to do so or when an explicitly religious emphasis was called for to deal most helpfully with the matter at hand.

The new professional discipline of religious education, which awakened expectations almost millennial shortly after the turn of the twentieth century, was charged through and through with this pastoral spirit. Informed by the new studies in psychology, infused with the hopefulness that characterized the spirit of the age, and sustained theologically by the liberal understanding of human possibilities, these educators centered their energies on the development of Christian personality in each person with whom they worked. Content, even biblical content, was taught not for its own sake but as a contributing element, along with others, in Christian growth. The leaders in this movement had remarkable gifts for spotting latent possibilities in young people and for guiding them in a relationship best described as pastoral.

The preaching of the nineteenth and early twentieth centuries, as we have already noted, took on a much more direct concern with the total range of problems that people face every day, not just the narrowly defined religious concerns of sin and guilt and fear of death. The fresh vitality in preaching, I suggest, grew out of the newer, broader pattern of the pastoral relationship.

In such a context it was natural for ministers to take a special interest in the emerging study of psychology. Already in the 1870s, as we have seen, preachers had begun to draw on the writers in this new field. The tremendous popularity of the work of William James and others soon after him who explored the psychology of religion, with special attention to the phenomena manifested in revivalistic conversion, posed many questions for informed laypersons. Educated preachers, especially those inclined toward liberalism, were eager to discuss these questions and to guide people toward what they considered a more wholesome understanding of conversion and the Christian life. Soon alert ministers were reading carefully the works of the pioneers in psychotherapy and finding helpful insights for members who came to them with personal problems.

Harry Emerson Fosdick, John Sutherland Bonnell, and other preachers who began to deal with such matters in their sermons discovered an overwhelming eagerness on the part of many to hear more discussions of this kind. The "psychological sermon" became an almost certain crowd-pleaser. It had the further advantage of not antagonizing persons who disliked the minister's theology or position on social issues. Norman Vincent Peale and later Robert Schuller drew huge congregations with a constant diet of pop psychology in the form of inspirational sermons.

Noting the overwhelming response to their readiness to address personal problems, some thoughtful ministers committed themselves to rigorous education in psychology and psychotherapy, followed by a program of clinical training under supervision. When persons like Anton Boisen, Russell E. Dicks, and Paul E. Johnson began to offer seminary courses in pastoral counseling, the most dramatic "growth stock" in the twentieth-century theological curriculum went on the exchange. Students by now had lost the earlier zeal for religious education and rarely, during their seminary years, clamored for much work in church administration. But pastoral counseling was something else! It became the strongest drawing card in the "practical field" and soon its elective classes outdrew courses in church history and even biblical studies; only theology or social ethics managed to stay close in popularity.

Work in counseling has proved the overwhelming first choice of pastors in continuing education. They could see a need in this area and along with a desire to meet it felt keenly their limitations in trying to do so. It also appears that the popularity of such courses among seminarians and pastors, as among college students generally, rests on the hope of finding greater self-understanding and help in dealing with immediate personal problems.

The entrance of some notably sensitive and capable scholars into the field has turned pastoral care from the offering of well-meant advice, which sometimes nevertheless was ill conceived, to a disciplined specialization with professional standards comparable to those of secular counselors—a vast army now with posts in high schools and colleges, the military, correctional institutions, industry, and private practice. The Counselor represents a significant response to needs that are widely felt in our time, offered according to a model with obvious secular parallels, yet with its own distinctiveness as a Christian ministry.

Ministers with the basic education now required for ordination in the mainline churches have had at least some introduction to the theory and practice of counseling. They are prepared to deal with the problems of most church members and others who come to them, and to refer to full-time professionals persons in need of long-term counseling as well as persons showing symptoms of psychosis. Many churches open their faciliies to Alcoholics Anonymous for their regular meetings, as well as to similar groups offering support to persons with problems of dependency. A good proportion of seminarians include a semester or more of clinical pastoral counseling, under supervision, as part of their program of study, thus enhancing their own self-understanding and their expertise in counseling. Some have enrolled in the Yale School of Alcohol Studies and other specialized programs. Churches with a staff of ministers frequently assign to one or more a full-time responsibility in counseling, and in many communities several congregations pool their resources to maintain a center with its own staff.

Reflections on the Counselor

How are we to respond to this trend? What does the concept say to us as we struggle with the problem of our own vocational self-definition? Significant reservations must be entered against making the Counselor the dominant determinant for a model of ministry.

What seems like an enlargement of pastoral ministry by furnishing it with a skill clearly recognized as professional may in fact diminish that ministry. For one thing, counseling requires an inordinate amount of time, a commodity that for most pastors seems even shorter than money. Time spent largely in one-to-one engagement reduces the time the minister can devote to other crying needs and responsibilities.[4] That represents a kind of narrowing.

A greater cause for concern lies in the narrowing of the concept of pastor itself. Despite its relatively late flowering, the concept of the minister as dependable and loving friend of each member of the congregation, caring enough to know each person at work and leisure, is an ideal with much to commend it.[5] Admittedly difficult to realize fully in metropolitan society, it is more needed now than when life moved at a more leisurely pace. It is sad to think of its being totally displaced by a scheduled session in a counseling room at the church.

Yet the pressures of ministerial practice today are making for a pattern of pastoral involvement with individuals limited to the following circumstances: 1) formal counseling sessions initiated by the "client"; 2) hospital calls; 3) calls on the recently bereaved; 4) other "crisis" calls in response to urgent requests; 5) interviews initiated by the minister, almost without exception to discuss an administrative problem in the congregation or to ask the person to accept a position of leadership; 6) chance meetings at a coffee shop or ball game where pastor and member have a friendly chat.

Ministers today commonly declare that they lack time for calling on members in their homes except in the cases named above. They also maintain that the pace of life and the patterns of metropolitan living make calling on families a virtual impossibility. Families are rarely at home and if they are, many have little or no time for an idle chat with the minister.

While not berating today's pastors for the condition of society, I lament the shrinking of the concept *pastoral* to refer only to the six circumstances listed above. In the minds of many seminarians it has shrunk even more. To them pastoral care means pastoral counseling and nothing more. Is this an indication that younger people today, even those who prepare for ministry, have had little or no experience in the kind of relationship with pastor as friend described earlier in this section? I hope not. It is too important a dimension of ministry to be lost.

Perhaps the most serious danger in the concept of minister as Counselor lies in a widespread tendency to reduce the total work of church and minister to an enterprise conceived as essentially psychological, with secular canons determining its norms. The old American subjectivism in religion now latches on to psychology as the discipline that speaks most certainly about one's inner trials. The pathological tendency to focus on individualistic troubles and to neglect the systemic problems of our society heightens the subjectivist preoccupation in American religion, diminishing both the significance of the church's message for the larger scene and the capacity to influence the reformation of social and economic structures.

Increasingly the popular vocabulary of psychotherapy replaces the language of scripture in public worship. The two vocabularies might well coexist in wholesome interaction helpful to both. What alarms is the tendency of trendy psychological jargon to replace the elevated language, concepts, and attitudes of traditional piety without anyone's seeming to notice or care. Instead of assembling the people in the presence of God, worship falls into a structured exercise in group therapy. Instead of focusing on the reality of the Eternal One and the divine purpose for the world in its agony and need, the prayers continue the preoccupation with self that for too many persons remains uninterrupted all through the week. Leaders seem to feel the need to jazz up an otherwise boring ritual with pop phrases and pompous assertions read in unison, rehearsing why we have come, who we are, and especially how we feel.

Much preaching also tends to take psychological notions more seriously than biblical ideas or theological concepts. Preaching that correlates responsible psychological insight with sound theology is much needed. What disturbs is the preacher who gives the impression that psychology is more interesting than the gospel, and whose biblical understanding and grasp of theology tend to show a sad deficiency.

A further peril is the temptation for the minister to allow the role of Counselor to divert her or him from other important tasks. Counseling makes heavy demands on one's time and patience and emotional resources, but "being needed" by someone who comes to one's office for help brings a sense of self-importance in a society that frequently seems to place little value on a minister's work. A pastor seldom receives criticism while counseling the bruises commonly acquired in administering the church. And this quiet ministry does not expose one to the fears and hostilities aroused when one deals with social issues.

These observations are not offered as a charge that the model of Counselor is invalid or even that the minister might not similarly find escape from responsibility in activity related to some other model that only partially defines the total task. But except for highly qualified persons in specialized ministries, the model of Counselor may be too limited a form to sustain an adequate concept of parish ministry.

Despite its parallelism with secular models and the high standards of training demanded for the pastoral Counselor, this recently developed form has not noticeably enhanced our standing as ministers in the eyes of the secular world. The stereotype of the minister as ignorant fundamentalist, purveying pious platitudes or harsh condemnations, still prevails too widely. The fact that Ann Landers, Dear Abby, and other such columnists have such a wide readership and receive so many letters indicates that many people who need help are not finding it where they live. The further fact that these writers feel repeatedly compelled to inform their readers that many ministers now have qualifications as counselors and are ready to help indicates also that the image of minister as Counselor has not deeply penetrated the public consciousness.

Yet the model of Counselor obviously carries important concepts for our understanding of ministry.[6] The minister as Counselor has replaced the emphasis on judgment and punishment (which so long dominated the cure of souls) with a mode of quiet acceptance, no matter how distasteful the client's story or how much self-hatred the client may carry in shame and sorrow for past behavior. Whether this more open attitude derives from the liberal theology of the nineteenth century, which began to take more seriously Jesus' teaching as to the parental nature of God, or derives from the openness of the secular therapist who is not shocked at anything, it represents an important gain. This is not to say that judgment on behavior is no longer needed. But no person who reaches for help is to be rejected.

The work of those who have done most to develop responsible education for the minister as Counselor has built an important bridge between Christian thought and a modern secular discipline. At a far more fundamental level than that of the shallow books offered in the popular market, members of seminary faculties with specialized competence in pastoral care, theology, and other "classical" disciplines have undertaken to relate responsibly the concepts of psychology and psychotherapy to those of the historic Christian tradition. Some secular psychotherapists have also written knowledgeably and not always unsympathetically about religious motivations and concepts. We might hazard the generalization that more work has been done on this particular bridge between Christian thought and a particular secular discipline than on any other area, except perhaps for the constant dialogue that theology sustains with philosophy. The gains from this particular engagement are instructive and should inspire the same high level of interchange in other areas of ministerial responsibility as well.

The model of the Counselor involves the minister with persons in crisis often at a time of desperate need. That involvement, along with the normal routine of pastoral ministry in calling on the sick and lonely and bereaved, functions as a constant reminder that every gathered congregation includes some persons who are hurting at the very time it is meeting. While we have maintained that Christian worship is more than formalized group therapy, the essential therapeutic element in worship must never be forgotten—the focus on the eternal goodness and love of God, the bidding to repentance, the invitation to cast our burdens on the Lord, the assurance of forgiveness, the reaffirmation of solidarity among the worshipers and with the whole Christian community, the call to a new life of uprightness and simplicity and service, the sending forth in the power of the Spirit with the abiding presence of God.

The church stands as the symbol of God's wholeness in a fractured world, and every element in its worship sends out intimations of the transcendent. Without the healing that comes to people week after week in the worship of God and the preaching of the gospel, we could expect the incidence of mental illness to increase.

People with personal problems are turning to the ministers of religion in impressive numbers. One recent study indicated that of those who seek out a pastor or other minister, four out of five find help in their counsel.[7] It can be argued that community programs in mental health follow an essentially pastoral pattern.

The model of Counselor keeps alive the honored tradition of the minister as shepherd, which flowered in a perception of the essence of the pastorate as friendship with the people in the spirit of Jesus Christ. As increasing numbers of secularized persons turn with their troubles to support groups, psychotherapists, and other certified counselors, this model represents a serious effort to retain for ministry an ancient service in a culturally relevant and methodologically responsible form.

Especially noteworthy is the development of the congregation as a caring community, its *koinonia* embracing the wounded and confused, not only within its own membership but in the community to which it ministers, and its sense of mission impelling it to evangelistic and social witness.[8]

Any concept of ministry that loses the concern for pastoral care will prove deficient in a realm that, according to the Gospels, held great importance in the work of Jesus. And pastors who prove inept in the area of counseling seriously reduce the effectiveness of their ministry.

Model 11

IMPRESARIO

Our next model has no long and honored Christian tradition behind it, though examples may be found again and again throughout the history of the church and quite commonly in pre-Christian times. It seems to flourish most luxuriantly in periods of religious uncertainty. It is the figure here designated as the Impresario—the minister who takes over the secular model of the celebrity and tries to employ it as a model of ministry.[1]

As used here, the term designates the founder of a religious cult and sometimes the designated successor or prominent disciple as well. It also refers to the guru, the authentic holy teacher from Hinduism or other historic Eastern religion come to these shores as a missionary of truth and enlightenment, and also the opportunistic imitator-of-the-guru who propagates a mishmash of metaphysical nonsense or psychological hogwash to a credulous and free-spending public. It applies to the self-made celebrity of the religious television circuit who, until the recent downfall of several leading superstars, had attracted so much notice from envious ministers of the forsaken mainline. It applies also to the big successful pastor of the supersuccessful congregation, commonly a "nondenominational" center, but sometimes an affiliate with one of the historic denominations.[2]

With all the terms used to designate the major models up to this point, I have tried to denote without implying a value judgment. My responsibility as historian obliges me to seek an accurate term. That responsibility also requires an assessment of the various models, with an honest effort to be fair. So my title of Impresario—foreign to the vocabulary of any of those it refers to, as far as I know—intends to designate accurately a mode of presenting religion that has such wide contemporary appeal that it must be listed among major twentieth-century forms of ministry.

159

Impresario is defined in Webster as "one who puts out or sponsors entertainment." For a synonym, try *producer*, in the Hollywood sense. The word *impresario* originated in Italy to denote the promoter of an opera company. In this book it designates the minister or other religious figure who turns religion into show business. Some here described will deny that that is what they do. Yet at the very least they use the techniques of show business to present their brand of religion. And often the demands of the show take priority over the claims of the sacred, especially over the integrity of the gospel.

Therein lies the problem with the model. Yet so many people in today's world have grown so accustomed to taking in every idea in their heads and nearly every emotion in their hearts through the media employing the techniques of show business that even the gospel of Jesus Christ—or what they are told is the gospel—satisfies them more fully when it comes to them in this guise than it does when presented in any other way.

The minister as Impresario is no producer-behind-the-scenes. Rather the Impresario is star and producer. That combination is the essence of the model. A person of obvious "charisma"—certainly in the vulgar, perhaps also in the biblical, sense—presents religion as the greatest show on earth, presiding at center stage, ostensibly making it all happen. This star has presence, flair, rapport with the "folks out there," and too often a shaman's readiness to connive in trickery and manipulation to give the people the thrill they so obviously crave. Even if a particular Impresario exercises the most rigid ethical self-discipline, this ministry still goes on within the framework of the show, and the demands of the show shape, even determine, the nature of the ministry itself.

While the Impresario is essentially a twentieth-century model of ministry, thriving in the breathless atmosphere provided by media hype, some of the subtypes have flared now and again across the American sky through much of our history.

The typical founder of a cult is the archaic shaman appearing once again in the modern world to declaim, "I TALKED WITH GOD." Secular society no longer provides the traditional cultural forms for such a ministry and the standard-brand denominations have difficulty in incorporating the primitive embodiment of holiness, who shows no disposition to submit to normal institutional procedures. As contemporary shaman the Impresario announces the vision and gathers such disciples as find the announcement convincing.

The content of the message and the lifestyle demanded by it differ markedly at some points from those inculcated by the old-line denominations. Otherwise the modern-day shaman would find no market. Accordingly, both the conventional religious leaders and the secular press tend to dub any such new religion a "cult." Legally, its standing is no different from that of any other religious body; its beliefs, worship, and perhaps distinctive dress are no business of government. Socially, members of the group feel the disapproval of society and particularly of their families. Such ostracism is the reverse side of the elation they feel at the uniqueness of the message that has changed their lives.

To maintain the morale of the group, to intensify its involvement in a distinctive way of life, and perhaps to give it greater visibility, the founder often gathers the community of believers into a new settlement. All this makes good copy for the press with its addiction to the bizarre. While being treated as "freaks" annoys some of the converts, it does not seem to bother the founder, who welcomes anything that calls attention to the cult. The founder tends to be an Impresario at heart, and this kind of religion is show business. Shamanic religion produced the first primitive spectacles of dance, music, and drama. The story line came from the mystical vision, but the shaman knew how to dramatize it, how to put on a show. So does the founder of a cult.

Such ministers have come on the American scene century after century. In 1774 Mother Ann Lee arrived in New York from England and soon began to broadcast glowing reports of her ecstatic visions, the joys of a new form of communal worship through dance, and the announcement of Christ's imminent second appearing as a female, namely herself. Soon colonies of Shakers sprang up in New England and the Midwest, given over to the simple life, hard work, pride in the elegant perfection of their handcrafts, lifelong celibacy for all, and the ecstasy of "shaking." Some of the colonies persisted into our time, their buildings still witnessing to the quieter ways of an earlier day.

An even more celebrated founder was Joseph Smith, whose visions, encounters with the angel Moroni, and report of discovering the Golden Plates in 1827 and of translating them from the Reformed Egyptian as the Book of Mormon, led to the establishment of the Church of Jesus Christ of Latter Day Saints. Hounded from New York to Missouri to Illinois, where the prophet was shot in 1844, the Mormons followed the successor, Brigham Young, across the desert to Utah. There they established the most spectacularly successful community ever founded by an American "cult." It prospered so remarkably and their missionaries gained so many converts that they outgrew the cultic designation. But they still stand apart from other religious bodies.

Throughout the twentieth century new religious cults have appeared on the American stage in even greater profusion. In Los

Angeles, Guy and Edna Ballard launched the I AM movement in 1930, announcing revelations from St. Germain and other "ascended masters." Later, Ballard reported, both the saint and Jesus Christ himself appeared to him on earth and sat to have their portraits painted. He offered copies of these for sale.

In New York City Father Divine served fried chicken dinners free to the poor people of Harlem during the Depression, rode in a chauffeur-driven Cadillac, and preached to adoring congregations as his heavy diamonds glittered with every gesture. In 1965 the Reverend Jim Jones moved his People's Temple from Indiana to California, then led a large colony of his followers to Guyana and at last to mass suicide in obedience to his commands.

The Reverend Sun Myung Moon came from Korea as the prophet of the Unification Church, which has gained the largest American following of any such group in our generation, along with extensive coverage in the press. From time to time he conducts massive rallies in an outdoor stadium or presides at weddings in which he solemnizes the vows of hundreds of couples whom he has paired.

Other lesser-known visionaries appear from time to time to become founders of new communities. The reporters rarely refer to them as shamans, but along with their word from the other world they also know how to put on a show.

A variation on the general model of ministerial Impresario is the guru. In the late nineteenth century a procession of Hindu swamis began coming to this country from India, astounding many Americans with their mysterious air of Eastern spirituality, their assurances of their way of serenity, and a brand of showmanship precisely suited to gaining maximum attention. For a time Madame Helena Petrovska Blavatsky, a Russian who arrived in New York in 1872, humbly basked in the glare of publicity, along with Swami Vivekananda who came from India in 1893. Swami Paramhansa Yogananda followed in 1914. At the midpoint of our century a new procession began, with one mahatma after another receiving the adulation of excited fans. (It *is* show business.) So many have come and gone that it is impossible to predict whether or not the influence of any of them will persist.

The guru or swami carries an air of mystical spirituality that unfailingly strikes the multitudes as holy, but majors in uttering metaphysical maxims of presumed profundity and rules for beatific living rather than the recounting of mystical visions. One can scarcely determine whether the product being retailed is religion or psychology. (The parallel with a good deal of contemporary preaching in the churches is striking.) Transcendental Meditation was a case in point. In the wake of the swamis followed the psychological gurus of the

'70s, displaying their wares in the same portentous procession. Their faddish gospels have flared and vanished with such rapidity that few of us can remember more than a few of their names, but new ones seem constantly to appear.

Both the metaphysical and the psychological gurus have majored in establishing centers of community. Some of the communes set up by small-time gurus of the counterculture in the 1960s were scruffy at best, and only a few still endure. The centers of serenity sponsored by the celebrity-gurus, sacred and secular alike, attract large numbers of well-heeled patrons to their luxurious grounds. People are willing to pay for this kind of show.

Exotic though the gurus may be with their high-sounding formulas for successful living so appealing to the modern ear, by far the lion's share of attention has fallen on the most spectacular type of Impresario—the television preacher or evangelist who plugs the old-time religion. Modeled on the secular celebrity right down to modulation of voice and modishness of hairstyle, this entrepreneur in religion is generally an independent operator who has built a private organization to finance a radio and television ministry. The obligations in trying to keep the program going require a constant stream of funds, and those whose flickering images have become the best-known ministers of our time have mastered the dual arts of show business and financial solicitation.

A seminarian engaged in research wrote to three of the best-known ministerial celebrities in the '80s, requesting "this week's free gift" in order to get her name on their mailing lists. Within ten weeks' time she was receiving from each of them a constant stream of "personal letters" that altogether ran to hundreds of pages. Most of them assured her of the Impresario's personal love and concern for *her*—though one of the computers took her name to be masculine and assured *him*—while plugging a line of religious merchandise purporting to carry a spiritual blessing with each item. Constant appeals to join prayer partnerships or form other tight spiritual bonds with the man of God boiled down to the simple matter of sending in a hundred dollars a month—or less if the listener could give no more.

Such personal attention strikes a responsive chord with many lonely people brought up on traditional religion. Faithfully they send in their money and offer their prayers for the support of the celebrity in presenting the gospel to the unsaved. How many of the latter actually listen to the programs and respond, it is difficult to say, but polls indicate that most of the viewers are traditional Christians past middle age.[3] In any case, the self-propelled Impresarios of the airwaves are virtually the only ministers of the 1980s and '90s, aside from the Pope and the Reverend Jesse Jackson, whose names and faces the general public recognizes. For the most part, the same condition prevails among church members. How many Protestant ministers outside their own immediate experience in congregation and youth camp or annual conference can the typical member of a mainline church even name today?

The virtual absence of the mainline churches from television is not hard to explain. It is not due to reluctance springing from alleged traditionalism. A Congregationalist minister, S. Parkes Cadman, pioneered the use of radio with a regular program of preaching, beginning in 1923. His style, while suited to the medium, was non-spectacular, representative of the better Protestant preaching of the day. Under the auspices of the Federal Council of Churches, Harry Emerson Fosdick, Paul Scherer, and Ralph W. Sockman preached to nationwide radio audiences for a generation, while pastors all over the country broadcast over local stations.

Television was another story. The big problem was money. The networks were not willing to offer large blocks of free time for ecumenically sponsored religious programs, as they had done with radio, and only a few local stations did so. Neither the councils of churches nor the single denominations found a way to raise the millions of dollars of new money necessary to sustain a continuing TV ministry. Furthermore, at the outset conventional wisdom held that preaching, the standard mode of address for a minister, was ill suited to television; people would not sit still for that.

A more serious problem was the contrast between denominational processes and the style of operation in the world of the media. A denomination functions by the cooperation and consensus of millions of members and thousands of ministers, but television needs a bright, particular star, a celebrity. How do you choose a potential star to represent the constituency of the National Council of Churches? Who does the choosing? Who knows that this fair-haired child will really draw on television? And how will the other ministers in the country feel about all the attention focusing on this one?

What began as a quiet series of broadcasts on a local station in the 1960s and '70s grew surprisingly into a national program with large audiences with Edward W. Bauman, a professor of New Testament at Wesley Theological Seminary, conducting Bible study on the passage for the week in the Uniform Lesson Series.[4] Otherwise, the mainline churches have not brought forth a TV celebrity by the process of denominational or ecumenical action. Missouri Synod Lutherans, Southern Baptists, and the Knights of Columbus, however, have sponsored regular programming, and in the early days of television the latter group brought forth a true celebrity in the person of Monsignor (later Bishop) Fulton J. Sheen.

A few mainline Protestant and Catholic ministers attained recognition, if not true celebrity status, by the nature of their ministry and a flair for attracting attention, at least for a time. These included Bishop James Pike, Malcolm Boyd, Eugene Carson Blake, the Berrigan brothers, Harvey Cox, Martin E. Marty, and William S. Coffin. Far ahead of all others in this class stood Martin Luther King, Jr. Though no more to be categorized as an Impresario than some of the other persons just mentioned, he knew how to make news by the preaching and acting out of the Christian gospel—as did these others also. King did not have to *buy* television time. Facing the police dogs and the fire hoses, he and his associates got full coverage on the evening news and interviews on the talk shows.

The typical ministerial celebrity, however, rises to stardom without denominational backing, approval, or even affiliation. The ascent is self-propelled. Billy Sunday, the last of the big-time evangelists, was a showman unabashed, to the consternation of proper religious types. Still clamoring for public attention after World War I, he depended on the newspapers to give it. The journalists' darling of the 1920s, Aimee Semple McPherson, also learned to use radio effectively. Billy Graham gained national recognition when old press lord William Randolph Hearst decided to puff the young evangelist. Graham mastered the art of radio and television programming, putting on enough of a show to attract a worldwide audience, using the publicity to draw attention to his evangelistic crusades, and struggling to retain integrity as a minister in the face of all the pressures attendant on being a celebrity.

The other big names in television evangelism have tended toward even more of a show-biz formula and to constant plugging of the old-time religion mixed with a heaping quantity of political conservatism. Sometimes the format included a healing ministry, such as brought fame to Oral Roberts and Kathryn Kuhlman. The TV minister who has departed farthest from the verbal cliches of revivalism, Robert Schuller, has kept the showmanship and added psychology, dispensing possibility thinking on his *Hour of Power* from the Crystal Cathedral. The television ministry of George Kennedy coming from a Presbyyterian church in Florida retains a setting of more or less traditional Reformed worship, but uses tried-and-true ploys of show business to present a gospel of theological and political conservatism.

Jimmy Swaggart, who commanded the largest viewing audiences of the 1980s,[5] surrendered his ministerial credentials in the Assemblies of God rather than submit to discipline imposed by the

Executive Presbytery after exposure of a moral scandal. Despite his confession, the "holiness" he so manifestly projects to a host of adoring followers—a holiness clearly shamanistic rather than ethical—overrides the force of any ecclesiastical endorsement or defrocking. For the Impresario, the loyalty of a personal following has far greater importance than any institutional validation of one's ministry. The ethos of free-enterprise capitalism that has entered so fully into American religion achieves the culmination of its influence in this twentieth-century model of ministry.

The local ministerial counterpart of the media celebrity, our last variation on the model of the Impresario, is the big successful pastor, the self-promoting religious entrepreneur operating from a congregational base. While possessing the essential skills of the Manager, this high-powered operator maintains the pose and mannerisms of the ministerial celebrity in every possible respect.

The local entrepreneur gathers the people in a converted theater or a spacious arena deliberately designed not to look like a traditional church,[6] making prominent use of all the electronic gear and other dazzling equipment of contemporary show biz. While serving as pastor in ministry to a local church, this form of Impresario makes sure to conform in every way to the stereotype of the star/producer. We first introduced the subtype in the chapter on model 4 as the contemporary heir of the Awakener, whose genius still influences the ethos and program of the nondenominational center. But the style is pure Burbank.

Just to be clear, it must be said that not every minister of a large congregation falls into this category, though nearly every one who keeps a big church going necessarily makes use of contemporary devices for communication. The difference between such a minister and the big successful pastor lies in the answer to the question: Which set of expectations dominates this ministry—the claims of authentic Christian faith or the demands of show business? The minister who cannot give a clear and honest answer turns out to be an Impresario. Even though the program is billed as a gospel ministry, the model for it is one of the least substantial forms of contemporary life—the media celebrity.

Reflections on the Impresario

To describe this form of ministry is almost assessment enough.[7] The minister who makes the model work reaps abundant rewards in the world that passes away. But some further reflection is in order.

The dangers of the model of Impresario are clear. It keeps the minister's personality front and center at all times and exploits her or his personal charisma to the full. No form of ministry is immune to this peril, to some degree, but this model rushes in to pick up the venomous serpent and down the deadly drug with a flair. It makes a point of keeping the minister in full control of the operation—a cardinal emphasis in the high-tuition seminar for pastors offered by Robert Schuller. This is an up-to-date form of priestcraft: the celebrity manipulates the mystery, producing a great show and a successful religious enterprise, while the people of God sit and gape.

The criticism hardest for the Impresario to deny is the accusation of exploitation. Transferring the most advanced techniques of fund-raising to the promotion of a religious institution that is one's personal domain, this "minister" trades on the needs and exploits the fears of people in trouble. The adroitness of the computer-processed letters in transforming an offer of spiritual help into a shakedown would have turned Boccaccio's Friar Onion or Chaucer's Pardoner green with envy. Perhaps a measure of this tendency lurks as temptation to any kind of religious leader. Karl Marx thought so. And all of us in ministry need to keep our consciences sensitive at this point. The impresario shrouds conscience in a bulletproof vest and rakes in the money.

The type of religion offered by the Impresario who serves up a succession of marvels, both technological and supernatural, at a rate no magician could match, seems to flourish in times of drastic social change when people have not yet learned to cope with a world no longer familiar. Driven by anxiety, they turn to any offer of security and assurance of personal significance. We believe that the gospel of Jesus Christ meets such needs. But not every nostrum that temporarily eases the pain by diverting attention from it is authentic gospel; Jesus rebuffed the temptation to cast himself from the pinnacle of the temple.

The world in which Christianity first appeared was full of gurus and fakirs and religious wonder-workers. They feared the Christians, for the believers who had found life in Jesus Christ delighted in exposing the trickery of these second-century Impresarios. Lucian of Samosata, himself a pagan, depicts a telling scene in his story of Alexander the Oracle-Monger. Before the celebrated religious star-and-producer began each show, he sent his assistants out through the crowd to cry: "Away, all Christians and Epicureans!" Those Christians were not gullible. Along with the skeptical philosophers, they saw through the trickery and exposed it to the public.

Some positive reflections on ministry arise from our consideration of the Impresario. It is not always wrong to enjoy church, and those of us who practice more conventional ministries would do well to make our offerings more interesting. The gospel is indeed *The Greatest Story Ever Told*. The Bible is high drama. Too often we have turned church life into a synonym for boredom, what with the dullness of our abstractions and the bleakness of our services. Without "buying" the model of the Impresario, we can pull out of our deadly rut and present the gospel once again with the excitement and power that our routines have so sadly concealed.

People are lonely. Massive inhuman structures rob them of any feeling of personal significance. Technological weaponry threatens instant annihilation. In such a world, thousands of ordinary folk reach out for a recognition and assurance they evidently have not found in the traditional churches, not in the measure they crave. Then the familiar face appears on the flickering screen. The well-known voice says, "I love you." In the mail comes a follow-up letter: "This is your friend, the Impresario. I am just sitting here thinking about you right now." Such tattered shreds of personal attention, mass produced and computer-coded, stir the hearts of thousands. People who ought to know better sit right down and write another check. We may well learn from the Impresario—not to exploit such loneliness, but to minister to it.

Some of the popular expectations raised for our ministry by the cultist, the guru, the television preacher, the local religious operator we need to take with utmost seriousness—not that we will respond to them in the manner of the Impresario, but that we will undertake to deal with them as we minister. At the same time we had best stay alert to the negative assumptions projected on us by people who have no personal knowledge of ministers beyond what they have seen on television. It is our responsibility to acquaint them with a nobler model of ministry.

TEACHER

To find the Teacher standing among the four dominant models of ministry in our times may bring a shock of surprise. In the twentieth century? The Teacher a major pattern?

When we reflect on the pervasive secularism and assertive paganism of the times, the anti-intellectualism of so much of the religion communicated through the media, the substantive emptiness of the pulpit scoldings from managerial ministers, the non-directive orthodoxy so long prevalent in counseling, the virtual abdication of educational responsibility on the part of many ministers, and the decline of the church school, we may well conclude that the ministry of teaching expired before our time. One of my most sympathetic and best informed critics, arguing with a heavy heart that today's ministers are no longer teachers, made a discouraging case.

The reasons for including the Teacher as a major form are four: (1) Despite discouraging developments, the most recent two decades or so do not make up the whole of the twentieth century, an era that earlier saw one of the more impressive ministries of teaching in the history of the church. (2) Today's ministry continues significant teaching functions, however unnoticed, and some pastors carry this responsibility with refreshing creativity, energy, courage, and high commitment. (3) Christian teaching is not limited to systematic instruction in discursive material, though it may starve intellectually without it, but also includes transmitting the tradition of story and symbol and life—and that still continues. (4) Despite ambiguities and counterpressures, the persistence of this ministry of teaching demonstrates wide recognition that the church desperately requires it, and justifies the inclusion of the form. I can think of no other model of ministry in our time, not yet treated in this study, that rivals that of

Teacher in the importance that thousands of ministers attach to it in actual practice.

The term suffers certain obvious limitations. To some ears "Teacher" sounds authoritarian and didactic and dull. Moreover, this image of ministry does not always seem clearly focused in the collective mind of today's ministers, church members, or "outsiders." Even so, the office retains a ritual importance in both Protestant and Catholic practice that, on examination, can hardly fail to impress.

The minister still appears before the people every week in the role of Teacher. (Recall that, in the precise use of the terms, preaching is addressed to outsiders, teaching to those within the Christian community.) For a period varying in individual instances from eight minutes to thirty, the minister presents a sermon employing an ancient method of instruction, the lecture. Increasingly, the minister reads from a manuscript, making the presentation a lecture in the literal sense!

The people listen more or less attentively. Even when the sermon is not particularly interesting, they assume it has to do with something they are supposed to know or to do something about. Granted that many ministers seem to follow no clearly planned curriculum, beyond the vague line offered by the Christian year or the lectionary, and that in individual instances some of them teach less than they harangue. Still, the opportunity, the function, the audience, and some kind of presentation are there, Sunday after Sunday throughout the year.

Most pastors also do a fair amount of occasional teaching or speaking to various groups in church and community. They conduct classes annually for persons preparing for membership. From time to time they plan special educational events. The teaching ministry continues.

The public influence of the pulpit has nevertheless sharply declined since the turn of the century. Because of the changes in society noted in our chapter on the twentieth-century setting, the Pulpiteer is no longer a public figure. The "great churches" where celebrated Christian orators held forth in splendor before audiences running into hundreds, in some cases thousands, either no longer stand or, for the most part, languish in melancholy remembrance of their former glory. With the fading of the great popular art form of the oration, the style and length of the sermon have been radically trimmed. At conventions of political parties or religious denominations one may still hear echoes of the old oratory, occasionally still at its windiest and most pompous. To listen to it at its best, one should seek out the leading black preachers.

Yet the essential function of the Pulpiteer remains as the essential function of the Teacher: to instruct in such a way as to persuade. Today's style is muted, the manner conversational, the range restricted, the challenge sometimes less exciting than in the age of romanticism. But the minister still has an opportunity to teach—and so to influence public opinion and popular behavior—offered to few others in our culture.

The art of the Teacher flourished spectacularly in the American church between the two World Wars. The most publicized preacher of the times was Harry Emerson Fosdick, who never failed to teach. Delivered from the misery imposed by a rigid traditionalism that insisted on denying the modern scientific worldview, he found freedom for the honest mind and spirit in the theological classroom of William Newton Clarke. Fosdick believed that people in the pews were also troubled by the questions of faith that had troubled him, and his pulpit attracted national attention simply because he brought into the open questions that too many preachers still try to sweep under the rug.[1]

In clear and persuasive manner he discussed the modern use of the Bible, the meaning of prayer, an honest faith, questions of personal ethics, and grave public issues. He made preaching interesting because he believed that people come to church with problems on which they want help, and Sunday by Sunday he would take on one problem or another with an intellectual clarity and moral earnestness that guided and inspired a generation.

Fosdick never backed off from an issue. When the attention given by the press to fundamentalism left many Americans with the impression that Christianity was an anti-intellectual hangover from the age of ignorance, Fosdick made news with his sermon, "Shall the Fundamentalists Win?"[2] Soon Clarence E. Macartney of Pittsburgh countered, "Shall Unbelief Win?" The debate between these two preachers, avidly reported in the press, involved the American public in a theological discussion that caused excitement across the land. It also produced widespread controversy.

If the adoption of Fosdick's method by other preachers failed to elicit the excitement his sermons produced, the reason is clear. Fosdick did not hesitate to provoke controversy, whereas most of us fear it like the plague. Granted, he enjoyed a kind of tenure in the backing of John D. Rockefeller, Jr. But that was not all.

As Teacher, Fosdick knew how to share the faith of an honest mind. When he felt compelled to attack a traditional religious idea, he did not leave the people holding an empty bag. He gave them a better idea that they could embrace with Christian integrity. And always he imparted a vital, vibrant faith, with evident devotion to Jesus Christ and to the purposes of God. He believed that his hearers wanted authentic religion without intellectual compromise. He preached in wholehearted commitment to Jesus Christ, offering the dedication of an active mind, willing to struggle with hard problems and to seek answers compatible with that commitment.

Thousands of listeners found that Fosdick gave far more than he might have seemed to take away, and that what he took away they had been on the verge of abandoning already, clinging to it only in fearful despair. What he gave instead permitted them to go on in freedom and honesty as "Christians unashamed."[3]

Fosdick was only the most notable of a generation of Christian preachers cast in the same mold, who taught with great effectiveness. Others include Charles Edward Jefferson, his older contemporary whose sermons at Broadway Tabernacle in the theater district of New York attracted consistent audiences for years; a company of luminaries who went from pastorates to leading posts in theological education without ever losing the ministerial ethos—Henry Sloane Coffin at Union Theological Seminary, Charles Reynolds Brown at Yale Divinity School, Willard L. Sperry at Harvard, and John Mackay at Princeton; the best-selling author and missionary who repeatedly returned from India to conduct preaching missions in this country, E. Stanley Jones; exciting biblical preachers such as George A. Buttrick, who found time as a pastor to write influential books and to preside over the editors and scholars who produced the *Interpreter's Bible* in twelve massive volumes of exegesis and exposition; Christian social critics such as Kirby Page, Ernest Fremont Tittle, and G. Bromley Oxnam; foremost preachers and educators who drew inspiration from their roots in the black community and whose influence reached far beyond it, such as Benjamin F. Mays and Howard Thurman; the eloquent preacher whose pioneering ministry in ecumenical journalism gained for *The Christian Century* a large audience within and beyond the church, Charles Clayton Morrison, and his colleagues W. E. Garrison, Paul Hutchinson, and Harold E. Fey. A generation of stirring and forthright preachers and editors adorned the American ministry with a quality of public teaching not seen since the Master of colonial times and rarely equaled in Christian history.

About mid-century, however, the age of the giants seemed to be passing. Then came Martin Luther King, Jr. His emergence on the public scene occurred in 1955 with the boycott of segregated buses in Montgomery, Alabama. Month after month, King pressed his civil rights marches through the South, into the cities of the North, to the nation's capital itself in the memorable Poor People's March on

Washington in 1963. All this time many people perceived King only as an agitator or activist, but he was first and foremost a Christian Teacher determined to help a sinful and divided nation discover the meaning of its fundamental commitments, political and religious.

In his preaching King dealt with the full range of biblical themes, handling each with spiritual insight to warm the heart of any believer, and always he declared the word of God carried in that Christian truth—to those living under racial oppression and to the oppressors as well. With the moral force of a Christian prophet he combined an appeal to the fundamental covenants of American freedom—the Declaration of Independence and the Constitution of the United States—with a deeper search into the meaning of familiar passages from the Bible. Night after night on the TV news, day after day in public address to groups of protesters, and now and again in a memorable speech that caught the ear of the entire country, he made his appeal to the hearts and minds of the people. And with his death he sealed his commitment to the lessons he taught. So fell the preeminent Christian Teacher in the history of the nation.

Meanwhile, almost unnoticed by the press, a quieter ministry of teaching was reaching new dimensions of importance. As a theological degree (B.D., then M.Div. or D.Min.) came to be the accepted requirement for ordination to ministry in the once free-wheeling "people's churches"—it had long been demanded by their more venerable neighbors with roots in the religious establishments of Europe—seminary faculties grew spectacularly. Few realized that the jump in numbers of students after World War II included a temporary bulge: veterans returning from several years of military service and ministers in midlife at last seeking a professional degree in order to measure up to the new standards. While the seminaries built new plants to accommodate their swelling enrollments, they also dramatically expanded their faculties, significantly increasing the number of theological scholars, most of them ministers, in the service of the churches.

About the same time, secular universities began giving new attention to religion as a proper area for impartial study, and new academic departments of religion came into being in most of the states. This enlargement of the teaching force meant that far more American scholars than ever before, the vast majority of them being Christian, were engaged in teaching and writing at an advanced level and that many students were encountering religion in a serious academic setting. These departments did not "teach the faith," clearly not the business of a tax-supported school, but they served to extend the knowledge and understanding of religion.

Among this vast company of scholars in both seminary and university, a few attracted wide attention, becoming teachers to the larger society. Chief among these were Reinhold and H. Richard Niebuhr in social ethics, and Paul Tillich, refugee from Nazi Germany, in theology. They themselves spoke to scholars, leaders in public opinion, and students, gaining a wide hearing for their reflections as Christian thinkers. Meanwhile, scores of their colleagues, some not as well known in society generally, engaged fully in the life of the churches, where many of their names became "household words." This great company of brilliant intellectuals provided leadership for American Protestantism across half a century. Besides names already mentioned here, it included John Knox, Georgia Harkness, Mary Ely Lyman, Kenneth Scott Latourette, James Muilenberg, Albert C. Outler, Henry Pitney Van Dusen, and many others.[4]

Most of these well-known Christian scholars were committed ecumenists and took a lively part in the dialogue. They immeasurably influenced the life of the churches. Their ideas were given broader currency by an impressive company of editors at *The Christian Century*, *Christianity and Crisis*, and the denominational journals, while *Christianity Today* entered the scene to project into the discussions an informed conservative voice. More recently *Sojourners* came on the scene with prophetic concern. Ours has been a century of impressive teaching.

The work of Teacher continues today as a major involvement of ministry, even when the familiar lineaments of this form are not clearly evident. The growing interest of ministers in liturgy is a case in point. On the surface we would seem to be seeing a revival of the venerable model of the Priest, and in many instances that is surely the case. Yet we observe that it is not primarily the sacramental character of priesthood, declared by the medieval church to be the essence of this form, that is coming back. Rather it is an equally ancient and equally essential aspect of priestly ministry that seems to dominate the contemporary trend—the work of the Teacher, the bearer of tradition.

Consider the most obvious signs of the liturgical revival: the recovery of the Christian year, the use of seasonal colors, reading and preaching from the lectionary, the designing of banners, marching in processionals and even breaking into dance, employing and interpreting old and new Christian symbols, composing hymns, writing liturgies, telling the story. All this is the work of the Priest as Teacher. It is the work of the Teacher in the distinctive vocabulary of religion—symbol and myth and tradition. Wherever the awakening of interest in worship makes for a renewed vitality of faith at the level of feeling or of the meta-rational, as long as it is integrated with honest Christian thought, it will be welcomed by all who value the Teacher's ministry.

Equally significant is the concern for advocacy shown by many socially conscious ministers today. The pastor or editor who speaks up on behalf of the poor, who challenges political decisions made at the expense of the least powerful, who commends public policies designed to level the playing field for the sake of the disadvantaged, whose mission is that of public champion for those with no one else to plead their cause—such a minister gives contemporary life to the model of the Teacher, not only by providing information that may not otherwise reach many church members and other citizens, but also by joining the prophets and Jesus and a great company of Christian leaders through the centuries in instructing the consciences as well as the minds of their contemporaries and in imparting a sense of compassion and commitment to the justice God wills.

Do not overlook the natural alliance between the authentic ministry of the Manager and that of the Teacher.[5] For any community of Christians to carry out its mission, the essential prerequisites are motivation and understanding. Providing these is the work of the Teacher. The pioneers of the "art of church management" a half century ago understood this well. The meeting of a congregational committee, or even a board, was envisioned as potentially an educational event, an exploration of some aspect of the church's task (worship, world mission, stewardship, evangelism). Often a committee or department would continue in systematic study through the year, so that its recommendations to the church might grow out of informed Christian understanding and conviction.

In such a setting the pastor's primary responsibility is not "selling a program" but seeing that learning takes place, whether through overt activity as a Teacher or through more quiet work in the background to help plan the process. Such an approach to management proceeds by developing within the congregation a corps of informed and motivated leaders, concerned and capable of planning and carrying out a program of action. This kind of work exemplifies the possibility of mutual support between two models of ministry, the Teacher and the Manager, as the strengths of both unite in an integrated understanding of the task.

Many ministers emphasize their work as Teacher by conducting a variety of special courses throughout the year. Such courses may include a series of sermons on a theme, meeting with a particular group in the church school for a period of weeks, presenting a program on a sensitive topic for one of the church organizations, or offering a short-term class. The special course provides opportunity to attract a self-selecting audience that may well include persons not drawn to conventional organized "classes" majoring in fellowship and projects.

One of our gravest sins in traditional programs of Christian education must be the habit of endlessly repeating the most elementary simplicities because we think that a "cross section of the congregation" is not ready for more advanced material. But like the good teacher in the old one-room school, some ministers have found a way to engage more mature Christians in a kind of study that makes for genuine intellectual growth in their knowledge of theology, biblical studies, social concerns, and other topics.[6]

Unlike church members of earlier generations who endured long sermons on doctrinal themes while sitting on very hard pews, and whose religious experience found a great deal of its charge in the excitement of denominational rivalry, today's Christians have little sense of historic identity. In a society that has pushed freedom of religion to its ultimate extreme and a culture committed to the subjectivism of doing one's own thing, many parishioners have no understanding of or commitment to the particular witness of the church to which they belong. That condition might cause little alarm if it were certain that they had a clear comprehension of the great tradition and were pledged unreservedly to it. But such is not the case.

Today's freewheelers and church shoppers have developed what Martin Marty calls a "pick-and-choose Christianity."[7] In such a context, the ministry of the Teacher is crucial, so that people may be informed about the basics of the faith: the grace of God in Christ, and the presence of the Holy Spirit in the life of the church, its power in the hearts of believers, the call to witness and serve. If a pastor is not engaged in work as a theologian and interpreter, it is time for a new job description.[8]

The entrance of large numbers of women into the seminaries during the 1970s and their ordination as ministers presents the church with significant new opportunities. In the past the main chance that most churches offered for women in ministry was in Christian education, with their role clearly understood as subordinate. Now that is not the case, as the old patriarchal structures start to give way. It may be hoped that as more and more women reach senior positions in ministry they will avoid the perils of some of the models we have described and, by emphasizing the nurturing aspect of the work, will bring new vitality to the model of Teacher.

The mode of the Christian Teacher today differs radically not only from the authoritarianism of the New England Master but also from the persuasiveness of the nineteenth-century Pulpiteer. In a "world come of age," many persons resist persuasion by another; they want to find out for themselves. Rather than coming on as a glamorous partisan to argue a case, the Teacher adapts to the new situation by playing the role of the *dis-coverer*, the one who humbly guides us in uncovering a truth so that we "find" it for ourselves. The dis-coverer quietly points out the way to those inquirers who will be satisfied only by tracing out the route themselves to see where it really does lead. Today's preacher teaches "as one without authority,"[9] raising questions, pointing to possibilities, hinting with stories, letting the hearer make the find—which no one else may really make for another.

Does not this "inductive method" for presenting the Christian faith seem to be strangely at odds with the demand for assurance, even for dogmatic certainty, that has arisen in many quarters in this age of insecurity? Clearly, it is. And conservative churches are growing because a portion of the population responds to the loud voice, the assertion of authority, and the stern demand for discipline. But can we believe that such a mode of witnessing to the gospel will continue to appeal to the minds and hearts of the late-twentieth and the twenty-first centuries? That is a serious question.

Perhaps the mind trained in technology alone, without exposure to the humanistic disciplines, responds readily to a tight system of doctrinal assertions or "laws" corresponding to the mechanistic understanding of technical processes. How radically different is such a mentality from the "enlightened minds" so lyrically predicted for the age of science! But surely the minds at the cutting edge of scientific inquiry, like those that continue to explore the realms of literature, history, philosophy, and the arts, will not be satisfied with such a constricted faith. The ministry of the interpreter, the Teacher without authority, is designed for them.

Liberal religion has its work cut out for it. It has vitiated its Christian witness by the same fault of which we accuse the Impresario and the Manager: It has accepted too blandly the assumptions of the prevailing order, without exercising sufficient concern to make sure of its own Christian integrity. The Teacher in these closing years of the century must be a woman or man fully as ready to dis-cover the abiding truth in the gospel as to ask how that gospel is to be understood anew in the light of new developments in secular thought.

Reflections on the Teacher

There is no need to argue an assessment of this model. Its forerunners in the priesthoods of antiquity, especially in Judaism, gave major attention to teaching, as did the sages in the schools of wisdom throughout the Middle East, the philosophers of the Greco-Roman world, and the great rabbis of early Judaism. The ideal was incarnated in the person of Jesus, the Great Teacher. It held a preeminent place in the work of the apostles and in the labors of ministers in every decisive era of Christian history, as well as in quieter times. It has appeared in every century of American religion, under a form particularly appropriate to the distinctive cultural context of that time. (Recall the Master, the Pulpiteer and the Builder.) And it yet holds a place of prominence among the dominant forms of twentieth-century ministry.

What expectations attend this concept? Too few people today have reason to await a sermon with the excitement that swept over a congregation when Fosdick or King stood up to preach. But are not the children of our generation as perplexed and as intelligent and as ready to act as the people who heard them, if only ministers more generally would recognize their teaching role and give it their best efforts?

In a single sermon the Counselor may offer understanding and encouragement to scores of persons, the Manager may awaken within them new motivations to Christian service more powerful than a dozen scoldings, and the Teacher may bring to life once again a greater wonder than any marvel in the Impresario's entire performance. For the Teacher tells anew the story that has changed the world and helps those who hear discover what it may change in their lives.

Having now almost reached the summit of the century's end and already able to look back over most of the terrain across which we have come, we must admit in all candor not only the greatness with which we have seen the Teacher modeled in our time by pastors, professors, editors, and denominational and ecumenical leaders, but also the absence of the model in vast, barren stretches of contemporary church life that need it so desperately.

It is not a pattern of ministry into which most of our members are likely to pressure us. They can see so much more readily the statistics that make the Manager look good or the spectacle staged by the Impresario; the time will come when many of them will seek us out as Counselor. But unless we (or our predecessors) have done a good job of teaching, most of them may never realize how little they know of the Christian faith, of the scriptures and the church's tradition, of Christian perspectives on the great issues of our time, of the resources in the gospel for directing and enriching our lives and for helping us establish closer communion with God.

Unaware of their ignorance and of the vast beyond that lies just over their limited horizon, they will not urge us to do a more solid job of education in our work as ministers. But unless we do so on our own initiative, we leave them with "hungers of the heart," pathetic moderns "who inhabit and enjoy but are not finally satisfied by liberal culture."[10] Our generation needs the Teacher.

If it is true that, in the life of our times, this model's "impact is felt by its absence,"[11] then all of us concerned for the well-being of the church need to turn again to the school of Christ and to model our ministry more faithfully after that of the Great Teacher.

Interlude: Perplexed, But Not in Despair

In January 1901 a new pastor in Chicago began publishing a weekly congregational calendar that included comments on some items of news. To a journalist's question whether the churches would survive through this twentieth century, the pastor responded that religion in the coming era might well be "a spiritual force working through literature and art, but without the familiar institutional forms." Still the hope prevailed "that religion would be more rational, more united, more Christian."[1]

Now at the end of the century we ponder the question and the young minister's response with a certain poignancy. It would be hard to argue that his hopes have come to any large fruition. In an era dominated by the mass media, religion has not mounted a significant force to compete with these new rivals that so largely form our culture. Yet we forget too readily the power of religion in sustaining the successful nonviolent campaign mounted by the masses in India under Gandhi's leadership when they won their deliverance from the British raj; in empowering the freedom movement led by Martin Luther King, Jr., in the United States in the 1960s; and in providing a forum for honest discussion that led to the great demonstrations for democracy in eastern Europe and the collapse of Communist rule in nearly all of them during the closing months of the 1980s.

But when it comes to the familiar institutional forms of religion, the perceptive young minister was correct. Most notably, the social structures and societal patterns that provided the churches in America a foundation of "cultural establishment" have given way, leaving those churches bobbing in the turbulent currents of secularism like houses swept away by a flood. For all their present irrelevance, denominations persist, unready to surrender their traditional mores and prerogatives within a united church designed for the present and the future. And when it comes to ministry, the old models, so well adapted to the conditions of earlier societies, have proved largely irrelevant to the emergent world, with its strange outlines that differ so menacingly from what we have known.

Within the enclosed little world of our congregations, church life in many cases seems to go on unperturbed. Ministers conduct the old familiar liturgies or major in contemporary worship; preach to the converted and, ever more rarely, to an occasional visitor; look forlornly over the flock trying to find a few more heads without gray, or in rare instances attract scores of baby boomers; do their best to retain a pastoral relationship on the basis of a snatch of conversation on Sunday morning and calling in time of crisis; and rally the troops to take on ever larger burdens of community service, as the federal government abandons responsibility for the homeless, the unfortunate, and the incompetent, and as the states find tax revenues falling short.

Even when congregational programs flourish, it becomes increasingly clear that, for the most part, they are serving a relatively small in-group—perhaps serving them well—but making little impression on the larger life of metropolis, on the materialistic value-system so insistently promoted by the media, on education, on the outlook of children and youth, on literature and art (despite the hopes of the young minister almost a century ago), or on national policy.

Here lurks the temptation to discouragement. The traditional models of ministry that once contributed so largely to the life of generations before us have lost their capacity, with rare exceptions, to influence the life of our society, the tone of the culture, even the affairs of our local communities. The Priest, the Master, the Awakener once could do all that. So could the Pulpiteer, the Revivalist, the Builder, and (in many situations around the world) the Missionary. But not the Manager or the Counselor, the one concerned with the survival of a local institution, the other largely with the personal problems of troubled individuals. The Impresario commands public attention, at least for a while, though it appears that, aside from devotees of the old-time religion, it comes from people wanting to see a show or from journalists spoiling to report an offbeat story or a cynical comment about mainstream churches. As for the Teacher, the model works with congregations or even denominations, but we find our ingenuity stretched to the breaking point in trying to extend its influence beyond the walls of the church.

Little wonder that in our century ministerial morale has sometimes run low. It seems to have sunk to its nadir in the late 1950s and early '60s, when bitter confessions on "Why I Left the Ministry" filled the pages of secular journals and the religious press alike.[2] The current generation of ministers appears tougher and less inclined to lose heart—perhaps because they were born into this kind of world and have few nostalgic illusions deriving from memories of earlier times. Moreover, they are well enough informed about the magnitudes of twentieth-century society and its problems to know that these are perplexing to all leaders—in education, politics, business, and all the professions—and that Christian ministry is not alone in the crisis.

Under the surface, nevertheless, discontent lurks, along with a general feeling of unease. Despite the stiff upper lip and cheery bravado, we have reason to suspect a widespread fragility of ministerial morale. It has been eroded, as pointed out in these chapters, by frustration over the church's loss of influence in the life of the nation and in the culture, over the seeming insignificance of the minister as a leader in community, denomination, or society at large, and over expectations, sometimes unrealistic, that run so high in the parish.

The weight of this larger malaise adds painfully to the more personal burdens and frustrations borne by most ministers: the common failure to receive recognition as a qualified "professional" (as reflected in salary scales or general confidence in one's knowledge of reality), the gap between the minister's vision and the mediocrity of day-to-day life in the parish, and the role-ambiguity and role-conflict with the movers and shakers in the congregation. Not long ago an intelligent pastor of tough inner fiber wrote an old friend, "Am in confused place about ministry here. $ things go well, people things so slow. And I am a people person."[3]

We today might be inclined to envy a description of a notable mid-century minister. Ralph W. Sockman, who gave strength to the model of the Teacher, was characterized forty years ago by a news magazine as "moving with relaxed urbanity through a round of activity that would faze most captains of industry."[4] Few of us can muster up a self-image of relaxed urbanity in the situation of ministry today. We feel closer kinship with the adjectives the great apostle used to describe his situation: "afflicted...perplexed...persecuted ...struck down...." Yet we hear him saying, "We do not lose heart" (2 Cor. 4:8-9,16).

We do not lose heart! Perplexed, but not driven to despair! Whatever causes for discouragement we may find as we undertake to carry on Christian ministry in the present complex of social and cultural conditions, they fall into perspective when we recall the long line of apostles and prophets and martyrs, of saints and priests and masters and awakeners, of pulpiteers and revivalists and builders and missionaries, of counselors and teachers who have gone before us and who stand beside us in the task today. The apostolic word describes them all: "as poor, yet making many rich" (2 Cor. 6:10). And so long as faith, hope, and love abide, we are content to have it describe us.

How then shall we find for ourselves an authentic model of ministry to serve the days ahead? To that question we address our final chapter.

Coming to a Conclusion:
OUT OF DISARRAY, CREATIVITY

Our inquiry began with the many, sometimes conflicting, expectations imposed on ministers today. The search for origins led us to examine the prevailing models of ministry in American history, and we have seen them all thrown into disarray by the dynamics of contemporary society. Our hope now is for the release of creative impulses in the church, to make for effective ministry in the days ahead.

This chapter will suggest some lines for thinking our way toward ministerial models, old or new, that will commend the gospel in this time of confusion, meet the needs of persons, and bring society into closer accord with God's will—models that we can claim with joy and maintain with integrity in the glad freedom of those who serve.

We concentrate on models, not on traits of character or financial schemes (such as a plea for bi-vocational pastors), nor specialized ministries limited to areas of particular expertise. We have in view the full range of responsibility assigned to a parish pastor.[1]

Standards for Evaluation

In assessing any model of ministry, consider three standards of judgment: 1) faithfulness to the gospel and mission entrusted to the church; 2) relevance, understood as responsiveness to the new situation in culture and society; and 3) creativity in working out new models for effective ministry.

Faithfulness

A faithful ministry will be God-centered, bearing the touch of holiness. In ordaining "certain of its members for the ministry in the name of Christ by the invocation of the Spirit and the laying on of

183

hands,"[2] the church appoints them to speak the word of God humbly and forthrightly into the present moment, and to guide persons into that inner knowledge of God that issues in a new manner of life, commitment to justice, and love for others. Complete ministry involves both contemplation and activism.[3]

Our concern for faithful ministry differs intentionally from the preoccupation with "order" that has loomed so large in twentieth-century ecumenical discussion, eventuating in the much-discussed consensus on *Baptism, Eucharist and Ministry*. A quick glance through that remarkable document shows an almost total introversion upon the internal life of the church. Fixation on order diverts attention from what really needs to be said and done about ministry today. Key rubrics ought to be servanthood, prophetic witness, relevance—genuine engagement of the gospel with the crucial issues affecting humankind. It is hard to suppress a monumental yawn at the straining diplomacy of this obsession with orders, continuity, authority—nervous ecclesiastical fretting over means made ends in themselves.

Our world waits for a demonstration of ministry that echoes the portrait of Jesus in the Gospels—a ministry concerned for the poor, the hungry, the outcast, the lonely, and the lost; a ministry joyfully offered with loving human touch to bring the knowledge of overflowing grace and eternal life as gifts from God. Do we not long with Carlyle Marney for a *person-centered* pastoral theology?[4]

A faithful ministry fulfills both apostolate and pastorate, the apostle being sent to the world outside the church, the pastor assigned to shepherd professing Christians and others who turn to the church for help.

The apostolic character of ministry appears in the New Testament image of *ambassador* (2 Cor. 5:20; Eph. 6:20). We see it in those ministries that reach beyond the familiar constituency of the church, to bring the good news of God, the call of Christ, and the challenge of the Kingdom to persons "on the outside." List among such apostles the missionary, the campus minister, the worker-priest or other bivocational minister whose job gives access for witness to others, the "street minister," the evangelist, the Christian social reformer, the religious broadcaster.

Many a pastor exercises apostolate through moving into the larger community in service or witness. A skill in athletics, communication, art, or music opens doors for contact with persons not related to one's own, or any, congregation. Include also those theologians who work at the point where Christian thought and secular thought intersect, who are "more concerned to address their culture than to squabble with other theologians."[5]

Save a place of honor for the movement in theological education to prepare students for "leadership in the public church—a community called by God to social responsibility."[6] In challenging the division between the public and the private spheres, Philip Devenish has characterized our situation as one in which "the problems of human life are more and more public and the religious responses to them are more and more private."[7] A pastor recently observed: "There is a demonic presence in our world—abused children and other victims of cruelty. We need to confront these evils. There is a need for conversion, and we need to address it."[8]

The cultural disestablishment of the churches has brought back the apostolic situation. In our schools and in the media "we've largely screened out the reality of religion in society. A youngster can watch fifteen years of children's TV and learn about the mailperson and the grocer but never see a rabbi, monk or minister."[9] The difficulty ministers encounter in gaining recognition along with other professionals and in exercising public influence derives, says an observer, from their position as "leaders of a marginal social institution. Unlike other professionals—educators, lawyers, doctors,—they do not have the society as a whole as their constituency. They lead a band of volunteers, offering 'services' no longer seen as social or life necessities in North American culture."[10]

We ministers do not relish such a marginal position, but it puts us where the apostles began: They too were outsiders. No one thought that they belonged or that their message was needed. Today 44 percent of our population have no formal tie with the church.[11] Though more and more Americans consider themselves to be religious, the polls show growing numbers who are not church-related. This situation should convince us that conversion is crucial, putting us in a properly apostolic frame of mind.

The pastoral dimension of faithful ministry is much more firmly institutionalized in the church than is the apostolic. In distinction from the latter's orientation toward the world, pastoral ministry is directed toward the building up of the church. It ordains persons to a ministry of Word, sacrament, and care—care for persons, for the Christian community, and for its institution. The dominant models of ministry in America have been essentially pastoral. Some that at first glance appear to have had apostolic intent—the Awakener, the Revivalist, the Impresario—were directed more toward people already in the church than is evident at first glance.

For faithful ministry both apostolic and pastoral commitments are essential. Both give expression to *agape*, God's unconditional love that Christians are called to live out in the world. Given the nature of the church as both community and institution, it is hardly a matter for wonder that pastoral concerns dominate its thinking. Even in the New Testament we see a shift, as time passes, from the "fisherman-missionary" to the "shepherd-presbyter."[12]

Faithfulness requires ministry both corporate and individual: 1) the corporate ministry of the church in which all Christians have a part as members of the body, and 2) the individual ministry of persons ordained to serve in and with and for the church in its mission of witness and service to all humanity. In reviewing a series of issues featuring six functional categories of parish work, the editor of *The Christian Ministry* observed:

> Totally absent was the supposition that the minister is the single source of wisdom and authority in matters of congregational life. The abiding problem of the clergy's authority and prerogatives *vis-a-vis* a participating laity has been by no means resolved, but we do sense at least an acknowledgment of the new dimensions of shared leadership in a parish.[13]

One of the high privileges as well as one of the chief trials of ordained ministry is its representative function. In a concentrated way the minister's life and work embodies what the church proclaims and what it stands for. Young families in the parsonage frequently feel that they are living in a fishbowl, but for a minister to be seen as more than a private individual comes with the vocation.

As a "representative character" the minister "is a kind of symbol," bringing together "in one concentrated image the way [Christian] people...organize and give meaning and direction to their lives." The "public image" projected by the minister "helps define...just what kinds of personality traits it is good and legitimate to develop." This person's life-and-work "provides an ideal...that gives living expression to a vision of life, as in our society today sports figures legitimate the strivings of youth and the scientist represents objective competence."[14] Thus both the Christian community and the outside world see the "vision of life" held by the church, and what it means by faithfulness.

We append to these reflections on faithfulness an observation: Virtually all the models of ministry are morally neutral or ambiguous, a possible exception being the Impresario. That model makes us uneasy precisely because it tilts toward the exploitative dazzle and celebrity-hawking of showbiz. But almost any model can function for or against the gospel, for or against people. The question then becomes: Which model most fully enables us to express our understanding of gospel and ministry for our time? Does a specific model offer opportunity to minister in faithfulness?

Relevance

A model of ministry appropriate to the church's situation today will hold out the prospect of relevance. It will fit the current scene, address the emerging new world in that world's own idiom, and work in ways that it understands.

Projections of the twenty-first century, some dazzling, some ominous, are already a dime a dozen, with the price dropping every day; no need for us to repeat or digest or analyze that plethora of prophecy. The issue before us is not forecasting the future, but stimulating alertness to the changes going on all about us and their implications for ministry.

Consider an example. Among the clear signs given by our emerging society, none is more obvious than the new place of women, and their altered relationship toward men, in the workplace. Women are no longer limited to subordinate posts. Changes have come rapidly in business, education, and the professions, more slowly in religion. But the church cannot hold them off much longer; a recent study indicates that 23 percent of all United Methodist clergy in the 25-29 age bracket are women,[15] and the situation is similar in other churches.

Though Rome opposes the ordination of women, it would be folly to prophesy what may happen even there. When Pope John Paul II put down in Alaska for a brief stopover during one of his recent tours, he was visibly surprised to be greeted by a woman in clericals, the priest of St. Jude's Episcopal parish at North Pole. Terminally ill with cancer and wanting to "proclaim by my presence that there are women priests in the church," the Rev. Jean Aubrey Dementi handed the pontiff a card on which she had written: "Your Holiness, we women priests bring a new dimension of wholeness to our Lord's ministry."[16]

That new wholeness should soon appear in mainline Protestantism, where the virtual monopoly of male pastors in leading congregations is necessarily nearing an end. Before another decade passes, one-fourth of the ministers available for such posts will be women. Willingly or grudgingly, the church will respond to the new situation.[17]

So to the many changes in the world around us, the church will make appropriate response or demonstrate its own irrelevance. It is not necessary or even desirable for the church to imitate the prevailing culture, as it is all too prone to do, in a way that compromises faithful witness to the gospel. But changes in society do require self-examination in the light of the gospel and of the new conditions. Particularly are today's Christians, so mired in the cultural traditions of a time now past, called on to give greater attention to the oncoming generation—its needs, its problems, its hopes, its modes of communication and expression, its potential for service to God and God's kingdom.

Probably nothing in our time has made society's elders less sensitive to the thought-world of younger adults than comfortable retirement on Social Security and their pensions. Bumper stickers on recreational vehicles proclaim, WE ARE SPENDING OUR CHILDREN'S INHERITANCE. Such a cavalier attitude toward the financial plight of everyone under fifty years of age does not characterize all retirees. But the feeling among the elderly that, apart from a few aches and pains, we now have things pretty much the way we want them and we can "let the rest of the world go by," is all too prevalent. And today's church—so dependent on its senior members for attendance, work as volunteers, financial support, leadership, and counsel—faces the temptation to take off in a nostalgic caravan down memory lane, leaving behind the working generations with their own more pressing concerns. If the church shapes its ministry to the irresponsible interests of older members, now in the majority, it will forfeit the prospect of relevance to the real world, and even of survival.

It now seems even harder than ever to remember the evangelist Luke's observation that "Jesus was about thirty years old" (3:23) when he began his ministry. It thrilled us in our youth. From it we inferred that most of his disciples must have been even younger, as well as many in the crowds that flocked to hear him. How many older members in today's church, we ask, would follow such an "immature" Teacher, or throw in with the neophytes in his company, to say nothing of confessing him as Savior and Lord? Perhaps the shock of dealing with such a question may open our eyes to the mentality of "modern maturity" that pervades so much church life today.

If we would find relevant models of ministry for tomorrow's world we will have to abandon the mindset of the "golden years" and seriously ask ourselves questions such as these:

How can the church engage the attention, interest, and commitment of the generations —
- who watched TV before ever they learned to read?
- who do not remember the Great Depression or FDR or even World War II?
- who never lived on a farm or visited grandparents in the country?

- who did not grow up attending revival meetings, Sunday school conventions, and Christian Endeavor rallies?
- whose value system has been shaped by the media far more profoundly than by church and home and school?
- who look back—the older ones among them—with nostalgia on the idealistic dreams espoused by the counterculture in the sixties?
- who regard common practices in public worship, along with its style, as quaint and do not understand the reasons for them?
- for whom conversation is a lost art, as is the memory of evenings spent in telling and retelling yarns?
- who have been so involved with uninterrupted TV, videotapes, Walkman, Muzak, and "boom boxes" that silence makes them uncomfortable?
- who have never learned how to relate to other persons in any relationship of depth because they are restless without the diversion of "something going on" in the background?
- who do not remember and cannot understand how proud we were, when we dedicated this church thirty years ago? (Or was it forty? or fifty? or more?)

After we have spent some time reflecting on such questions and letting the import of the answers soak through our consciousness we may reach a frame of mind to recognize that it is *their* world in which the church is now called to minister, not the world that so largely shaped the habits of the church as we know it.

Only after such an exercise are we likely to raise any question about our disposition to regard the way the churches now do things as normal. Only then will we begin to take seriously the world as it now is, and is becoming, as the world to which today's Christians must respond with relevance. Only then are we likely to call forth much creativity in projecting new models of ministry.

Scary? Perhaps. But if so, mainly to the old and mentally arthritic.

A young California minister in one of our discussion groups on new models of ministry spoke of engaging the new situation with delight, despite the risk. Then he suggested the image of surfing. "If you're going to do it, you have to get out to the waves. You have to lean into the waves and then ride them out. The ocean is not kind. It's not always fair. But you have to take it on." Such an image doubtless appeals more to youth than to the gray heads now doing so much of the church's thinking. But it should shake us out of our somnolence and open our eyes to new possibilities.

A Creative Process

How then shall we find creative possibilities for ministry that may move us beyond perplexity and disarray? By calling upon our imaginations. By submitting new ideas to hard analysis and revising them in the light of criticism. By putting a new model into practice to test its viability. And then, probably, by turning over further experimentation to another generation!

The task requires openmindedness, with a readiness to examine both traditional models (either in pure form or with adaptations) and new ones, avoiding doctrinaire inflexibility, for in rapidly changing situations no ideal form can be perfectly followed. Whatever model we advance, it may be necessary to claim for it essential features of other models also. In this quest, sensitivity and modesty are virtues, as well as imagination and daring. Above all, the task requires willingness to come to terms with the full implications of each proposal and to explore its possibilities for a complete ministry of Word, sacrament, and care. Any trial model that comes up wanting at this point must be regarded as incomplete, a form of specialized ministry.

None of the "classic" models we have examined came into being as the product of individual genius. Rather, each of them emerged in the intuitive response of a faithful church to the spirit and the need of the times.

Sometimes in the past, however, an individual stroke of genius has produced a new form of ministry. In the late Middle Ages, St. Francis of Assisi adapted the monastic ideals of poverty, chastity, and obedience to a new kind of order that, instead of withdrawing to the desert, would deliberately cast its lot with the people of the newly emerging towns to care for the poor and the sick, to preach to the crowds, and (very soon) to fight the intellectual battles of the faith in the newly chartered universities. The Friar, the Little Brother of the Poor, entered the scene. All honor to St. Francis, St. Dominic, St. Ignatius Loyola, Mother Teresa, and any other genius with a mind to match a major new need with a significant new model of ministry.

The enterprise is one for many thoughtful ministers, "brainstorming" together, experimenting individually with promising proposals, engaging in cooperative drafting of new plans and in joint testing, evaluation, and redesign. Not only ministerial groups but the church at large will be involved, especially pioneering congregations, with thoughtful contributions from the laity. Scholarly leadership from the seminaries will be essential, as well as ecumenical studies and denominational processes.

Above all, the task will require imagination. An official in the government of France named "the worst crime an intelligence chief can commit"—"a lack of imagination."[18] Is it not also true of ministry?

Imagination will keep an eye out for potential value—in the oldest of forms, or in models yet untried, like the householder in the parable who brought from his vault treasures old and new (Matt. 13:52).

Assessing Relevant Models

A Scheme for Analysis

In attempting to evaluate any model of ministry, it is essential to take note of its positive elements, its limitations in the past and on the current scene, and any lingering expectations, appropriate or inappropriate, associated with it. During the feudal era, when prelates were accounted princes of the church, they affected courtly pomp and ceremony, and pious Christians honored them with the customary medieval gestures of fealty. The story is told of the late Roman Catholic Archbishop of Bombay, Thomas Roberts, who abhorred all such vestiges of an undemocratic age. To a woman who asked if she might kiss his ring he is said to have replied, "Madam, you may if you wish, but I must warn you that it is in my hip pocket."[19] In urging on today's church the threefold ministry, it would be highly inappropriate to link episcopacy with the etiquette of feudalism.

To be acceptable, any proposed model of ministry should manage to stand up to such questions as the following:

- Is it rooted in the ministry of Christ and committed to the corporate ministry of God's people?
- Is it egalitarian in spirit, relying on instruction, persuasion, and free consent rather than resorting to arbitrary exercise of authority?
- Is it responsive to the needs of the poor, the marginalized, those who have no one to speak for them or awaken the dignity given them by God?
- Does it offer an effective means of confronting today's world with God's prophetic judgment, free grace, and insistent demand for personal uprightness and public justice?
- Can it faithfully fulfill the ministry of Word, sacrament, and care?
- Is it equally open to members of all races, to women and men?
- What in it is *essential* to the life and ministry of the church?

Contemporary Models

With a mind to relevance we do well to ask: What are the commanding and influential forms or models that point directions in our secular society? And might any of these provide possibly useful analogues for ministry? Some are relatively easy to dismiss—politician, bureaucrat, arbitrageur—though they have their imitators within the church. Other secular models have profoundly influenced twentieth-century models of ministry, as we have seen—manager, counselor, celebrity, entertainer. Others offer possibilities for our reflection—teacher, scholar, consultant (in this information age), engineer (working up detailed plans), one or another of the "caring professions." It would be profitable to spend some time in reflection on emerging forms of secular influence and what they may suggest for the practice of ministry.

We briefly comment on three prominent secular models that invite our further exploration.

In this secular, scientific age, the *storyteller* enjoys truly amazing prominence. As actor, scriptwriter, director, producer, advertising agent, lyricist, novelist, short story writer, artist, dancer, mime, rapper, raconteur, or stand-up comic—to name only a few contemporary incarnations—the storyteller offers the hope of something to fill the great void in our lives, our longing for meaning and color and excitement and a happy outcome. The gospels suggest that a major source of Jesus' appeal to the crowds was his gift for telling parables; twenty centuries afterwards we cannot get them out of our minds.

A "theology of story" enjoys a current vogue, and it has much to commend it (though some of its proponents seem better at theologizing about it than they do at telling stories). Congregations can scarcely restrain their delight when a preacher shifts from abstract propositions to storytelling, though some who affect the art show little interest in any story but their own; a small sheaf of sermons would provide a ghostwriter with more than enough material for an "autobiography" of the preacher. Such ministers need to learn that there are other stories with perhaps even greater fascination for their hearers. Most of all, the preacher needs to know and visualize and love and tell *the* story, from which all Christian preaching springs.

Equally prominent in giving voice and direction to people's commitments and in providing the information on the basis of which they make their decisions is the *reporter-commentator*. As newscaster on the radio and television networks, sports announcer, host on the succession of talk-shows that exploit current issues, journalist writing for newspaper or newsmagazine, master of the exposé who rushes into print with a book within weeks of a major event, inside source who can spice every conversation with the latest information about the company or the city council or the White House, tattletale child, or back-fence gossip, the reporter-commentator informs us what is going on and helps establish our attitude toward it.

Every Sunday the minister is given the opportunity to tell the good news of God made known in Jesus Christ. But let it always be remembered that the minister is a reporter, not a historian: The proper business of the pulpit is not archaeology, delving in the annals of antiquity, but newscasting, letting people know what has happened lately in God's dealings with us. Not only is the preacher a reporter but also a commentator, with the opportunity to answer our question, "What does it all mean?"

To the minister struggling with discouragement and a sense of professional insignificance, it may come as a jolt to be offered a model from the world of games, the *sports star*. In this age of exaggerated machismo, what profession does the popular imagination hobble with the image of the wimp (unjustly, to be sure) more than the ministry? To the cheering, jeering crowd gathered for the fight, the minister appears more like the lad David struggling to put on King Saul's armor than like the mighty Goliath, at whose tread the earth shook. (Doubtless he pumped iron for an hour every day.)

Given the excitement with which schoolboys collect baseball cards, the size of the sports staffs on the metropolitan dailies, and the mania of a community's involvement with a winning team and its heroes, should there be any wonder about the boredom people suffer in church? A city goes wild with excitement over an athletic contest that is ultimately irrelevant except as a test of skill and spirit, but people go to sleep in church. Why? Because they see no contest there. Church leaders fear controversy like the plague; they want a pastor whom Joseph Sittler characterized "a combination of master of ceremonies and soothing friend."[20] Such a minister may be "nice," but hardly exciting.

Contrast with this pale and placid propriety the athletic imagery in the New Testament, which stirs the blood with images of boxing, wrestling, racing, and combat, with accounts of perils escaped and sufferings endured, and which concludes with a book of promises to the one who overcomes. Recall the thumping excitement, even if sometimes contrived, of a nineteenth-century revival meeting, with its crowds and color and lively music, the air electric with expectancy. Watch the dramatic contest against indifference and sin and even the devil, the stirring accounts of other victories in other places and of some victories already won here, the vivid story of Golgotha and its cross and the victim who became the victor winning eternal life for all.

Then see the payoff as the evangelist invites the hearers to confess Jesus Christ as Lord. Hear the melting music of the invitation hymn, as people from all over the great tent or tabernacle press to the front to take the preacher's hand and claim God's forgiveness and the gift of new life.

The Christian life is, of course, more than the first step. Still we must ask: Does today's minister challenge people to the difficult contest and coach them so that they can win significant victories? Congregations today still know excitement when a group of members finishes a project for Habitat for Humanity, when a caravan of young people returns from their mission to Mexico, when people make personal decisions for Christ, and the minister can celebrate these without betraying confidences. It is a time of elation when a church dedicates a new building or unit, when it burns the mortgage, when it celebrates the high days of the Christian year, especially Easter, or when members rally behind a venture in social action. Nearing retirement, a minister remembered the day when he was serving in the Army and God called him with the mandate, "Bill, I am putting you in charge of trumpets."[21] A brass band spurs on a team, and a minister can incite people to good works and celebrate Christian victories.

Biblical Paradigms

We need to match up any model we consider against the biblical paradigms of ministry for the essential elements they contain. No need to elaborate here, with Bible dictionaries so readily available. Enough to enter a reminder of the most important forms.

The figure of the *servant* clearly sets forth the intention and spirit of all ministry; it is inclusive and determinative for all models.[22] Every minister is called to look to Jesus Christ, who came not to be served but to serve. His ministry stands as a reminder to every minister that "God's way is not the way of upward mobility,"[23] but of service.

The biblical *prophet* spoke by direct inspiration of the Spirit of God, a power that most ministers do not claim. The true prophet, moreover, was not salaried by the religious institution (at least, not for being a prophet), but instead turned aside from the mundane job to declare the message received from God. In Israel, the prophet spoke to the king, having an access to power closed to most ministers today. After Pentecost the prophet addressed the church, as today's minister is appointed to do.

The figure of the *shepherd* commonly applies in the Hebrew scriptures to the king, anointed to guide and protect the people. Applied in the New Testament most often to Jesus Christ, it is also used for the Christian minister, under the title *pastor*. The pastoral directives in the New Testament have to do not so much with "handholding," however, as with sustaining the morale of a Christian counterculture (Col. 4; Rom. 12:2). The pastors in the ancient church exhorted their people to be faithful to death, and many themselves suffered martyrdom. Care for persons remains a fundamental responsibility of ministers, not only in times of crisis, but in guidance and support through all the stages of life. In a time when the numbers of persons going into the helping professions lags and "Compassion is a term of derision in the circles of the *au courant*,"[24] shepherding ministry remains a pressing need.

The figure of the *teacher* found expression in biblical times in the ministries of the priest, the sage, and the rabbi.[25] The persistence of the teaching function in leading models of ministry throughout biblical history and in our twentieth-century model of the Teacher points up an essential element in the church's leadership.[26]

The recurring image of the *soldier* in the epistles of the New Testament is in no sense an incitement to militarism, much less to intolerance, but rather a clear reminder that the Christian gospel leads to conflict with many secular forces—power as domination over others, consumerism as self-indulgence in a world of crying need, nationalism as idolatry, racism and tribal strife, patriarchy and the exploitation of the weak. The church is called to spiritual conflict, not just to easing the minor pains that people sustain.

Any sufficient model of ministry will not only relate to the world it seeks to serve, but will also fulfill the essential functions of these basic biblical forms of ministry.

Our "Classical" Models

Each of our "classical models" from the life of the American church originated as a response to the needs and conditions of a particular time. Most of these have now passed, along with the age whose needs they came into being to serve. Nevertheless, though the model itself may be obsolete, each gave prominence to certain basic concerns that ought never be lacking from ministry. In brief space, let us call to mind these essentials.

In the Saint we see that holiness that derives from the experience of direct encounter with God, the assurance of personal vocation as a humble servant who belongs without reservation to God, the humility that lives out one's service without either fanfare or denial of one's life with God. We see a human spirit sustained and disciplined by solitary prayer, unafraid of standing against the glitter of mammon and the gore of Mars, and unpretentious and joyful in the Christian life.

From the Priest we learn the necessity of the religious institution with a disciplined order of ministers, who lead the people in the time-tested rites of the faith, who in praying join their supplications with the prayers of the whole church, who teach the people the essentials of Christian faith and life and conduct, who by their ministry invoke the blessing and assurance of God on every critical moment of life and at time of death, who warn us of God's judgment and who declare God's forgiveness to every penitent spirit.

In the eighteenth-century Master we see embodied the intellectual and spiritual faithfulness of the minister who brings responsible biblical, theological, and ethical scholarship to preaching and pastoral care, who addresses the members of the congregation in their crucial spiritual need, and who confronts the world of public affairs with unwavering concern for God's intention and the moral law.

The Awakener arose to confront both religious lethargy and spiritual despair with reliance on God's animating Spirit and the assurance of amazing grace, reminding every minister to stir up the gift of God within.

The Pulpiteer of the nineteenth century knew how to make the proclamation of the gospel exciting and compelling, giving voice to the biblical word in direct engagement with the chief concerns of the times, making effective use of the chief means of communication and earning for religious leadership a place of respect among the devotees of culture and the arts.

The Revivalist awakened popular excitement about religion, dismantled the negative aspects of Calvinist doctrine, drew the unchurched to the gospel and the faith, renewed the spirits of Christians, and established a new mode of religious music, the gospel song.

The Builder did the steady, usually quiet, and often uncelebrated work of establishing and strengthening congregations, founding secular institutions to serve the new communities, brought millions of "westering" Americans and immigrants into solid relationships with the churches, and launched hundreds of schools, colleges, and other educational and benevolent institutions, local and national.

The Missionary responded to the commission to carry the gospel into the whole world; learned the languages and cultures of nations and tribes around the globe; translated the Bible; baptized converts; established churches, schools, hospitals, orphanages, and printing presses; brought into being a worldwide Christian community; and laid the foundations for the modern ecumenical movement, while setting an example of unreserved self-giving for the cause of Christ.

The Manager adapted the methods of business to the administration of the church, rationalized methods of congregational work that had been sporadic or altogether neglected, educated church officers in principles of leadership and in understanding the tasks of the Christian mission, and helped members develop orderly processes for establishing goals and for reaching them.

The Counselor appropriated and synthesized with Christian understanding the new psychological and therapeutic wisdom from academia, using it to deal individually with the fears and confusions and other psychic needs of people in trouble, to energize preaching by dealing with such concerns, and to make the church a center for support groups to serve people with addictions and other special needs.

The Impresario adopted the techniques of show business employed by the secular celebrity on television and undertook to use them in reaching outsiders with the gospel. Sad to report, the best-known practicians of the form, consumed by the demands of the medium, fell into compromise and moral disgrace. Even so, they took up a major mode of contemporary communication that the mainline churches have for the most part not managed to employ.

The twentieth-century Teacher, in a time that had lost its taste for eloquence, still made preaching exciting by engaging forthrightly the modern ideas that threatened traditional religious thought and by working out from the pulpit a contemporary Christian formulation of theology, prayer, ethics, and public policy. The Teacher as theologian gained attention from secular thinkers, and as activist for civil rights led our generation in removing many of the old barriers of racial segregation, thus changing the face of American society, politics, and higher education.

With no inclination to minimize the weaknesses mentioned in our full discussion of the various forms, we nevertheless conclude that each of our twelve "classical" models had strengths not to be ignored or casually forfeited, even though few ministers could measure up to the full expectations of any one of them. Taken together, a listing of their strengths, no matter how brief, indicates something of the possibilities in Christian ministry and the positive expectations that members of congregations entertain in projecting their hopes on any woman or man who comes to serve as their minister.

"Varieties of Ministries"

These twelve, along with such emergent new models as may be adapted from contemporary society or worked out in ecumenical experimentation, confront us with more "varieties of ministries"[27] than the apostle Paul must have ever imagined. But they need cause us no more confusion than he allowed in the realization that the varieties of gifts come from the same Spirit and the varieties of services are offered to, and empowered by, the same Lord.

Focusing Expectations

Even the briefest reflection brings the recognition that, for fullness of ministry, the various models in any given century need each other; at least each needs to be supplemented with positive elements emphasized by the others. Since it has been clear from the outset that any of our models is an "ideal type," it follows that, however idealistic one's intentions, "No one individual can fit any one of the 'ideal' categories or types."[28] To some extent, moreover, the various models will mingle in the work of any one minister. A church historian and educator of ministers writes:

> Each pastor must undertake duties that are similar to those types described in the book....It is important to decide where one has the greatest gifts and abilities, but at the same time not neglect the other areas of ministry which are often called for by a congregation. One of the glories of the ministry is its diversity. That is also its curse.[29]

The minister who stands at the brink of the twenty-first century dare not surrender to dismay over the disarray into which the rapid changes of recent years have cast contemporary social institutions, including, of course, American ministry. Even though the way ahead is not clear, we are called to follow the road with strong heart and faithful mind, rendering the best service of which we are capable.

It falls to each of us in ministry to think through as best we are able the model of ministry that, given our particular abilities and inclinations, will enable us to make our largest contribution. We may take over or adapt one of the "classical" models. Or we may opt for a new emergent worked out with others in a manner suggested earlier in the chapter.

Once committed to a particular model, each of us is obligated to candor and fairness in drawing the covenant with the church. That means respectful openness with one's conference board or denominational commission on ministry, a readiness both to witness and to learn. It means an equal openness with a pastoral search committee and members of a congregation when one is being considered for a call. And it will require deliberate effort on the minister's part to extend such an understanding among members of the larger community where one serves, so that they may not be unduly confused by one's failing to meet certain expectations, and that, among those with whom there is readiness for such a ministry, there may be a knowledge of what one hopes to be about.

Even so, there will always be some tension between the minister's "want to be" or "want to do" and the "have to" imposed by the expectations and demands of those who have called him or her as their minister and who pay one's salary.

Freedom to Serve

In any such situation of tension the minister can expect no easy way out. Ministry is by definition a lived-out offering of self to God and to those one seeks to serve; consequently, it must be sustained by prayer in its very essence, namely a total giving of self to God's good purpose and holy will.

We come back to the question with which we began: What is a *good* minister? We answer: One who has joyfully received the forgiving love of God made known most fully in Jesus Christ, who has in grateful return given one's own life back to God for service to the church and the world, who has carefully thought through one's concepts of ministry in open dialogue with the church, who does not try to please everybody but rather to please the Lord, and who day by day undertakes to carry through one's ministry with integrity, commitment, imagination, and gladness for the privilege.

> So deeply do we care for you that we are determined to share with you not only the gospel of God but also our own selves (1 Thess. 2:8).

> May it be so!

NOTES

PREFACE

[1]Ronald E. Osborn, *In Christ's Place: Christian Ministry in Today's World* (Bethany Press, 1967), deals with the ministry of Jesus Christ, the corporate ministry of all Christians, and the special ministry of the ordained. It moves from study of the New Testament to theological reflection on contemporary church life in an ecumenical context.

[2]The paper was one of several written by various members of the faculty of the School of Theology at Claremont as part of the dialogue out of which came the book by Joseph C. Hough, Jr., and John B. Cobb, Jr., *Christian Identity and Theological Education* (Scholars Press, 1985).

THE PROBLEM OF MINISTERIAL IDENTITY

[1]David S. Schuller, Merton P. Strommen, and Milo L. Brekke, eds., *Ministry in America: A Report and Analysis* (Harper & Row, 1980), p. 25f. For other surveys, see Ronald E. Osborn, *The Education of Ministers for the Coming Age* (CBP Press, 1987), p. 74f.

[2]Samuel W. Blizzard, "The Minister's Dilemma," *The Christian Century*, April 25, 1956, p. 508f.

[3]Saint Ambrose, *Letters*, tr. Sister Mary Melchior Beyenka, O. P. in *Fathers of the Church* (Fathers of the Church, Inc., 1954), vol. 26, p. 51. Ambrose to Horontianus, 276 (cf. p. 58). Ambrose to his clergy, 317-20.

[4]"Why Clergy Are Fired," *The Christian Century*, Dec. 10, 1980, p. 1215.

[5]Donald Light, Suzanne Keller, and Craig Calhoun, *Sociology*, 5th ed. (Alfred A. Knopf, 1989), p. 20.

[6]Mircea Eliade, *Shamanism: Archaic Techniques of Ecstasy*, tr. Willard R. Trask (Princeton University Press, 1964), chaps. I-IV. Cf. *Black Elk Speaks: Being the Life Story of a Holy Man of the Oglala Sioux*, as told through John G. Neihardt (Flaming Rainbow) (University of Nebraska Press, 1961), in passim.

[7]Chalmers McPherson, *Disciples of Christ in Texas* (Standard Publishing Company, 1920), p. 20, as quoted by Colby D. Hall, *Texas Disciples* (Texas Christian University Press, 1953), p. 199.

[8]Corbett H. Thigpen and Hervey M. Cleckley, *The Three Faces of Eve* (Fawcett Popular Library, 1957).

[9]*Ten Faces of Ministry* by Milo L. Brekke (Augsburg, 1979) had effectively preempted my proposed title.

[10]*Sociology*, p. 20.

[11]Alasdair McIntyre, *After Virtue: A Study in Moral Theory* (University of Notre Dame Press, 1981), pp. 26-29. I am indebted to my former colleague, Dean Joseph C. Hough, Jr., for this reference. See also Hough and Cobb, *Christian Identity and Theological Education*, p. 5, n. 12.

¹²Consider the approach, for example, in the consensus statement, *Baptism, Eucharist and Ministry* (World Council of Churches, 1982). I would argue that the issues there discussed are hardly the central concerns which ought to be addressed in a theology of ministry, but the prominence and recalcitrance of a few doctrines pertaining to "order" have consumed ecumenical energy for more than two generations. It may be suggested that a theology of ministry springing from reflection on the ministry of Jesus Christ and on such historical realities of ministerial practice as this book addresses might well put the interminable disputation over matters of order in proper perspective.

¹³For a study combining theological and historical analysis, though with minimal attention to the American scene, see Bernard Cooke, *Ministry to Word and Sacraments: History and Theology* (Fortress Press, 1976).

¹⁴It may have been Dorothy Sayers who, in her essay on Dante Alighieri, made such a comment regarding the *Divine Comedy*. Whatever the source of the observation, it has proved quite illuminating in the reading of that epic and in reflecting on the human scene.

THE EIGHTEENTH-CENTURY SETTING

¹See "A Public Declaration to the Tribal Councils and Traditional Spiritual Leaders of the Indian and Eskimo Peoples of the Pacific Northwest," an apology on behalf of their churches, signed by ten bishops and denominational executives of churches in the region, *The Christian Century*, Dec. 9, 1987, p. 1115.

²Henry Mitchell, *Black Belief: Folk Beliefs of Blacks in America and West Africa* (Harper & Row, 1975).

MODEL 1 SAINT

¹For an exploration of "saintliness," broadly conceived in American history, see Dumas Malone, *Saints in Action* (Abingdon Press, 1939).

²Eliade, *Shamanism*.

³Albert J. Raboteau, *Slave Religion: The "Invisible Institution" in the Antebellum South* (Oxford University Press, 1978), pp. 128-150. Cf. Henry Mitchell, "Two Streams of Tradition," in C. Eric Lincoln, ed., *The Black Experience in Religion* (Anchor Press/Doubleday, 1974), pp. 69-75.

⁴Recall the protests of Native Americans to Pope John Paul II during his visit to California in 1988, against the beatification of Fr. Junipero Serra, founder of the California missions. See "Serra—Saintly or Not?" *The Christian Century*, Oct. 19, 1988, p. 921.

⁵Phyllis M. Jones and Nicolas R. Jones, eds., *Salvation in New England: Selections from the Sermons of the First Preachers* (University of Texas Press, 1977), p. 180.

⁶Consult Janet Whitney, ed., *The Journal of John Woolman* (Henry Regnery Co., 1950).

⁷See Herbert A. Wisbey, Jr., *Pioneer Prophetess: Jemima Wilkinson, the Publick Universal Friend* (Cornell University Press, 1964).

⁸For the text of the sermon, see H. Shelton Smith, Robert T. Handy, and Loefferts A. Loetscher, *American Christianity: An Historical Interpretation with Representative Documents, Vol. I, 1607-1820* (Charles Scribner's Sons, 1960), pp. 321-328.

⁹Langdon Brown Gilkey, *How the Church Can Minister to the World Without Losing Itself* (Harper & Row, 1964).

[10]For a serious attempt by the United Methodist Church through its Academy for Spiritual Formation, see Gregory S. Clapper, "Spiritual Formation in a Part-time Monastery," *The Christian Century*, April 10, 1991, pp. 388-390.

MODEL 2　PRIEST

[1]See, e. g., *Popol Vuh: The Mayan Book of the Dawn of Life*, trans. Dennis Tedlock, with commentary based on the ancient knowledge of the modern Quiche Maya (Simon & Schuster, 1985).

[2]Åke Hultkrantz, *The Religion of the American Indians*, trans. Monica Setterweall (University of California Press, 1979), pp. 125-128.

[3]*A History of the Expansion of Christianity* (Harper & Brothers, 1939), vol. III, p. 370.

[4]Bernard Bailyn, *The Ideological Origins of the American Revolution* (The Belknap Press of Harvard University Press, 1967), pp. 249-263, 268-271. Robert Frederick West, *Alexander Campbell and Natural Religion* (Yale University Press, 1948), pp. 12-19.

[5]Because of the representative character of ministerial office, I believe it appropriate that an ordained minister should normally preside at the eucharist, but also that occasional symbolic variations from this rule serve to demonstrate important ecclesiological truths and values.

[6]For an earlier argument as to the importance of such a ministry, see Charles Clayton Morrison, *The Social Gospel and the Christian Cultus* (Harper & Brothers, 1933). For a current exposition of biblical thought, see Walter Brueggemann, *Israel's Praise: Doxology against Idolatry and Ideology* (Fortress Press, 1988).

MODEL 3　MASTER

[1]Urban T. Holmes III, *The Future Shape of Ministry: A Theological Projection* (The Seabury Press, 1971), chaps. 2-4.

[2]Orpha [Caroline] Ochse, *The History of the Organ in the United States* (Indiana University Press, 1975), ch. I, "The Spanish Missions."

[3]Moses Coit Tyler, *A History of American Literature, 1609-1765*, p. 85, quoted in D. Duane Cummins, *The Disciples Colleges: A History* (CBP Press, 1987), p. 9.

[4]*New Englands First Fruits* (London, 1643), as cited in H. Shelton Smith, Robert T. Handy, and Loefferts A. Loetscher, eds., *American Christianity: An Historical Interpretation with Representative Documents* (Charles Scribner's Sons, 1960), vol. I, p. 123f.

[5]Baldwin, *The New England Clergy and the American Revolution* (Duke University Press, 1928). Cf. Clinton Rossiter, *Seedtime of the Republic: The Origins of the American Tradition of Political Liberty* (Harcourt, Brace and Company, 1953) and Bernard Bailyn, *The Ideological Origins of the American Revolution* (The Belknap Press of the Harvard University Press, 1967).

[6]John Wingate Thornton, *The Pulpit of the American Revolution: or the Political Sermons of the Period of 1776*, with a Historical Introduction, Notes, and Illustrations (Gould and Lincoln, 1860), pp. 401-520.

[7]Jones and Jones, eds., *Salvation in New England*, pp. 12-16.

[8]See Ola Elizabeth Winslow, *Meetinghouse Hill, 1630-1783* (The Macmillan Company, 1952). Cf. David D. Hall, *The Faithful Shepherd: A History of the New England Ministry in the Seventeenth Century* (University of North Carolina Press, 1972).

[9]See Sacvan Bercovitch, *The American Jeremiad* (The University of Wisconsin Press, 1978).

[10]H. Richard Niebuhr, in collaboration with Daniel Day Williams and James M. Gustafson, *The Purpose of the Church and Its Ministry: Reflections on the Aims of Theological Education* (Harper & Brothers, 1956), p. 81.

[11]Jonathan Edwards, *Basic Writings*. Selected, Edited, and with a Foreword by Ola Elizabeth Winslow (New American Library, 1966), p. 173.

MODEL 4   AWAKENER

[1]Used by the biographer Albert D. Belden to characterize the great English evangelist in his book, *George Whitefield—The Awakener* (Cokesbury Press, 1930), the term is here applied to his American contemporaries who modeled their ministries after his. For a study of forerunners, see G. R. Owst, *Preaching in Medieval England: An Introduction to Sermon Manuscripts of the Period c. 1350-1450* (Cambridge University Press, 1926).

[2]This paragraph condenses the thesis advanced by William G. McLoughlin in his *Revivals, Awakenings, and Reform: An Essay on Religion and Social Change in America, 1607-1977* (The University of Chicago Press, 1978).

[3]Jonathan Edwards, *The Great Awakening*, ed. by C. C. Goen, *The Works of Jonathan Edwards*, John E. Smith, General Editor (Yale University Press, 1972), vol. 4, pp. 97-211.

[4]Albert C. Outler, ed., *The Works of John Wesley*, vol. 2, *Sermons II 34-70*. Sermon 53, "On the Death of George Whitefield." The Bicentennial Edition of the Works of John Wesley, Frank Baker, editor-in-chief (Abingdon Press, 1985), p. 335.

[5]See Model 1: Saint, p. 25f. For the text of the sermon, see Alan Heimert and Perry Miller, eds., *The Great Awakening: Documents Illustrating the Crisis and Its Consequences* (The Bobbs-Merrill Company, 1967), pp. 71-99.

[6]See McLoughlin, *Revivals, Awakenings, and Reform*.

[7]For an analysis of the current "missionary situation" of the churches in Europe and America, see Lesslie Newbigin, *Foolishness to the Greeks: The Gospel and Western Culture* (World Council of Churches, 1986).

[8]John Greenleaf Whittier, "The Preacher" [an encomium honoring George Whitefield and the other Awakeners], *The Complete Works of John Greenleaf Whittier* (Houghton Mifflin Company, c. 1894), pp. 70-73.

THE NINETEENTH-CENTURY SETTING

[1]A generation ago, W.A. Visser't Hooft tried with little success to goad ecumenical theologians into reflection on the ecclesiological significance of councils of churches. For attempts by this author, see "The Church of Christ, the Denomination, and the Council of Churches: An Essay in Ecclesiology," *Encounter*, 20:1, pp. 72-93, and "The Role of the Denomination: An Essay in Ecclesiology," *Encounter*, 22:2, pp. 160-174.

[2]See "The Shape of Ministry" in Frederick A. Norwood, *The Story of American Methodism: A History of United Methodists and Their Relations* (Abingdon Press, 1974), pp. 133-144. Ronald E. Osborn, "The Eldership among Disciples of Christ: A Historical Case Study in a 'Tent-Making Ministry,'" *Mid-Stream*, VI, 2 (Winter, 1967), pp. 74-112.

[3]Robert N. Bellah, "Civil Religion in America," *Daedalus* 96:1 (Winter, 1967), pp. 1-21; Elwyn A. Smith, ed., *The Religion of the Republic* (Fortress Press, 1971); Russell E. Richey and Donald G. Jones, eds., *American Civil Religion* (Harper & Row, 1974); Sidney E. Mead, *The Nation with the Soul of a Church* (Harper & Row, 1975).

⁴The pattern recurs in the narratives recounted in the *Book of Mormon*.

⁵See Richard Hofstadter, *Anti-Intellectualism in American Life* (Alfred A. Knopf, 1963).

⁶Cummins, *The Disciples Colleges: A History*, p. 14.

MODEL 5 PULPITEER

¹See *Frances Lea McCurdy, Stump, Bar, & Pulpit: Speechmaking on the Missouri Frontier* (University of Missouri Press, 1969).

²Barnet Baskerville, *The People's Voice: The Orator in American Society* (The University Press of Kentucky, 1979).

³Dana Greene, ed., *Lucretia Mott: Her Complete Speeches and Sermons* (The Edwin Mellen Press, 1980). Mary Earhart Dillon, "Willard, Frances Elizabeth Caroline," in Edward T. James, Janet Wilson James, and Paul S. Boyer, eds., *Notable American Women, 1607-1950: A Biographical Dictionary* (The Belknap Press of Harvard University Press, 1971), vol. III, pp. 613-619.

⁴Quoted by Quintilian, *Institutio oratoria*, XII, I, 1 (LCL, vol. IV, p. 354f.) The sexist language of the definition constituted no barrier for competent women who demonstrated their mastery of the art.

⁵"The author's chief indebtedness for help has been to Aristotle, Cicero, and Quintilian, and to Whately and Vinet." John A. Broadus, *A Treatise on the Preparation and Delivery of Sermons*, New (Thirtieth) Edition, edited by Edwin Charles Dargan (Hodder & Stoughton, George H. Doran Company, 1898), p. xii.

⁶Cicero, *De oratore*, II, lxxvii, 310. Cf. Augustine, *De doctrina christiana*, IV, 12, (27).

⁷Some students of the Bible continued to insist on the distinction. See Alger Morton Fitch, Jr., *Alexander Campbell: Preacher of Reform and Reformer of Preaching* (College Press Publishing Company, 1988), pp. 29-32.

⁸For insight into the power of the black tradition in preaching, see James Weldon Johnson, *God's Trombones: Seven Negro Sermons in Verse* (The Viking Press, 1927).

⁹Selections from *The Life Experience and Gospel Labors of the Rt. Rev. Richard Allen* (Philadelphia: Martin & Boston, 1833) are reprinted in Milton C. Sernett, ed., *Afro-American Religious History: A Documentary Witness* (Duke University Press, 1985), pp. 135-149.

¹⁰Four sermons by John Jasper are included in Clyde E. Fant, Jr., and William M. Pinson, Jr., eds., *Twenty Centuries of Great Preaching: An Encyclopedia of Preaching* (Word Books, 1971), vol. 4, pp. 237-257.

¹¹Phillips Brooks, *Lectures on Preaching* (1876-77) (Zondervan Publishing House, n.d.), pp. 5-34.

¹²See the analysis of the preaching of Billy Sunday in Douglas Frank, *Less Than Conquerors: How Evangelicals Entered the Twentieth Century* (William B. Eerdmans Publishing Company, 1986), pp. 173-195.

¹³See Fant and Pinson, *Twenty Centuries of Great Preaching*, vol. 5, p. 280f.

¹⁴Daniel Calhoun, *The Intelligence of a People* (Princeton University Press, 1973), pp. 259-291.

MODEL 6 REVIVALIST

¹For nineteenth-century revivalism, see William Warren Sweet, *Revivalism in America: Its Origin, Growth, and Decline* (Charles Scribner's Sons, 1944), Timothy L. Smith, *Revivalism and Social Reform in Mid-Nineteenth-Century America* (Abingdon Press, 1957), William G. McLoughlin, Jr., *Modern Revivalism: Charles Grandison*

Finney to Billy Graham (The Ronald Press company, 1959), and William G. McLoughlin, *Revivals, Awakenings, and Reform* (The University of Chicago Press, 1978).

2For the Great Western Revival, see *The Biography of Eld. Barton Warren Stone, written by himself*: with Additions and Reflections by Elder John Rogers (Published for the Author by J. A. & U. P. James, 1847), pp. 34-42.

3John Bach MacMaster (1852-1932), in his multi-volume work, *A History of the People of the United States from the Revolution to the Civil War* (New York, 1883-1913), gave an extended account of the Cane Ridge Revival, based on contemporary reports in the secular press.

4In addition to the sources listed in note 1 of this chapter, see Charles G. Finney, *Revivals of Religion* (New York, 1868; reprint: Moody Press, 1962).

5The Revivalists managed to find theological justification both for the intentional use of human means to fulfill the divine purpose of conversion and for the freedom of a believer to claim salvation without waiting for a miraculous experience. It must be remembered that their achievement took place within a context of ebullient democracy in which the people were arguing for their right to decide political issues for themselves. "Political Arminianism—a sovereignty of the people that is explicitly, definitively free in the profane sphere, and manifest in its works—called forth an Arminian liberation in the sacred sphere as well." So writes George Armstrong Kelly, "Faith, Freedom, and Disenchantment: Politics and the American Religious Consciousness," in Mary Douglas and Steven Tipton, eds., *Religion and America: Spiritual Life in a Secular Age*, (Beacon Press, 1983), p. 214. For a more extended discussion of this dynamic, with emphasis on the populist aversion to Calvinism, see Nathan O. Hatch, *The Democratization of American Christianity* (Yale University Press, 1989).

6George M. Marsden, *Fundamentalism and American Culture: The Shaping of Twentieth-Century Evangelicalism, 1870-1925* (Oxford University Press, 1980), pp. 11, 28.

7Mary Ellen LaRue, "Women Have Not Been Silent...: A study of women preachers among the Disciples," *Discipliana*, January, 1963, p. 88, citing a biography by Earl T. Sechler, *Sadie McCoy Crank* (Hermitage, Mo.: The Index, 1950), p. 35.

8See John Holmes Acornley, *The Colored Lady Evangelist: Being the Life, Labors and Experiences of Mrs. Harriet Baker* (New York, 1892). Cf. Amanda B. Smith, *An Autobiography* (1893), The Schomburg Library of Nineteenth-Century Black Women Writers (Oxford University Press, 1988).

9For Jesse Bader, see LaRue, "Women Have Not Been Silent...," *Discipliana*, January, 1963, p. 89, citing *World Call*, 19 (March, 1937), p. 29. For Harold E. Fey, see his *How I Read the Riddle: an Autobiography* (Council on Christian Unity, 1982), pp. 27-29; he did not remember the revivalist's name.

10Marsden, *Fundamentalism and American Culture*, p. 45.

11The retelling of the story is from an undated news clipping from the Eugene (Oregon) *Register-Guard*, circa 1950.

MODEL 7   BUILDER

1A sculpture in the McMaster Divinity College Building at McMaster University, Hamilton, Ontario, commemorates "the host of almost forgotten ministers who by selfless devotion and godly labor brought the church of the Canadian Baptist fellowship into existence during the formative years of Canadian history." It depicts "eight different aspects of the pioneer Baptist minister's life and work: his [sic] ordination, his Christian family life, his pastoral visitation, his administration of the ordinances, his teaching ministry, his pulpit ministry, his studies, his prayer life." Quotations are from the leaflet, "The Unknown Baptist Minister," kindly provided to me by Principal William H. Brackey of McMaster Divinity School, and are used by his permission. The sculpture is by Adlai Hardin, a minister's son. For the memoirs of such a minister among American Congregationalists, see Rev. Sherlock Bristol, *The Pioneer Preacher: Incidents of Interest and Experiences in the Author's Life*, with an introduction and notes by Dewey D. Wallace, Jr., illustrated by Isabelle Blood, 1887 (University of Illinois Press, 1989).

[2]See Bernard Cooke, *Ministry in Word and Sacraments* (Fortress Press, 1976), Part One: "Ministry as Formation of Community." Cf. Donald G. Mathews, "The Second Great Awakening as an Organizing Process, 1780-1830," in Mulder and Wilson, *Religion in American History*, pp. 199-217.

[3]Joseph J. Ellis, review of *Jedidiah Morse and New England Congregationalism* (Rutgers University Press, 1982), in *American Historical Review* 89:2 (April, 1984), p. 516.

[4]Colby D. Hall, *Rice Haggard: The American Frontier Evangelist Who Revived the Name Christian* (Fort Worth, Texas: University Christian Church, 1957), p. 26.

[5]Stephen J. England, *Oklahoma Christians: A History of Christian Churches and of the Start of the Christian Church (Disciples of Christ) in Oklahoma* (Printed for the Christian Churches in Oklahoma by the Bethany Press, 1975), pp. 78-80, 89.

[6]Robert S. Michaelsen, "The Protestant Ministry in America: 1850 to the Present," in H. Richard Niebuhr and Daniel Day Williams, eds., *The Ministry in Historical Perspective* (Harper & Brothers, 1956), p. 265f.

[7]Arnold S. Nash, *Protestant Thought in the Twentieth Century: Whence and Whither?* (The Macmillan Company, 1951), p. 181f.

[8]Consider Henry Ward Beecher's sermon, "Christian Life, a Growth" (published in a two-volume collection of his sermons in 1871), in Fant and Pinson, *Twenty Centuries of Great Preaching*, Vol. IV, pp. 329-342.

[9]The film was based on the book by Hartzell Spence, *One Foot in Heaven: the life of a practical parson* (New York: Whittlesey House, 1940), written about his father, a Methodist minister at the turn of the century.

[10]England, *Oklahoma Christians*, pp. 55, 90. Randi Jones Walker, unpublished research on Protestantism in territorial New Mexico.

[11]Quoted by LaTaunya M. Bynum, "Opening the Doors," *The Disciple*, July, 1988, p. 9.

[12]*Ibid.*

[13]Mary Ellen LaRue, "Women Have Not Been Silent," *Discipliana*, January, 1963, p. 88.

[14]Angie Debo, *Prairie City: The Story of an American Community* (Tulsa, Oklahoma: Council Books, Ltd., [1944] 1985), p. xxvii.

[15]Norwood, *The Story of American Methodism*, p. 334.

[16]Sidney E. Mead, *The Lively Experiment* (Harper & Row, 1963), p. 103.

[17]Theodore Maynard, *The Story of American Catholicism* (The Macmillan Company, 1941), p. 218f., quoting John Gilmary Shea, *History of the Catholic Church in the United States*, 4 vols. (New York: 1886-1892), Vol. II, p. 495. The passage concludes Maynard's chapter entitled "Under Construction."

[18]T. Furman Hewitt, review of *Women and Temperance: the Quest for Power and Liberty, 1873-1900* by Ruth Bordin (Temple University Press, 1981), in *Church History*, Vol. 52, No. 1 (March, 1983), p. 100.

[19]See, for example, Jasper T. Moses, ed., *Helen E. Moses of the Christian*

Woman's Board of Missions: Biographical Sketch, Memorial Tributes, Missionary Addresses by Mrs. Moses, Sonnets and Other Verses (Fleming H. Revell Company). Cf. Barbara Brown Zikmund and Sally A. Dries, "Women's Work and Woman's Boards," in Barbara Brown Zikmund, ed., *Hidden Histories in the United Church of Christ*, (United Church Press, 1984), Vol. II, pp. 140-153.

[20]William Warren Sweet, *The Story of Religion in America* (Harper & Brothers, 1939), p. 484.

[21]Winthrop S. Hudson, *The Great Tradition of the American Churches* (Harper & Brothers, 1953).

[22]Washington Gladden, *Present Day Theology*, as cited by John Coleman Bennett, "The Social Interpretation of Christianity," in Samuel McCrea Cavert & Henry Pitney Van Dusen, eds., *The Church through Half a Century: Essays in Honor of William Adams Brown* (Charles Scribner's Sons, 1936), p. 116.

[23]See pp. 69f.

MODEL 8 MISSIONARY

[1]The title was bestowed by Kenneth Scott Latourette in his monumental work, *A History of the Expansion of Christianity* (Harper & Brothers, 1941); see vol. IV, "The Great Century in Europe and the United States of America." Latourette used it also for vols. V & VI, which dealt with Christianity in the rest of the world during the nineteenth century.

[2]For an eloquent sample of the emotion associated with the missionary cause, see the conclusion of an address on the theme, quoted in Ronald E. Osborn, *Ely Vaughn Zollars, Teacher of Preachers, Builder of Colleges: A Biography* (Christian Board of Publication, 1947), pp. 104-106.

[3]In its early decades, of course, Protestantism had its great examplars of ultimate devotion. cf. John Foxe, *The Acts and Monuments of the Church*, known since the 16th century as "Foxe's Book of Martyrs." Recall also New England's "Visible Saints," the Puritans.

[4]See, e. g., Randi Jones Walker, ed., *Kept by Grace: A Centennial History of First Congregational Church of Pasadena* (Pasadena, CA: Hope Publishing House, 1986), p. 17. Cf. Dan Bryant, *In Mission and Service: Disciples in Pomona, 1883-1983* (Pomona, CA: First Christian Church, Hundredth Anniversary Committee, 1983), pp. 26, 36, 45.

[5]D. March (1816-1909), "Hark! the Voice of Jesus Crying," in Charles Clayton Morrison and Herbert L. Willett, eds., *Hymns of the United Church* (The Christian Century Press, 1925).

[6]The distinguished novelist Pearl S. Buck, daughter of China missionaries, depicted their lives with insight and power in *The Exile* [her mother] and *Fighting Angel: Portrait of a Soul* [her father] (Reynal & Hitchcock, 1936).

[7]A. F. Beard, *A Crusade of Brotherhood* (Boston, 1909), p. 121, quoted by Winthrop S. Hudson, *Religion in America: An historical account of the development of American religious life*, 3rd ed. (Charles Scribner's Sons, 1981), p. 224f.

[8]E. Lyman Hood, "New Mexico and Arizona," *The Home Missionary*, 63 (March, 1890), p. 484, quoted by Randi Jones Walker, *Protestantism in the Sangre de Cristos 1850-1920* (University of New Mexico Press, 1991), p. 58.

[9]As one example of openness to the culture into which a missionary had come, consider E. Stanley Jones, *The Christ of the Indian Road* (Abingdon Press, 1925). Cf. the same author's *Christ at the Round Table* (Abingdon Press, 1928).

[10]E.g., James Michener's novel and the film, *Hawaii.*

[11]Robert Pierce Beaver, *All Loves Excelling: American Protestant Women in*

World Mission: History of the First Feminist Movement in North America (Eerdmans, 1968).

[12]Jane Hunter, *The Gospel of Gentility: American Women Missionaries in Turn-of-the-Century China* (Yale University Press, 1984), quoted by reviewer Trudy Bloser Blosh, *The Christian Century*, Nov. 14, 1984, p. 1074.

[13]Blosh, *The Christian Century*, Nov. 14, 1984, p. 1075.

[14]See Jaroslav Pelikan, *Jesus through the Centuries: His Place in the History of Culture* (Yale University Press, 1985), chap. 18, "The Man Who Belongs to the World."

[15]John Bunyan Hunley, *A Spiritual Argosy: The Romance of Fifty-Eight Years in the Christian Ministry* (The Christopher Publishing House, 1958), p. 230.

INTERLUDE: Confused Expectations

[1]Peter Farb, *Man's Rise to Civilization as Shown by the Indians of North America from Primeval Times to the Coming of the Industrial State* (E. P. Dutton & Co., 1968), pp. 280-284. Cf. Weston LaBarre, *The Ghost Dance: Origins of Religion* (Dell Publishing Company, 1970).

[2]Recall John G. Neihardt, *Black Elk Speaks*: the references to "The Good Red Road" and the concluding pages.

THE TWENTIETH-CENTURY SETTING

[1]For further reflection on the impact of twentieth-century social forces on church and ministry, see Osborn, *The Education of Ministers for the Coming Age*, chap. 1, "The World Rushing Toward Us."

[2]James M. Wall, "A Few Kind Words for Billy Graham," *The Christian Century*, 99:19 (May 26, 1982), p. 619.

[3]Richard Schickel, *Intimate Strangers: The Culture of Celebrity* (Doubleday, 1985).

[4]Richard M. Merelman, *Making Something of Ourselves: On Culture and Politics in the United States* (University of California Press, 1984), pp. 1-3.

[5]Wade Clark Roof and William McKinney, *American Mainline Religion: Its Changing Shape and Future* (Rutgers University Press, 1987), p. 51.

[6]Robert S. Paul, *The Church in Search of Itself* (William B. Eerdmans Publishing Company, 1972), p. 197, n. 98.

[7]See pp. 101-103.

[8]Peter Berger, *The Social Reality of Religion* (Faber, 1969), pp. 137-149: "Religion on the Market."

[9]In a word-study of the Book of Acts and the New Testament epistles, I have not found one clear-cut instance of the use of the title *minister* as a synonym for disciple or member of the church. The term is ambiguous in that it can mean just *servant* in a general sense. But all three of the Greek nouns commonly translated *minister* in the New Testament designate someone bearing public responsibility in the church; in everyday speech they denote an officer in an organization, its official public representative, not just any member. Instance after instance recurs in the New Testament in that official sense, as the context makes clear. See Ronald E. Osborn, *In Christ's Place: Christian Ministry in Today's World* (The Bethany Press, 1967), pp. 60-70. For an influential argument maintaining the position here repudiated (i.e., the idea that every Christian is a minister), see Arnold B. Come, *Agents of Reconciliation* (Westminster Press, 1960).

[10]Lester G. McAllister, *Thomas Campbell: Man of the Book* (The Bethany Press, 1954), p. 147.

[11]Martin Luther, *Selections from His Writings*, edited with introduction by John Dillenberger (Quadrangle Books, 1961), pp. 78f., 159f.; Hendrik Kraemer, *A Theology of the Laity* (Westminster Press, 1958).

[12]For a careful analysis of the meaning of the term *professional*, with its implications for ministry, see Paul M. Harrison, "Religious Leadership in America," in Donald R. Cutler, ed., *The Religious Situation: 1969* (Beacon Press), pp. 957-979.

[13]The paper that grew into this volume proposed the twelve models developed here. Since its completion, I have come upon other authors who, not known to me at the beginning, had already designated the Manager and the Therapist (Counselor) as representative "characters"in our time. See MacIntyre, *After Virtue*, pp. 26-29, and Robert A. Bellah et al, *Habits of the Heart*, pp. 44-47.

MODEL 9   MANAGER

[1]Hudson, *Religion in America*, p. 232.

[2]See, e. g., Clarence Day, *Life with Father* (Knopf, 1957) and *Life with Mother* (Knopf, 1957). Ask any minister who lived through the early part of the century or anyone who belonged to a minister's family.

[3]As late as 1929, when Daniel Fox concluded a twenty-year pastorate at First Congregational Church in Pasadena, with a large ministry of community service and a major building program, he still followed his custom of coming to the church office only on Wednesday mornings from 10:00 until 12:00. The rest of his time he spent in study and calling. See Walker, *Kept by Grace*, pp. 15-20. His pattern of work was not unusual among urban ministers in the first decades of this century, but the pattern rapidly changed in the '20s, '30s, and '40s.

[4]It currently appears as *The Clergy Journal*, with the original name as a subtitle.

[5]Clarence E. Lemmon, *The Art of Church Management* (Christian Board of Publication, 1933).

[6]The term *pastoral theology* is now enjoying a comeback. See Thomas C. Oden, *Pastoral Theology: Essentials of Ministry* (Harper & Row, 1983); Edward Farley, *Theologia: The Fragmentation and Unity of Theological Education* (Fortress Press, 1983); Don S. Browning, ed., *Practical Theology: The Emerging Field in Theology, Church, and World* (Harper & Row, 1983), pp. 187-202: "Pastoral Theology in a Pluralistic Age."

[7]H. Richard Niebuhr, *The Purpose of the Church and Its Ministry*, pp. 27-47.

[8]See, e.g., Allen J. Hinand, "The Pastor as Enabler for Lay Ministry," *Pastoral Psychology*, 22:6 (June, 1971), pp. 21-26.

[9]For an account of an evangelical change agent, see Randall Balmer, *Mine Eyes Have Seen the Glory: A Journey into the Evangelical Subculture in America* (Oxford University Press, 1989), pp. 138-154.

[10]See Angie Debo, *Prairie City*, pp. 163-172, "The Sheeted Terror." Though written under a thin disguise of fictional names, this history of Marshall, Oklahoma and the surrounding area is based on solid research by a master historian. See also Frank Elon Davison, *Thru the Rear-View Mirror* (The Bethany Press, 1955), pp. 75-79, "My First Baptism of Fire."

[11]Harold E. Fey, ed., *Kirby Page: The Autobiography of a 20th Century Prophet for Peace* (Fellowship Press, 1975), p. 111.

[12]For essays on the involvement of the churches in public affairs, see Mark A. Noll, ed., *Religion and American Politics: From the Colonial Period to the 1980s* (Oxford University Press, 1990). For thoughtful reflection by fundamentalist

authors on the recent incursions of conservative Christians into American politics, see Ed Dobson and Ed Hinson, *The Seduction of Power: Preachers, Politics and the Media* (Revell, 1989); reviewed in *The Christian Century*, Nov. 1, 1989, p. 992f.

[13]"A Holy Helicopter," *Time*, March 13, 1989, p. 27.

[14]Norwood, *The Story of American Methodism*, p. 413f.

[15]"Congregations had their minds on matters other than the city," observes a sociologist and historian in discussing the inability of a metropolitan council of churches to deal adequately with the urban problems of the 1960s. See Edwin L. Becker, *From Sovereign to Servant: The Church Federation of Greater Indianapolis, 1912-1987* (The Church Federation of Greater Indianapolis, 1987), p. 69.

[16]Barbara Brown Zikmund's comments in an address some years ago started my thinking about this development. See Robert W. Lynn and Elliott Wright, *The Big Little School: Sunday Child of American Protestantism* (Harper & Row, 1971), pp. 71, 77ff.

[17]Undated flyer advertising the *Clergy Desk Book* by Manfred Holck, Jr., with Ashley Hale. The author "is an ordained Lutheran minister, Certified Public Accountant, author of more than a dozen books, and publisher-editor of *The Clergy Journal.*"

[18]Alasdair McIntyre writes of our secular society, "The manager treats ends as given, as outside his scope; his concern is with technique, with effectiveness." See *After Virtue*, p. 29. For the importance of centering on specific Christian missional objectives in programming, see Kenneth L. Callahan, *Twelve Keys to an Effective Church: Strategic Planning for Mission* (Harper & Row, 1983).

[19]See T. J. Peters and R. H. Waterman, Jr., *In Search of Excellence: Lessons from America's Best Run Companies* (Harper & Row, 1982).

[20]For reflections on the moral insufficiency of the managerial model in secular society, with its "criteria of effectiveness shaped ultimately by the market," see Bellah et al, *Habits of the Heart*, pp. 44-46.

[21]Peter Drucker, interview with *Leadership*, quoted in item entitled "Church Management," *The Christian Ministry*, Vol. 20, No. 4 (July-August, 1989), p. 4.

[22]A frequent comment to ministerial students made by Ross J. Griffeth, long-time president of Northwest Christian College.

[23]A positive view that seeks to refine and commend the concept is set forth in David S. Luecke and Samuel Southard, *Pastoral Administration: Integrating Ministry and Management in the Church* (Word Books, 1986).

[24]The director of the Office of Pastoral Services for the Wisconsin Conference of Churches reports troubling results, with statistics, in the case of ministers with unrealistic expectations of the "megapastor" model—an exaggerated variation of the Manager. See G. Lloyd Rediger, "What Has Happened to the Megapastor Model?" *The Christian Ministry*, January, 1984, p. 17f.

MODEL 10   COUNSELOR

[1]Jean Caffey Lyles, "Reporter's Notebook: The NCC in Cleveland," *The Christian Century*, Nov. 25, 1981, p. 1223.

[2]See John T. McNeill, *A History of the Cure of Souls* (Harper Torchbooks,1951); William A. Clebsch and Charles R. Jaekle, *Pastoral Care in Historical Perspective: An Essay with Exhibits* (Prentice-Hall, Inc., 1964); Thomas C. Oden, *Care of Souls in the Classic Tradition* (Fortress Press, 1984).

[3]Richard Baxter, *The Reformed Pastor* [1656], ed. William Brown, abridged, 1829 (Edinburgh: The Banner of Truth Trust, 1989).

[4]"When the minister becomes a therapist, the congregation loses a pastor instead of gaining one," said A. M. Pennybacker at his installation as professor of homiletics at Lexington Theological Seminary. See the *Lexington Theological Seminary Bulletin*, XVII:2 (April, 1991), p. 1.

[5]See Frank D. Rees, "Pastoral Care: Accountability or Availability?" *The Christian Ministry*, January-February, 1989, pp. 8-10.

[6]See particularly John Patton, *Pastoral Counseling: A Ministry of the Church* (Abingdon Press, 1984).

[7]The information came to me in a memo from my one-time colleague Howard C. Clinebell, emeritus professor of pastoral counseling at the School of Theology at Claremont, who assisted me throughout my efforts to identify and evaluate the Counselor model of ministry.

[8]For insights into the life of such a congregation, see Robert K. Hudnut, *This People, This Parish* (Zondervan Publishing House, 1986).

MODEL 11   IMPRESARIO

[1]Recall the discussion of the celebrity in the chapter on the twentieth-century setting, pp. 126-128.

[2]For a description of such a big successful pastor, see Balmer, *Mine Eyes Have Seen the Glory*, pp. 71-91: "Phoenix Prophet"; see also p. 117.

[3]Mark R. Halton, in "Evangelical Broadcasters: Preaching to the Choir?" *The Christian Century*, April 12, 1989, p. 375, describes the typical listener to religious TV as "a woman over 50 who did not attend college, who is married to a blue-collar worker, who lives in the South, and...who is predisposed to evangelical messages and attends a local church." Halton credits Peter G. Horsfield, *Religious Television: The American Experience*, for this profile.

[4]Study guides for the Bible telecourses were published by Educational Communication Association in Washington, D.C., and later by Bauman Bible Telecasts in Arlington, Virginia.

[5]Ray Formanek, Jr., "Swaggart thumps his way to become king of TV preachers," *The Oregonian*, March 3, 1985, p. A26f.: "According to Arbitron Rating Service, 'The Jimmy Swaggart Telecast' reaches nearly 2 million households each week over more than 500 stations." William F. Fore, "Religion and Television: Report on the Research," *The Christian Century*, July 18-24, 1984, p. 711, adduces reasons for concluding that the actual number of listeners to religious broadcasts is about one-half (or at most, three-fourths) of the Arbitron estimate.

[6]David Gates and Daniel Shapiro, "The Superchurches of Houston," *Newsweek*, Oct. 24, 1983, p. 117; Barbara Dolan, "Full House at Willow Creek," *Time*, March 6, 1989, p. 60. Cf. Balmer, *Mine Eyes Have Seen the Glory*, pp. 72, 117.

[7]For reflections on the type of ministry we have here discussed, see Balmer, *Mine Eyes Have Seen the Glory*, pp. 227-235: "Epilogue."

MODEL 12   TEACHER

[1]For a graphic account see Harry Emerson Fosdick, *The Living of These Days: an Autobiography* (Harper & Brothers, 1956).

[2]For the text of these sermons, with an introductory commentary, see Allan H. Sager, "The Fundamentalist-Modernist Controversy, 1918-1930" in DeWitte Holland, ed., *Sermons in American History: Selected Issues in the American Pulpit 1630-1967* (Abingdon Press, 1971), pp. 332-364.

[3]From the title of one of his sermons, "On Being Christians Unashamed," in Harry Emerson Fosdick, *Successful Christian Living: Sermons on Christianity Today*

(Harper & Brothers, 1937), pp. 75-85.

[4]Dean K. Thompson eloquently recalls the significance of these ministers (all in the role of Teacher), and calls them "perhaps the most outstanding single generation of leaders in the history of the American churches." See his article, "A Pre-eminent Generation of Protestant Leaders," *The Christian Century*, January 7-14, 1976, pp.13-16. See also, "There *Are* Women Theologians!" *The Christian Century*, August 28, 1963, pp. 1053-54.

[5]See Iris V. Cully, "The Pastor as Teacher," *The Christian Ministry*, March, 1982, pp.13-16; note the section headed "Administration Involves Teaching," p. 15.

[6]See Eugene C. Roehlkepartain, "What Makes Faith Mature?" *The Christian Century*, May 9, 1990, pp. 496-499.

[7]Kenneth L. Woodward, "Pick-and-Choose Christianity," *Newsweek*, Sept. 19, 1983, p. 82.

[8]For a strong statement of this position, see Clark M. Williamson and Ronald J. Allen, *The Teaching Minister* (Westminster/John Knox, 1991).

[9]See, e.g., Fred B. Craddock, *As One Without Authority: Essays on Inductive Preaching*, revised and enlarged edition (The Phillips University Press, 1974).

[10]Martin E. Marty, "Filling in the Gaps of Liberal Culture," *The Christian Century*, Nov. 8, 1989, p. 1022.

[11]Quoted from a comment by Rod Parrott after reading an early draft of this chapter.

INTERLUDE: *Perplexed, But Not in Despair*

[1]Van Meter Ames, ed., *Beyond Theology: The Autobiography of Edward Scribner Ames* (The University of Chicago Press, 1959), p. 70.

[2]Susan Harrington DeVogel, "Clergy Morale: The Ups and Downs," *The Christian Century*, December 17, 1986, pp. 1149-51.

[3]Robert Wessman, letter to the author, March 29, 1987.

[4]"Practical Pastor," *Time*, January 23, 1950, p. 53.

OUT OF DISARRAY, CREATIVITY

[1]For reflections on ministry in the future, see Henri J.M. Nouwen, *In the Name of Jesus: Reflections on Christian Leadership* (Crossroad, 1989); Rosemary Ruether, "Ministry in the Church of the Future," in Sloyan, *Secular Priest in the New Church*, pp. 2322-249.

[2]*Baptism, Eucharist and Ministry*, Faith and Order Paper No. 111 (Geneva: World Council of Churches, 1982), p. 30.

[3]Consider, for example, such twentieth-century ministers as Harry Emerson Fosdick, Georgia Harkness, E. Stanley Jones, Rufus M. Jones, Kirby Page, Howard Thurman, and Ernest Fremont Tittle—each committed as a Christian to the struggle for justice and peace and equally devoted to a life of prayer and communion with God.

[4]John J. Carey, *Carlyle Marney: A Pilgrim's Progress* (Mercer University Press, 1980), p. 37.

[5]Leander E. Keck, *A Future for the Historical Jesus: The Place of Jesus in Preaching and Theology* (Abingdon Press, 1971), p. 265, referring specifically to the work of Shailer Mathews and Shirley Jackson Case.

[6]W. Clark Gilpin, "The Public Church and Its Ministry: The Focus of Ministry Studies at Chicago," *DDH Bulletin* (The Disciples Divinity House of the

University of Chicago), Vol. 59, No. 2, Fall, 1988, p. 1.

[7]Quoted by Gilpin, p. 4.

[8]Observations of a minister in a continuing education seminar, as reconstructed from a transcript by Rod Parrott.

[9]"A Conversation with the Rev. Martin Marty," *U. S. News & World Report*, September 24, 1984, p. 46.

[10]Janet F. Fishburn, "Male Clergy Adultery as Vocational Confusion," *The Christian Century*, Sept. 15-22, 1982, p. 923.

[11]Church Membership Down," *The Christian Century*, August 3-10, 1988, p. 696.

[12]R.E. Brown, "Peter," *The Interpreter's Dictionary of the Bible: Supplementary Volume* (Abingdon Press, 1976), p. 657.

[13]Robert Graham Kemper, "Summing up 1972: A Fresh Look at the Functional Categories of Ministry," *The Christian Ministry*, November, 1972, p. 2.

[14]Bellah, *Habits of the Heart*, p. 39. See also p. 319, n. 21, for comment on the necessity of social role to a sense of identity. In the passage quoted, "representative character" is used, in reflecting on de Tocqueville's "this American, this new man," in the sense established by Alasdair McIntyre in *After Virtue*, pp. 26-29. But in a real way, part of the minister's calling (in which no minister completely succeeds) is to represent through one person's life and work the essence of the Christian community and its commitments. Read from that slant, the passage just quoted says something of profound importance about ministry.

[15]"Women Pastors Accepted," *The Christian Century*, October 5, 1988, p. 864. Cf. Edward C. Lehman, Jr., *Women Clergy: Breaking through Gender Barriers* (Transaction Books, 1986). For accounts of women in contemporary ministry, see Pauli Murray, *Song in a Weary Throat* (Harper & Row, 1987).

[16]Mary Lou Suhor, "Woman Priest, St. Jude, and the Pope," *The Witness*, June, 1984, pp. 12-14.

[17]For reflections on this new situation, see Lyle E. Schaller, ed., *Women as Pastors* (Abingdon Press, 1982).

[18]"'A Lack of Imagination,'" *Newsweek*, October 27, 1986, p. 6.

[19]"Events and People," *The Christian Century*, March 31, 1976. p. 303.

[20]Linda-Marie Delloff, "Joseph Sittler and the Theater of Human Existence: An Interview," *The Christian Century*, February 1-8, 1984, p. 114.

[21]William G. Shoop, "Notes from the Pastor," *Webster Groves Christian Church Witness*, Vol. 16, No. 35 (Oct. 24, 1989), p. 2.

[22]Ronald E. Osborn, *In Christ's Place*, discusses the ministry of the Servant as fundamental and, as subsidiary to it, Prophet, Priest, and Shepherd.

[23]Henri J. M. Nouwen, "On Radical Prayer," adapted from the *New Oxford Review*, advertisement in *The Christian Century*, Oct. 2, 1985, p. 873.

[24]Martin E. Marty, "Martin Luther King's Inner Spiritual Church," *The Christian Century*, Jan. 21, 1987, p. 44.

[25]For a commendation of the role-model of the *rabbi*, see Clark M. Williamson, *Has God Rejected His People?* (Abingdon Press, 1982), p. 115. For further reflection on the rabbi and on study as worship, see Clark M. Williamson, *When Jews and Christians Meet: A Guide for Christian Preaching and Teaching* (CBP Press, 1989), p. 115. Cf. John Tracy Ellis, "The Priest and the Intellectual Life," in Gerald S. Sloyan, ed., *Secular Priest in the New Church* (Herder and Herder, 1967), pp. 186-218.

[26]For historical observations and reflections on the current scene, see Richard Osmer, *A Teachable Spirit* (Westminster/John Knox, 1990). Cf. Joseph Hough, Jr., and Barbara G. Wheeler, eds., *Beyond Clericalism: The Congregation as a Focus for*

Theological Education (Scholars Press, 1989); Michael Kinnamon, "The Fourth Era," *Lexington Theological Quarterly*, 24, 3, (July, 1989), p. 85. On religious and moral illiteracy, see Daniel R. Heischman, "Transmitting a Vision: Religion in Independent Schools," *The Christian Century*, April 19, 1989, pp. 417-419. For current implications of Alexander Campbell's conception of the teaching responsibility of the pulpit, see Ronald J. Allen, "'Worship among Disciples: Literature and Practice'—Some Further Considerations," *The Disciples Theological Digest*, Vol. 3, 1988, p. 27.

[27]The Greek phrase *diaireseis diakonion* in 1 Cor. 12:5 is rendered "varieties of services" (or something similar) in all the twentieth-century versions I have consulted, but the word in question often refers more specifically to the "ministries" offered by the duly appointed and recognized public ministers of the church. See Osborn, *In Christ's Place*, pp. 67-70.

[28]President John M. Mulder of Louisville Theological Seminary, letter to author, March 6, 1985.

[29]*Ibid.*